HUMAN GROWTH
AND DEVELOPMENT

SAGE was founded in 1965 by Sara Miller McCune to support the dissemination of usable knowledge by publishing innovative and high-quality research and teaching content. Today, we publish over 900 journals, including those of more than 400 learned societies, more than 800 new books per year, and a growing range of library products including archives, data, case studies, reports, and video. SAGE remains majority-owned by our founder, and after Sara's lifetime will become owned by a charitable trust that secures our continued independence.

Los Angeles | London | New Delhi | Singapore | Washington DC | Melbourne

THIRD EDITION

HUMAN GROWTH
AND **DEVELOPMENT**

CHRIS BECKETT AND HILARY TAYLOR

Los Angeles | London | New Delhi
Singapore | Washington DC | Melbourne

Los Angeles | London | New Delhi
Singapore | Washington DC | Melbourne

SAGE Publications Ltd
1 Oliver's Yard
55 City Road
London EC1Y 1SP

SAGE Publications Inc.
2455 Teller Road
Thousand Oaks, California 91320

SAGE Publications India Pvt Ltd
B 1/I 1 Mohan Cooperative Industrial Area
Mathura Road
New Delhi 110 044

SAGE Publications Asia-Pacific Pte Ltd
3 Church Street
#10-04 Samsung Hub
Singapore 049483

Editor: Kate Wharton
Editorial assistant: Lucy Dang
Production editor: Katie Forsythe
Copyeditor: Bryan Campbell
Proofreader: William Baginsky
Indexer: Gary Kirby
Marketing manager: Tamara Navaratnam
Cover design: Lisa Harper-Wells
Typeset by C&M Digitals (P) Ltd, Chennai, India
Printed and bound in Great Britain by Ashford
Colour Press Ltd

First edition published 2004. Reprinted 2005, 2006, 2007
(twice) and 2009
Second edition published 2010. Reprinted 2011, 2012, 2013,
2014 and 2015

This 3rd edition first published 2016

Library of Congress Control Number: 2015955562

British Library Cataloguing in Publication data

A catalogue record for this book is available from
the British Library

ISBN 978-1-4739-1625-8
ISBN 978-1-4739-1626-5 (pbk)

At SAGE we take sustainability seriously. Most of our products are printed in the UK using FSC papers and boards.
When we print overseas we ensure sustainable papers are used as measured by the PREPS grading system.
We undertake an annual audit to monitor our sustainability.

We would like to dedicate this book, with much love, to Hilary's sons, Owen, Evan and Hywel, and Chris's children, Poppy, Dom and Nancy. Between them they have taught us so much about human growth and development.

CONTENTS

About the authors   viii

Preface to the third edition   ix

Introduction   x

1   The Birth of a Human Being: What makes us who we are?   1

2   The Balancing Act: Psychodynamic insights   20

3   A Secure Base: The importance of attachment   45

4   The Emergence of Reason: The developing ability to understand   67

5   Making Connections: Ideas from behaviourism   85

6   Who Am I Going to Be? Adolescence, identity and change   105

7   Acting like a Grown-up: Challenges of adulthood   130

8   Access to Adulthood: Growing up with a disability   150

9   No Man is an Island: Family systems and their life cycle   169

10   It Takes a Village: A sociological perspective   189

11   Coming to a Conclusion: Dimensions of old age   207

12   That Good Night: Death, dying and bereavement   222

References   239

Index   257

ABOUT THE AUTHORS

Chris Beckett divides his time between being a senior lecturer in social work at the University of East Anglia, and a writer of fiction. He studied psychology at Bristol University and qualified as a social worker at Bangor in 1980, going on to work for eighteen years as a social worker and social work manager, mainly in the children and families field, before moving into academic social work. He has published six books of fiction, and won prizes for his short story collection *The Turing Test*, and his novel Dark Eden.

Hilary Taylor trained as a social worker after studying English at Oxford University, qualifying in 1973. At the beginning of her career she worked with all service user groups, and later in adult social care, mental health, group therapy and family mediation. She then moved into social work training and education, teaching at Anglia Ruskin University and also working as an independent practice teacher. She also trained as a psychoanalytic psychotherapist, and now has a private counselling and psychotherapy practice.

Other SAGE books published by the author

- Chris Beckett and Nigel Horner, Essential Theory for Social Work Practice, Second Edition, 2016
- Chris Beckett and Andrew Maynard, Values and Ethics in Social Work, Second Edition, 2012
- Chris Beckett, Assessment & Intervention in Social Work: Preparing for Practice, First Edition, 2010
- Chris Beckett, Child Protection: An Introduction, Second Edition, 2007

PREFACE TO THE THIRD EDITION

Inevitably, the authors of a book begin to notice things they'd like to change about it pretty much from the day it finally leaves their hands. We are grateful for the opportunity to have a third go at this particular book, revising it not only in the light of our own fresh perspectives, but also in response to some very helpful and detailed comments, commissioned by the publishers, from users of the book from a range of disciplines – nursing, social work, occupational therapy – and from several countries. All of the chapters have been reworked to a greater or lesser extent, with new material added and old material reshaped, and we have made a small change to the order of the chapters. However, the book begins and ends in the same way, and its overall structure remains the same, as does the general approach set out in the Introduction.

Chris Beckett and Hilary Taylor

2016

INTRODUCTION

This is an introduction to human development written specifically for people studying for careers in the helping professions, such as nurses, social workers, occupational therapists, teachers and counsellors. It is written by a social work academic and novelist, who previously worked in child and family social work, and a psychotherapist and former social work academic who used to work in the field of social work with adults. The book very loosely follows the shape of a human life, beginning with a birth and ending with a death, but many of the chapters deal with ideas and topics that are relevant at many different stages of life, such as bereavement, attachment and learning. Its focus throughout is on *psychosocial* development – that is to say, psychological development within a social context – rather than physical development, though it is impossible to talk about the former without at least some mention of the latter.

The book does not pretend to be an exhaustive summary of cutting edge research in the field (though we have tried to keep it up to date!) but rather a collection of ideas about human growth which we think is useful for people whose job requires them to think about human development, not as an academic subject, but as a practical matter: 'What might A be struggling with at the moment?' 'Why does B always behave in this way?' 'How might C's childhood experiences affect the way she sees the world now?' There is no exact science to answer these questions. In practice we have to rely to a considerable extent on imagination and experience, but there *is* a body of knowledge that can enrich and deepen our thinking, and we try to give some sense of it here, offering suggestions for further reading at the end of each chapter for readers wishing to look more deeply into the topics discussed.

Interspersed in the text are 'activities' which invite readers to pause and consider the topic under discussion in relation to hypothetical situations, or in relation to their own lives. These can be used in a variety of ways. For instance, they can be extracted from the text and used as classroom exercises. Many readers may simply choose to read through them as part of the text.

One final point. All books reflect, to a large extent, the character, experience, background and preoccupation of their authors. This book is no exception, and the authors themselves have noticed a shift in the emphasis of the book from its first edition, written by Chris Beckett alone when he was in his forties, to the current edition, written by two authors around retirement age. While we have tried as far as possible to enter into the experience of people different to ourselves, we freely acknowledge that our own perspective is necessarily shaped by what we ourselves have seen of the world, and perhaps by what we have not seen.

1 THE BIRTH OF A HUMAN BEING

WHAT MAKES US WHO WE ARE?

- Ideas, theories and prejudices   2
- Nature and nurture   6
- Free will versus predetermination   16
- Events, transitions, resilience   18

In a delivery room in a maternity hospital, a mother is about to give birth after an eight-hour labour. There are four people present: the mother herself, the baby's father, a midwife and a doctor. Everyone is trying to encourage the exhausted mother ('Keep pushing!', 'You're almost there!', 'Don't forget your breathing!').

Then the father shouts out excitedly, 'I can see its head!'

Suddenly, a fifth human being is in the room, a stranger, a new being that no one has ever seen before (though across the world four new babies are born every second).

'It's a girl!' says the midwife.

It's about the only thing they can tell about her at this stage, though soon they will weigh her and then there will be another fact to tell the relatives over the phone. If she had some obvious physical abnormality – a missing limb, a harelip, a spinal deformity – that would of course be another thing that they could see, and something that might drastically alter their initial response (see Chapter 9). But apart from that, what else can they know about her?

Even her future appearance can't really be discerned from the wizened ancient-looking little face (however much they may tell themselves she has her father's eyes, her mother's chin), let alone her future personality, her future abilities, her future life story.

What will she become? Will she be the prime minister or an office cleaner? Will she be happy? Will she be healthy? Will she be loved? Will she win honours or commit crimes? Will she one day be in a place like this bringing her own baby into the world?

It is impossible to tell.

What is it that determines what sort of person we become? Is a child's future personality already determined at birth, or is a newborn baby like a blank sheet, waiting to be written on by life? Is our personality determined by *anything*, or do we choose for ourselves who we are, create ourselves out of nothing? These are important questions, not only from an academic point of view, but also from a very practical one, because our views on these questions radically affect the way we see the world, our attitudes to other people and the way we work with other people.

In this chapter we will provide an overview of the sorts of questions that we will be exploring in this book. To begin with, we will ask you to look at your own ideas and assumptions about what makes people who they are, as it is really those ideas and assumptions which will either be validated or called into question by what you read here. We will also offer a 'health warning' about theories. Fortunately or unfortunately, no theory about human life can ever be completely objective or value free. Trying to see ourselves completely objectively is a bit like trying to catch a glimpse of your mirror image when it's not looking at you.

We will then look at two very old questions. The first of these can be summed up as 'nature or nurture'. To what extent is who we are determined at birth and to what extent are we shaped by the environment we live in? And we will discuss the factors, both inherited and environmental, that contribute to human development, and consider how these factors interact. The second question has been debated by philosophers for thousands of years: the question of 'free will' versus 'predetermination'.

Finally, we will mention the events that typically mark the turning points in our lives, the transitions that we all have to go through as we adjust to new circumstances and new life stages, and we will touch on the concept of personal resilience.

Ideas, Theories and Prejudices

It isn't only psychologists and philosophers who like to come up with theories about what makes people who they are. All of us have been studying other people all our lives, for we need to understand other people in order to work out how best to deal with them. How to make friends, how to bring up our children, how to get others to cooperate with us, how to get over painful experiences – all of these everyday questions, and many more, require us to have ideas about 'what makes people tick'. And most of us find this a fascinating question anyway. Why else do we watch and talk about reality shows on TV, or about people we know, or the characters in novels and films? But our ideas about 'what makes people tick' don't come from nowhere and they are not really our own original thoughts. All our lives we are exposed to the ideas of others and to the 'accepted wisdom' of the society in which we live. So we all have an enormous store of ideas, theories, information and, undoubtedly, misinformation in our heads about what makes people what they are.

The following activity is intended to highlight some of your own personal ideas and assumptions about what shapes people's lives.

ACTIVITY 1.1

The following are some types of dangerous or antisocial behaviour which you might encounter, either directly, or in the news. Why do people behave in these ways? Jot down a few thoughts for each:

- two parents spend almost all the family income on heroin, leaving hardly any money for food or clothes for the children
- a woman violently assaults her husband
- a 12-year-old boy gets hold of a gun and goes on a shooting spree at school with the intention of killing as many of his fellow-pupils as he can
- an adult breaks the arm of a toddler in an outburst of rage
- a young man becomes a suicide bomber and kills himself and 20 others in a railway station
- a group of men rob a bank at gunpoint, seriously injuring a bank employee
- an adult deliberately torments a child by threatening him with humiliation and violence
- a man violently assaults his wife
- an elderly woman steals from a shop
- a politician accepts a bribe
- a child sets a cat on fire
- a soldier has himself photographed with his foot on the head of a naked prisoner of war
- an adult sexually abuses a child.

COMMENTS ON ACTIVITY 1.1

If you look at your answers, you may find that they fall into a number of different categories. In some cases, your answer may constitute a moral judgement: 'greed', 'selfishness' and so on. (A lot of people might describe corrupt politicians as greedy, for example, and regard that as sufficient explanation for their behaviour.) In other cases, you may have explained the behaviour in quasi-medical terms, without any moral judgement. (You might describe the boy who goes on a shooting spree as being emotionally disturbed or having some kind of mental illness, or the drug-abusing parents as having their thinking distorted by addiction.) Or, in some cases, you may use past events to account for behaviour. (You may have thought that a child who torments animals has probably been mistreated in some way herself, or that the woman who assaulted her husband may be responding to cruelty or mistreatment on his part.)

(Continued)

(Continued)

In short, in some cases, you will have been inclined to say that there is a reason which accounts for the behaviour and to some extent 'excuses' it, whereas in other cases you will have been more inclined to say that the behaviour is simply 'bad'.

Actually which behaviour we choose to view in purely moral terms, and which behaviour we choose to understand in terms of external or internal causes, is probably quite an arbitrary distinction which is as much to do with our own personal circumstances as anything else. If you are a smoker, or if you use or have used illegal drugs, you may find drug addiction relatively easy to understand. Whether you are a man or a woman may well affect your attitude to several of the behaviours described. Parents are often more understanding than non-parents,of people who injure their children in a rage, because most parents have experienced such rages, even if they have not acted on them.

Most of us are more tolerant of 'crimes of passion' than of premeditated crimes, such as sexually abusing children or accepting bribes. And yet if we have experience of compulsive behaviour of some sort (even if it is only, say, a compulsion to buy cigarettes or play computer games), we may have personal experience that tells us that a person who appears to act coldly and rationally may in fact be driven in some way. A corrupt politician who accepts bribes is greedy, yes, but why are some greedy in that way and others not at all? If it is sufficient explanation to describe the corrupt politician as 'greedy', why is it not sufficient explanation to describe the child who torments animals as simply 'wicked'? Our personal theories and ideas about why people are as they are and behave as they behave, are often quite inconsistent and arbitrary, based on our own experience and on our own needs.

A 'health warning' about theories

Our own personal interests influence the way we see the world. We are more likely to condemn behaviour which we ourselves are not guilty of, and excuse behaviour which we understand from our own personal experience. And this is true not just on an individual level but on a much wider level too.

We use ideas and theories to help us understand what makes us become what we are. But ideas and theories themselves grow and change and are shaped by circumstances. No theory about human beings, whether it is a homespun one we made up ourselves or one that is in a textbook, can be value-free. Things look different depending on our perspective, and on the dominant ideology of the society in which we live. For example Sigmund Freud, who we discuss in the next chapter, is sometimes criticised for basing a theory largely on the neuroses of middle-class Austrian Jewish women at a particular point in history, seen from the perspective of a middle-class Austrian Jewish man.

What is a Theory?

In the text we have used the words 'idea' and 'theory', often together. What is the difference between an idea and a theory? And how exactly do we apply theory to the messy realities of everyday life?

A theory is an organised, coherent set of ideas that offers an explanation for something we observe or experience. In science, a theory can be tested against evidence to see if the explanation it offers is an adequate one. Some theories are easier to test against evidence than others, and all sorts of problems and questions arise. What constitutes evidence? Who is collecting it? What assumptions do they bring with them? How is it collected? What is the context? How is it interpreted?

A theory is useful because it offers a map, a way of making sense of something. But the map is not the same as the territory. Consider the London Underground map, which has helped generations of Londoners and visitors to navigate their way around the capital since it was designed by Harry Beck in 1931. It is a classic of graphic design and clarity, but in order to achieve this it simplifies and distorts the actual geography of London. If one wants to really get to know London, as opposed to passing through it easily, one needs to walk its streets. Theory is a helpful guide and an orientation to the newcomer, but it cannot be mapped directly onto practice. We also need to learn through experience.

In this book we will look at theories which offer explanations of different aspects of human development. Research and thinking in this area is ongoing, especially in neuroscience and genetics, and is moving so fast that we cannot claim to be able to cover all the newest developments. But we will examine classic theories which have proved useful and influential in the past, and encourage you to think critically about what they can teach us today.

All the ideas and theories we are going to discuss in this book contain assumptions which can be challenged. Among the assumptions you will notice and may wish to question, you will find:

- assumptions about the roles of men and women
- assumptions that take heterosexuality as the norm and do not recognise that there are many different ways in which sexuality can be expressed (these can be termed 'heteronormative' assumptions)
- assumptions that North American/European society is somehow the norm for the whole world (these are called 'Eurocentric' assumptions)
- assumptions that ideas derived from the study of prosperous middle-class people are necessarily relevant to people from different backgrounds.

As authors we try to avoid biases of this kind – or at least to acknowledge them – but we are doubtless guilty of them all the same. We offer a male and a female perspective, but we are both white, middle-class, middle-aged and British. (When revising the text for the third edition, we wondered whether one of us, having reached the age of 65, could still really be described as 'middle-aged', but found ourselves reluctant to change the wording because of the assumptions we perceive as being attached to words like 'old' or 'elderly', which might make us less likely to be taken seriously.)

Many ideas have been widely accepted in the past, which we now would regard as obviously untrue. For instance, well into the twentieth century, there was a wide consensus among men in Britain, America and many other countries that women should not be allowed to choose the government of their own country. Sexism is still with us in many forms, of course, but there are very few people in any of those countries now who would seriously argue that women should not have the vote. Yet, less than a century ago, this was seen by many as a perfectly sensible and reasonable position to take.

An idea can become generally accepted and even regarded as 'common sense', when it suits vested interests in society to accept that idea as 'true':

> Each society has its regime of truth, its 'general politics' of truth: that is, the types of discourse which it accepts and makes function as true; the mechanisms and instances which enable one to distinguish true and false statements ... the status of those who are charged with saying what counts as true. (Foucault, 1980: 131)

It is naïve to think that, while everything people thought in the past was mistaken, what we think now is simply 'the unvarnished truth', for doubtless many of the things we think of today as being self-evidently true will also seem quite obviously untrue from a future perspective. And even at a single point in time, there is not one generally accepted truth, but many different ones. What seems self-evident in one cultural context does not necessarily seem so in another. *Any* idea serves a purpose and we should always consider what that purpose might be – and whose purpose it is. This applies to ordinary and everyday ideas, including your own, as well as to the more systematic organisation of ideas that we call a theory, and to the big ideological systems which constitute political, religious or moral philosophies.

The so-called 'nature or nurture' question, which we will now consider, demonstrates very well how ideas can be used to serve such purposes – and it provides some examples of how different ideas have been used for political ends, as well as of how ideas may be used by individuals on a day-to-day basis to justify their own position.

Nature and Nurture

What determines who we are and what we become? Biological inheritance ('nature')? Or the environment we grow up in ('nurture')? As soon as we begin to think about this question, it becomes obvious that it is a crudely oversimplified one, and we cannot answer it by coming down either on one side or the other. But there is a long-running argument about the relative importance of inheritance and environment. As well as being a philosophical and scientific question since classical times, this is also a *highly* political question. 'Nature' or 'nurture' theories can both be used by vested interests – at the level of society at large and at the individual level – to justify their position or their actions.

But before we go on, here is an exercise to explore where you yourself stand on the nature–nurture question.

ACTIVITY 1.2

At the beginning of this chapter we described the birth of a (fictional) child, and wondered what kind of person she would become: prime minister or office cleaner?

1. Suppose her parents were Mr and Mrs Smith. One was an office cleaner, and the other was long-term unemployed. Neither has any educational qualifications. What does that make you think about her chances of becoming prime minister?
2. Suppose her parents were Mr and Mrs Jones. Both came from distinguished, wealthy families. One is a world-famous economist, the other a TV personality. How likely is it that she will become an office cleaner?
3. Suppose her parents were Mr and Mrs Smith, but both died in a tragic accident straight after her birth – and she was then adopted and brought up as their own by Mr and Mrs Jones. How do you see her future prospects?

COMMENTS ON ACTIVITY 1.2

You will probably agree that – at least in the world as it now exists – the child of Mr and Mrs Smith is likely, on average, to have rather more modest career prospects than the child of Mr and Mrs Jones. There are many exceptions of course but, by and large, successful people are the children of other successful people, while poor people are the children of other poor people. But why is this? Is it because successful people are born with above-average abilities – and pass these abilities on to their children through their genes? (That would be a 'nature' theory.) Or is it just because successful people are able to provide their children with a better education, a more stimulating environment, better contacts and so on? (That would be a 'nurture' theory.)

Where you stand on these questions will be indicated by your answer to question 3. Do you think that the child of Mr and Mrs Smith, if adopted by Mr and Mrs Jones, will perform just as well, in terms of career achievements, as a natural child of Mr and Mrs Jones would do? (If so, you take a 'nurture' view on the question of career success: you think it's mainly about upbringing and social circumstances.) Or do you think that the child of Mr and Mrs Smith, even if exposed to all the advantages that Mr and Mrs Jones can offer, will still probably not be a high-flyer, because it is likely that her natural parents were not of especially high ability and she is likely to have inherited their abilities? (If so, you lean towards a 'nature' view on this question: you think it's mainly about genes.)

Of course career success is only one of a vast number of things that distinguish one person from another. Some of the differences between us are quite obviously the products of genetic inheritance, while others are undoubtedly the products of environment. Few would dispute that hair colour is the result of genetic inheritance, or that the ability to speak Slovenian is a product of environment. No one is born with the ability to speak Slovenian. The ability is acquired either by growing up in a Slovenian-speaking environment, or by being taught Slovenian by someone else who speaks it. On the other hand, the ability to acquire language as such *would* seem to be the product of genetic inheritance, since no other species is known to be able to acquire language, whatever the environment. (Although some chimpanzees have been trained to use a relatively small vocabulary, they do not acquire language in the human sense.)

But when we come to discuss things such as personality traits, moral character, intelligence and abilities, then the argument becomes more difficult – and often more heated.

The 'nature' viewpoint

Although few of us have any difficulty with the idea that our genetic inheritance determines our basic physical characteristics, to many it seems far-fetched – and perhaps also distasteful – to think of genes determining our personality and behaviour as well. There are, however, countless examples in the animal kingdom of very complex and specific behaviours which are inherited rather than learnt. Spiders build intricate webs without being taught. Cuckoos, which are not even raised by their own parents, still know how to lay their eggs in the nests of other birds, just as their parents did. It seems clear that at least some behaviour patterns are encoded in the genes just as are physical characteristics, which means that, like physical characteristics, they will have evolved over time through the process of natural selection.

Studies of twins are one way in which researchers have explored the influence of genetic inheritance on personality and other individual characteristics. There are two kinds of twins. So-called 'fraternal' twins are conceived at about the same time and grow together in their mother's womb, but are no more closely related than any other pair of siblings (that is to say that they share, on average, about 50 per cent of the same genes). Fraternal twins do not necessarily look alike and may not be of the same gender. 'Identical' twins, on the other hand, result when a single fertilised egg divides and the two resulting parts start growing into separate individuals. Such twins are not always *absolutely* identical because environmental factors – in the womb, at birth, or subsequently – may result in some differences. But they certainly look very alike – and they are *genetically* identical: they both have exactly the same set of genes.

Occasionally it happens that identical twins are separated at birth and this event allows scientists to look in reality at the kinds of questions that you considered hypothetically in

Activity 1.2. Is it the genetic parents, or the environment and the adults who actually *raise* a child, who have the most powerful influence on the child's development? It is also possible to compare fraternal twins with identical twins.

Twin studies have shown that there are often surprising similarities between the lives, preferences, careers, and so on, of twins who have been separated. Oskar and Jack were twins raised respectively as a Nazi in Czechoslovakia and a Jew in Trinidad, yet when they finally met as middle-aged men, both wore the same kind of shirt, and both had the same odd habit of flushing the toilet before and after using it (Steen, 1996: 25). Recent research has tended to conclude that inheritance is the major factor in intelligence. The Minnesota Study of Twins Reared Apart concluded that variations in intelligence are 70 per cent related to inheritance, and only 30 per cent to all the environmental factors such as family circumstances, schooling, nutrition, and so on (Bouchard et al., 1990).

But there is a whole range of methodological difficulties with such studies, which should make us cautious of placing too much weight on such precise conclusions (Steen, 1996: 26–32). Even extraordinary stories, such as that of Oskar and Jack just mentioned, should be treated with caution. Naturally people are amazed when they notice similarities like this and want to tell the tale, just as we all do when we encounter coincidences. We do not get to hear of instances where there are no such similarities, just as we do not tell the tale of the countless occasions in our lives when coincidences do not occur.

There can be no doubt that genetics play an important role in making us who we are. But exactly how important a role this is continues to be a subject of debate. There have been claims in recent years, for example, that genetic causes have been identified for schizophrenia or autism, both of which have also been said to have been caused by childhood upbringing. It has even been suggested that a 'gay gene', making it more likely that a person will become homosexual, has been identified (see Steen, 1996: 185 ff). Recent research in genetics is bringing new insights to the nature–nurture debate. The Human Genome Project, completed in 2003, mapped and sequenced all the genes of human beings for the first time, and as this material became available to researchers it opened the door to new understandings of the causes of human diseases, conditions and behaviour. However, the science of genetics is extremely complex, and when new findings are reported in the popular press to a non-scientific public they are often over-simplified.

'Nature' ideas in everyday life

In common parlance the idea of the importance of inheritance is encapsulated in phrases such as 'blood will out', 'the apple doesn't fall far from the tree' and 'the leopard can't change its spots'. The following exercise illustrates how 'nature' theories about human behaviour can crop up in a very direct way.

ACTIVITY 1.3

MATTHEW

You're a school teacher visiting a lone-parent family, to discuss the problem of the son's poor attendance at school, and his poor work when he is there. The boy – Matthew, aged 13 – is getting in increasing trouble with the law as well as missing most of his schooling and he is staying out at nights. Matthew's father left the family home when Matthew was just a year old, and now has no contact with him at all.

Matthew's mother says his father was violent towards her and constantly in trouble with the police. She says, 'Matthew takes after his father. There's nothing I can do about it.'

What is your reaction to this comment?

COMMENTS ON ACTIVITY 1.3

Matthew's behaviour may be similar to his father's in some respects, but, as you may have observed, this doesn't necessarily mean that this is some sort of unavoidable fate carried in the genes. There are all kinds of environmental reasons why Matthew might behave in the same sorts of ways as his father. For example, both Matthew and his father may have grown up in a community where there was a strong cultural expectation for boys to be tough and 'hard' and where a low value was placed on schooling. There may be a long family history of fathers abandoning their families and for sons feeling hurt and angry as a result, so that they find it difficult in turn to stay in a stable family relationship when they grow up. You may well have thought of other reasons.

But one can see how it may be easier for Matthew's mother to take a 'nature' view of this by blaming his problems on his father's genes than to face her own part in causing them. Her anger with Matthew's father is being transferred onto his (and her) son as he grows up and reminds her more and more of his father. This makes it difficult for her to engage constructively with the problems that he is facing.

'Nature' ideas in the political arena

A 'nature' viewpoint can result in a rather fatalistic attitude – 'That's the way things are and there's nothing we can do about it!' – and it can have the attraction that it lets people off the hook. We suggested earlier that it's important to think carefully about why ideas become current and whose purposes they serve. You can see that 'nature' theories can be attractive not only to people like Matthew's mother in the above activity, but also to those in positions of privilege and power, because they can be used to argue that the status quo is inevitable. They seem to justify inequality and it is no accident that 'nature' ideas tend to be more popular with the political right. For example, the word 'aristocracy' comes from the Greek and means the 'rule of the good'. The concept of an aristocracy was based on the idea that the upper class enjoyed more privileges and power because they were *innately superior* to other people. Racist theories are also 'nature' theories, as are ideas that women are innately inferior to men (or vice versa). And if those in positions of power can tell themselves that the poor are poor because they are 'by nature' incapable of earning a good living, or that criminals are criminals because they have criminal genes, then they can feel that they are absolved of responsibility.

But this is not to say that 'nature' theories have no validity. It can hardly be disputed that many of our characteristics are inherited: and there is certainly good evidence that genetics plays an important role in intelligence, personality and predisposition to some mental illnesses as well as to physical ones. Nor is it right to say that 'nurture' theories are necessarily less oppressive, as we will see below.

The 'nurture' viewpoint

The word 'nurture' refers in particular to the care received by a child from her parents. Nurture in this sense is one important part of the environment in which human growth takes place and few would argue that nurture in this sense does not make a difference to the kind of person we become. But when we speak of 'nurture' in the context of the nature–nurture debate, we are talking more generally about *any* kind of environmental influence, which may include anything from events before, during and after birth, to factors as diverse as cultural expectations, nutrition, education, political circumstances and so on. In short, for the purposes of this discussion, the word 'nurture' will cover all the factors other than biological inheritance which might make a difference to who we are and what we become.

In Chapter 5 we will look at the ideas of *behaviourists* (or 'learning theorists'), starting with Pavlov and his famous dogs. As we will see, this strand within psychology accumulated impressive evidence that the environment shapes behaviour according to certain predictable rules.

Marxism, hugely influential on the history of the twentieth century, sees human thought and consciousness as being shaped by the society in which it took place. In particular, Karl Marx proposed that societies, including the roles that people play in them, their beliefs and their value systems, are the product of *economic* forces. The 'means of production' – the way that the economy is organised – was the determining factor, so that a certain set of values, ideas and behaviours would prevail in, say, feudal society, and another set in capitalist society:

> Consciousness is, therefore, from the very beginning a social product, and remains so as long as men exist at all. (Marx, 1986 [1845]: 176)

You will find similar assertions in the writings of many who look at human life from a sociological perspective (see Chapter 10), whether they are inside or outside the Marxist tradition.

In the next chapter we will look at psychodynamic theories, originating with the ideas of Sigmund Freud. In some respects, Freud's ideas could also be described as 'nurture' theories, both in the wide and the narrow sense of the word 'nurture'. They place a great deal of emphasis on early childhood experience, including very basic things like toilet training, as a determining factor on how human beings grow and develop (although Freud also placed a huge emphasis on instinctive drives which he saw as biological, inherited and present from birth).

'Nurture' theories in everyday life

Just as you find 'nature' theories not only in academic texts, but also in everyday life, so also do you find 'nurture' theories. The following activity gives one example:

ACTIVITY 1.4

LIZ

You are a probation officer and you are meeting a new client, Liz, aged 19, to talk to her about a pre-sentence report which you've been asked to write (in which you will comment on the reasons for her offending and the likelihood of her offending again). Liz is charged with a series of violent assaults, using knives and other weapons, on other young women.

When you ask Liz about the reasons for her offending, she shrugs:

> I can't help myself. I just see red and then my mind goes a blank. I was beaten myself as a child, you see. My dad used to beat me and then my stepdad. My mum pretended she didn't know it was going on. I was taken into care when I was 6 and my stepdad was sent to jail for assaulting me, but my mum got back together with him again when he came out. So I suppose that was it. It's just what was put into my head when I was a child and I can't help it.

What might your response be to Liz and what could you put in your report?

COMMENTS ON ACTIVITY 1.4

It may have struck you that if Liz doesn't take some more responsibility for her own actions, she is going to have difficulty persuading a court to be lenient with her. More seriously, she is going to have difficulty in changing her behaviour or progressing with her life if she doesn't see herself as having any kind of control over it.

There can be little doubt that violent and unhappy relationships in childhood can predispose people to crime and other deviant behaviour in adult life (in Chapter 3, we will consider some reasons why this is), so Liz is not wrong in seeing her childhood abuse as a major contributing factor in her present problems. But in the long run it is not going to help her if she insists on seeing her problems in such a fatalistic way, even though in the short run it may seem easier to 'let herself off the hook' by blaming her unhappy childhood.

('Nurture' as well as 'nature' can be used to let ourselves off the hook, particularly for those, like Liz, who are genuinely the victims of mistreatment.)

But you could also argue that if it is possible to learn violent behaviour, then it must also be possible to learn another way of acting!

You could even argue that Liz's fatalism is in itself a learnt behaviour, which could likewise be unlearnt. (See the discussion on 'Learnt Helplessness' in Chapter 5.)

'Nurture' ideas in the political arena

Historically, 'nature' theories have been used as the rationale for oppression of various kinds, as we've noted above, and they tend to be associated with the political right. The idea that human beings are shaped by their environment, on the other hand, has always been attractive to the political left, which sees the poor as being poor not because of their innate qualities, but because they have not been given access to the advantages enjoyed by the rich.

However, the idea that human beings are entirely the product of their environment has also been used in extremely oppressive ways by the political left. The infamous Pol Pot regime in Cambodia in 1975, for example, justified the horrors of its notorious Year Zero, with its death toll of around 2 million, with the idea that it was possible to change people by totally wiping out the influence of the past, and those individuals seen as responsible for transmitting that influence, and retraining an entire population to start again.

Much closer to home, parents of schizophrenia sufferers, or of children with autism, might well complain about 'nurture' theories, fashionable in the 1960s and 1970s, that blamed them for their children's problems. For instance, it was suggested that parents could make their children schizophrenic by putting them in 'double binds', giving them contradictory messages (Bateson, 1973: 201 ff). From the perspective of a parent, such theories must feel much more oppressive than theories which propose a genetic origin for these problems.

Beyond nature and nurture

It is too simplistic to reduce the various factors that make people what they are to 'nature' and 'nurture', and no one would seriously suggest that it is all one or all the other. In reality a whole range of different factors contributes to making us what we are, some of which could be described as nature, some as nurture, and some of which could be assigned to either category. It is more helpful to see nature and nurture as acting together, 'nature via nurture' (Ridley, 2004). Recent research in genetics and neuroscience shows us in increasing detail how this happens, and more is constantly being discovered. Rather than seeing genes as a blueprint, we need to understand them differently:

> Genes are cogs in the machine, not gods in the sky. Switched on and off through life, by external as well as internal events, their job is to absorb information from the environment at least as often as to transmit it from the past. Genes do more than carry information; they respond to experience. (Ridley, 2004: 229)

In Chapter 3, when we look at attachment, we will see how neuroscience is helping us to understand how brain development is critically affected by the kind of nurture a child receives in the early years. And it is not just in the early years that environmental influences can shape the brain. Research into neuroplasticity (the ability of the brain to change) is showing that brain development can continue throughout life. For example, scans of musicians' brains show that clear differences emerge with time and practice compared to the brains of non-musicians. For string players, the area controlling the left hand expands significantly, and in trumpeters the neurons that respond to 'brassy' sounds enlarge (Elbert et al., 1995; Pantev et al., 2001, cited in Doidge, 2007: 289).

So a complex interplay between inherited and environmental factors is at work. Some of these factors are:

- genetic inheritance
- other physical factors such as nutrition, health, physical injury, not only after birth, but from conception onwards – for example, a baby's growth may be inhibited if a mother drinks or smokes during pregnancy, and serious brain damage can be caused by complications during the birth itself
- upbringing, early relationships, position in the family (older children have a different experience from middle and youngest children, for example), traumatic and/or positive experiences
- cultural factors – nationality, social class, geography (whether one grows up in the country or a town, for example), ethnic background, time in history
- random life events (car accidents, lottery wins, chance meetings …).

One could think of many more. But the important thing to note here is how all these factors interact with one another. What sex we are, for example, *is* a matter of genetic inheritance and it has (of course) many purely physical implications: women can give birth and breastfeed, men can't; boys are more likely to suffer from certain inherited conditions (haemophilia, colour-blindness); men and women have different hormones in their bloodstream – and so on. But the way in which the sexes are viewed, the expectations of them, the roles and behaviour which are considered appropriate and inappropriate, will depend on cultural factors. (There is a further discussion on gender roles in Chapter 5.)

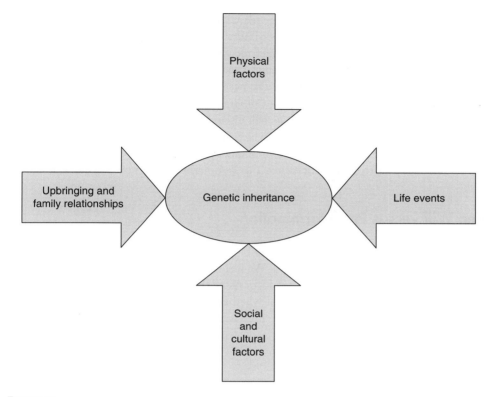

FIGURE 1.1

To give another example: physical appearance might seem a purely inherited feature at first glance, but in fact a whole range of environmental factors can affect physical appearance. In rare cases a child's physical growth can be affected not only by malnutrition but by emotional abuse and rejection ('psychosocial short stature': see Iwaniec, 2004: 52). And the *significance* attached to physical appearance will depend very much on culture, as can be seen from the fact that plumpness and white skin have been regarded as beautiful and desirable in some societies at some stages in European history, while thinness and sun-tanned skin have been the ideal at others.

Existential questions

We would suggest too that, in addition to the interacting influences of nature and nurture, our thoughts and beliefs are shaped by the fact that life poses certain unavoidable questions – 'existential' questions – which would be faced by any thinking being, even, hypothetically, an alien from another planet or a sentient machine (for a fictional example of the latter, see Beckett, 2010).

For example, there is the fact of *death* (see Chapter 12). Our lives are finite. Even for an extraterrestrial alien or a robot, the possibility of non-existence would be an inevitable corollary of existence. And there is the fact too of *individuality*. The fact that we exist as individuals means that there are other things in existence which are separate from us. So, as well as being limited in time, our lives are also necessarily located in space. (The way that we come to terms with the concept of 'self' and 'others' is something that is of particular interest to the object relations theorists whom we will discuss in the next chapter and in Chapter 3, and to theories of cognitive development, which are the subject of Chapter 4.)

Another existential aspect of being a conscious being, and not merely an automaton, is that we feel ourselves to be making *choices*. This is something we'll now discuss further.

Free Will versus Predetermination

As human beings, we don't feel ourselves to be passive passengers of bodies which simply respond to our genes or our environment. We feel as if we are constantly making decisions, and often difficult and painful ones. As old, or older, than the nature–nurture question, and even more fundamental is the question of whether or not we have free will. Here it is, for instance, in Chaucer's *Canterbury Tales*, written in the fourteenth century:

> But I kan nat bulte it to the bren …
>
> Whether that Goddes worthy forwiting
>
> Streyneth me nedeley for to doon a thyng …
>
> Or elles, if free choys be graunted me
>
> To do that same thyng, or do it noght. (Crawley (ed.), 1992: 470)
>
> (Rough translation: 'But I can't sift the grain from the chaff … [as to] whether God's worthy foreknowledge constrains me necessarily to do a thing … or else, if free choice is granted me to do that same thing or not do it.')

All the writers we have quoted so far in this chapter assume that there are causes for human behaviour, whether those causes are genetic or otherwise. Yet most of us also believe that there is such a thing as choice and personal responsibility. The French existentialist Jean-Paul Sartre wrote: 'I am condemned to be free … we are not free to cease being free' (2001 [1943]: 184). When people like Liz (in Activity 1.4) blame their behaviour on external factors outside their control, Sartre would say that they were acting in 'bad faith' by denying the existence of their own capacity to choose. Most of the world's religions see human beings as making choices between good and evil and ultimately taking the consequences of those choices.

Here is one more activity, based on a real-life case, for you to consider where you stand on this issue:

ACTIVITY 1.5

In England in 1993, Jon Venables and Robert Thompson, then both aged 10, were found guilty of the murder of a toddler, James Bulger, whom they had picked up in a shopping mall, taken to a railway line and beaten to death by hitting him with bricks. Many have said that these boys committed this appalling act because they were 'evil', while others have suggested that there must have been distressing events in their previous childhood that caused them to act in this way. What is your own view about why they might have done this and how they should be seen?

COMMENTS ON ACTIVITY 1.5

If you incline to the view that these boys were indeed evil (and few would dispute that evil is an appropriate word for what they did), you need to ask yourself precisely what you mean by that. Are you saying that they were born with a propensity to do bad things (a nature theory) and, if so, how can they be blamed for what they did any more than a person born blind can be blamed for not being able to see?

Or are you saying that we all make choices between good and evil, and these boys chose evil of their own free will? If so, we'd have to ask you whether, at 10 years old, you were ever tempted to kidnap and murder a small child, and had to resist that temptation? If not, clearly this was not just a matter of choice.

Or are you saying that these boys became evil as a result of something in their upbringing? If so, you are really agreeing with those who say the act must have been the result of environmental factors (a nurture theory). The obvious question then is why do other children, from similar or worse environments, not commit such crimes? One answer might be that no two environments are exactly alike and we can never know all the subtle influences that might tip a person one way or the other. Another might be that no two individuals are born exactly alike, so the environment never affects any two people in exactly the same way.

Clearly, whether we believe in free will or not can have huge implications for how we act and how we view other people. In fact, as we noted earlier, people tend to make moral judgements in some cases and look for causes in others – and don't necessarily do so in a very consistent way. But we are not here going to attempt any sort of resolution of this question that has troubled great thinkers for several millennia, beyond offering a pragmatic compromise.

We don't wish to dissuade anyone from believing that they make real choices in their lives. We also believe that the idea of personal responsibility is necessary for society to function. But if you look at the things that you think of as free choices, and consider why other people make different choices from yours, it is hard to avoid noticing that there is a pattern.

As we've discussed, evidence exists that people with the same genes are more likely to make the same choices. We also know that people can be trained to act differently by rewarding or punishing different behaviours – and that people with the same childhood experiences often have the same kinds of problems in later life.

Ridley (2004), citing the work of neuroscientist Walter Freeman (1999), proposes that 'free will is entirely compatible with a brain exquisitely prespecified by, and run by, genes'. By moving away from a linear view of cause and effect and taking account of how feedback influences behaviour from moment to moment it is possible to begin to see how this apparently contradictory statement could make sense. There is evidence that genes behave in this circular way, being switched on and off by events in the external world, and by each other (Ridley, 2004: 275).

We may not be automatons, but we are *shaped*, if not controlled, by our history and by the world around us. We suggest that this requires us to try not to judge other people in a moral sense, and to try to understand the reasons why people act as they do. And yet at the same time we cannot function without taking some responsibility for our own actions, and expecting others to take responsibility for theirs.

Events, Transitions, Resilience

It can be an interesting exercise to draw a line representing the course of your own life, marking on it what you see as the high and low points, the times of rapid personal change and the times of stability. You will probably find that most of the turning points you notice will be related to *events* of different kinds: births, deaths, moves, the beginnings and endings of relationships, leaving school, changes of job, retirement, accidents, windfalls … Some of these events might seem to you to have been freely chosen (you choose to get married, to change your job, to go to college). Some of them may have been unexpected (a lottery win, a bereavement, an unplanned pregnancy). Some of them may have been outside of your control, but nevertheless expected (going to secondary school, leaving school, becoming an adult, growing old). Some of them may have been expected but not inevitable (you become a parent, you enter the world of work, you get a home of your own). Human growth and change can be understood as a complex interlocking web of such events, some of which we choose, and some of which we have to adjust to whether we like them or not. We have to change within ourselves in order to get to places that we want to reach, or even just to cope with the places in which we find ourselves.

In this book we will often come back to this theme, when we discuss the transitions which life requires us to make (becoming an adult, growing old …) and the challenges which life faces us with (bereavement, the birth of a child, disability …). One interesting question is how it is that people cope so differently with these things. Some are ground down by adversity, and find even small changes difficult to handle. Some seem to be much more resilient, manage change much better, and move on much more easily from painful experiences. Resilience too, a big question in the study of human growth, is another topic we will be coming back to later in Chapter 6.

Chapter Summary

- The chapter began with an account of the birth of a child and looked at some ideas about what will shape her as she grows and develops. But ideas themselves are not fixed, so we began by giving a warning about ideas and theories. They are not neutral. People use them for their own ends.
- In particular, we looked at the debate about the extent to which our identity is determined by our genes and by environmental factors (the 'nature and nurture' debate). We looked at the way this debate has very practical implications, both in daily life and in politics, and we proposed that we need to see human growth as being the product of a number of interacting factors, of which genetic inheritance is one.
- We considered another very ancient subject of debate – between free will and predetermination – and looked at the issues this raises.
- Finally, we discussed the way our growth and development over our lives is marked by a series of events, some chosen, some not, some expected, some completely unexpected, some welcome, some not welcome at all. We looked at the transitions that we have to go through in the course of a lifespan, and at the fact that some people are much better at coping with changes than others: some are more resilient.

In the next chapter, we will look at the ideas of Freud, who saw human personality developing as the result of our having to try to strike a balance, from the moment of birth onwards, between instinctive drives, the external environment and previous learning.

Further Reading

Doidge, Norman (2007) *The Brain That Changes Itself.* London: Penguin.

Ridley, Matt (2004) *Nature via Nurture: Genes, Experience and What Makes Us Human.* London: Harper Perennial.

And for a brief overview of recent developments in genetic research and their implications for child development policy and practice, see National Scientific Council on the Developing Child (2010) Working paper 10: Early experiences can alter gene expression and affect long-term development. Accessed online Oct 2015 at http://developingchild. harvard.edu/resources/reports_and_working_papers/working_papers/wp10

2 THE BALANCING ACT

PSYCHODYNAMIC INSIGHTS

● The unconscious   22
● The structure of personality   24
● Psychosexual stages   29
● Developments of Freud's ideas   33
● Object relations and ego development   34
● Criticisms of Freud and his successors   41

In the last chapter we discussed various factors – some innate, some environmental – that might play a part in human development. We want to look now at a view of the human mind that sees human development as the product of a dynamic process incorporating both innate and environmental forces. From this psychodynamic viewpoint, we are shaped by our experience as infants as we seek to get our basic needs met when we are completely dependent for survival on our carers. Through these earliest experiences, we begin to learn about the world outside ourselves and how it meets, or doesn't meet, our urgently felt innate needs. We develop psychological strategies, both conscious and unconscious, to deal with situations in which our needs go unmet – a lifelong balancing act between our inner world and the world outside. Strategies adopted in childhood are carried into adult life, where they may sometimes be maladaptive, and cause problems for the individual concerned, unless she can get help in unravelling the patterns laid down in the past.

Although this theoretical model has been developed, modified and expanded in many different directions, and although it had historical antecedents, Sigmund Freud is certainly its most well-known exponent. Freud, who was born in Austria in 1856 and died in London in 1939, remains a controversial figure. Like Marx and Darwin, he played a pivotal role in the history of ideas, changing the way in which we see the world, and the terms on which we debate fundamental issues. Many criticisms can be levelled against him – and we will discuss some of them later – but he has left an important legacy which we now almost take for granted. Many of his ideas, in fact, have entered the language and we use them without thinking about their origin. In particular, the Freudian tradition has offered the possibility of new insights into the way that apparently irrational things – madness, dreams, obsessions, jokes, slips of the tongue – have a kind of deep logic of their own, rooted in the fears and longings of childhood and, even before that, in our biological origins. It has also given us a way of understanding how family relationships in childhood lay down a template for our later functioning as adults.

Many people approach Freud's ideas with some fairly strong preconceptions. Even if you don't think you know much about his ideas, you will probably react to his name and the term 'Freudian' with some thoughts, feelings and associations and you may find it useful to be aware of these as your own starting point.

Sex is often the first thing that comes to mind when Freud's name is mentioned; people will say that 'he was obsessed with sex', 'he thinks everything is to do with sex'. You could argue that one of the legacies of Freud was to make sex something of an obsession in modern society. Whether that is really a legacy of Freud, or whether it owes more to broader social and economic forces, is of course another question – and a big one. What we will see, though, is that Freud's use of the term 'sexual' was fairly broad.

You may also be aware of the therapeutic technique known as psychoanalysis which Freud developed, which has spawned a thousand cartoons featuring couches and Freud lookalikes with pencils and pads. Certainly, a lot has been written about the efficacy or otherwise of psychoanalysis and its potential for abuse. We will not be covering this in any detail here, because this is a book about psychosocial development and not about therapeutic techniques. But it does rightly form a large part of most people's image of what Freud was 'all about'.

You have probably also come across the idea of 'the unconscious' as a driving force within us but outside our control which underlies the aspects of our behaviour that seem to defy rational explanation. Freud described the aim of psychoanalysis as to make the unconscious conscious, and his theories about how the unconscious worked were developed through his experience of the practice of psychoanalysis, and the case histories he recorded.

And you may be aware of doubts about Freud's claim to be offering a genuinely scientific or objective theory, or concerns about Freud's attitudes and assumptions (particularly towards women) or about whether his ideas can be generalised in the way that he did generalise them. These are important questions which will be discussed later in this chapter.

Many people also find some of the language in which Freud's ideas are expressed rather off-putting, or even at times a bit absurd, though many of them have passed into everyday speech ('penis envy', 'phallic symbol', 'anal personality'). It is important to try to look behind the language and the sometimes startling imagery and try to get some sense of the underlying ideas.

We will now attempt to sketch out some of the main themes in Freudian thinking, with the warning that this is necessarily a very partial account of a rich and complicated set of ideas which Freud himself changed and developed repeatedly during his lifetime, and which has been developed further in many different ways since his death.

The Unconscious

Freud didn't begin his professional career in psychiatry but in the field of pathological medicine and neurology. At the age of 29, while working in Paris with a French physician called Charcot, he encountered the treatment of 'hysteria' using hypnosis. At that time 'hysteria' was a term used to refer to physical symptoms which had no apparent physical cause. Freud was impressed by the fact that observable physical symptoms could be caused not only by infection or by injury, but simply by distressing *ideas* in a patient's mind. And he was impressed by the fact that unconscious thoughts could be accessed and patients apparently treated by talking to them under hypnosis to neutralise these powerful ideas.

When being treated by hypnosis, the patient listens while the doctor talks. Freud turned this on its head by developing a form of therapy in which the patient talks while the therapist listens. In other words he moved on to what a patient of his early collaborator, Josef Breuer, described as 'the talking cure' (Freud and Breuer, 1955 [1895]: 30). This is now the basis of the practice of many helping professionals who would not regard themselves in any way as Freudians. He then developed this further into a technique which encouraged the patient to 'free associate' in order to allow exploration not only of the patient's conscious thoughts, but of connections of which the patient herself may not be consciously aware.

Free Association

In free association, the patient is asked to respond to a word or an idea with the first thing that comes into her head, without thinking about it and without holding anything back. It's a bit like the parlour game 'elbow tennis' except that the patient is not required to demonstrate a connection between one word and the next. On the contrary, the technique is based on the assumption that there will always *be* some link, though the patient may not be aware of it.

When one of the authors was giving a lecture on this subject one Christmas, he tried hard to think of two completely unrelated words and came up with 'tangerine' and 'anger'. Later he realised that there *was* a Christmas-linked connection for him between these words. He does not like tangerines but his parents always put one in the very toe of his Christmas stocking. After the unwanted and unexciting tangerine, there were no more presents.

Another more obvious connection has since been pointed out to us: that the word 'anger' is actually embedded in the word 'tangerine'. And this is a good example of the kind of punning word play that Freud saw, along with 'slips' and jokes, as a clue to unconscious meaning. He believed that, by exploring the links that our minds make without us being consciously aware of it, we obtain glimpses of the contents of the unconscious.

As a result of his explorations, Freud became convinced that his patients' neurotic problems were rooted in traumatic events in infancy, and that these events were basically sexual. Again and again they seemed to be telling him that their fathers had sexually assaulted them.

He came to the conclusion that most psychological problems in adulthood were caused by what we would now call sexual abuse in childhood. This theory is known – rather inappropriately – as the *seduction theory*.

When Freud presented this theory to a distinguished scientific audience in 1896, it met with a chilly reception, and he found himself ostracised and professionally isolated. His views later changed, as they did about many aspects of his theory, in the light of further work with patients and of the analysis of himself which he carried out. He recognised his own sexual fantasies about his father and his daughter, but knew that these were not related to actual abuse (Gay, 1988: 93–4). This led him to reject the view that all 'hysteria' was caused by sexual abuse, and to explain it more in terms of the fantasies arising from unconscious wishes and desires, and the view that sexual feelings are present and active from the earliest infancy. From the last part of the twentieth century, as the prevalence of sexual abuse has become more widely recognised, Freud has been criticised for changing his mind over the reality of the events described by his patients, most notably by Masson (2003), as will be discussed later.

Suppressed desires

As a result of changing his mind over the seduction theory, Freud moved on from his original perspective that 'hysterics' suffered mainly from reminiscences, to the idea that the primary problem was not so much memories – or suppressed memories – as suppressed *desires*. His view was that we have all kinds of desires, not all of which can actually be met, and some of which we cannot even safely admit even to ourselves. Desires which we are aware of but which we don't allow ourselves to act upon we *suppress*. Other desires we *repress*, which means that we push them right out of our conscious mind altogether.

But Freud believed that unconscious desires could not be completely contained. It is as if we were to put the lid on a pan of boiling water, so that we can no longer see its contents. We may have put the lid on the pan but we are nevertheless made aware, in various ways, of the heat and pressure inside. The contents of the unconscious, Freud thought, emerged in disguise in various ways: in jokes, in slips of the tongue (the famous 'Freudian slip') and in dreams. The technique of 'free association' is supposed to provide a means of tapping into them.

It was certainly not a new idea of Freud's that we are not always aware of all the contents of our mind. If you reflect on this for a moment you will see that this is actually self-evident. We are not always thinking about everything that is in our memory. If someone mentions your last summer holiday, it is probable that, until they mentioned it, it was not in your thoughts at all. At times we may even be unable to retrieve something from our memory and into consciousness, even though we know quite well that it is there. 'It's on the tip of my tongue', as we say.

But such memories are like library books which are not currently being read, and which may occasionally be hard to find if we can't remember what subject they were filed under. In Freudian terminology these things are *preconscious*, rather than unconscious. Freud's conception of the *unconscious* was much more dynamic than this. He saw the unconscious not as a kind of static library or storehouse but as a powerful, active player in the dynamic system that was the human mind. It was a source of energy, and it contained things which were in some sense dangerous. Desires, unlike memories, have urgency about them. And the unconscious is timeless – it does not distinguish between past and present.

The Structure of Personality

Freud moved on again from being primarily interested in the distinction between conscious and unconscious, to making a new distinction between parts of the mind known in English as the *ego* and the *id*. (Freud's translators used these rather technical-sounding Latin terms for the everyday German words 'ich' (I) and 'es' (it) which Freud himself used.) In this new model, the *id* – or 'it' – contains the instincts: the inherited part of ourselves, our basic biological drives, and it operates on the *pleasure principle*. It is:

> a cauldron full of seething excitations … It is filled with energy … but … has no organisation … only a striving to bring about the satisfaction of instinctual needs subject to the observance of the pleasure principle … (Freud, 1964 [1933]: 73)

The *ego*, or 'I', is a part of ourselves that develops from the id as a result of experience, and is the part of ourselves where conscious thought takes place.

> …The ego is that part of the id which has been modified by the direct influence of the external world…The ego represents what may be called reason and common sense, in contrast to the id, which contains the passions… in its relation to the id it is like a man on horseback, who has to hold in check the superior strength of the horse… (Freud (1961 [1923]: 25)

According to Freud, the ego operates on the *reality principle*. It deals not only with the powerful instinctual demands arising from the id, but also with the demands of the external world, and with what it has learnt through experience. One of the jobs that the ego does is the job of *repressing* desires which cannot safely be allowed into consciousness. The part of the ego that does this job is necessarily itself unconscious. This meant that Freud's previous model of the mind as being made up of separate layers, of conscious, preconscious and unconscious, could no longer convey the complexity of the relationship he now saw between the conscious and unconscious parts of the mind.

In order to explain how the unconscious part of the ego decided what must be repressed, Freud introduced the idea of the *superego* ('uber-ich' – over-I – in German). The *superego* is a kind of 'deposit' left behind in our minds from our childhood relationship with our parents and others who were in charge of us. It contains rules and restrictions which a child would originally have received from adults ('That's naughty', 'You mustn't do that', etc.), but which in due course become internalised. The superego is therefore the seat of conscience and self-criticism. To give a simple example of how this process of internalisation operates: a small child does not think to wash her hands after using the toilet. She has to be told to do so, and starts to do so in order to conform to adult wishes. By the time we are adults, however, we wash our hands not to please others, but because it feels uncomfortable not to do so.

To understand more clearly how these different parts of the mind work together, try this activity:

ACTIVITY 2.1

Imagine you see something in a shop that attracts your attention; perhaps an expensive piece of clothing that you think would really suit you, or the latest electronic gadget. You really want to possess it; in that moment it has become the object of your desire. Think about how you might respond to this, and the part the id, ego and superego might play in your response. What might you do if the id dominates? The superego? The ego? What kind of response is most likely for you? If you do this activity with others, you will probably notice a different range of responses.

COMMENTS ON ACTIVITY 2.1

The id will draw you towards instant gratification of your desire without thinking about the consequences. At worst, this could lead you to shoplifting! More likely you will reach for your credit card without thinking about how much you already owe on it, or whether you can afford to spend the money. You will make an 'impulse buy'.

The superego will speak to you in the voices of your parents, and frame your internal debate in moral terms. Perhaps, 'That's far too extravagant. How could you think of spending all that money on yourself?' Or 'That's too showy. You can't go out dressed like that.' Or conversely, 'You deserve it', or 'That's the kind of thing that will convey the right image, the sort of thing that people like us wear/own.'

The ego will be aware of the voices of the id and the superego, and will try to balance them out, and look at the reality of your situation. Do you need it? Would you wear/use it? Can you afford it? Do you have to buy it today or would it be better to go home and think about it, and perhaps do some more research? And so it will help you to make a considered decision.

Returning to the language of nature–nurture: the superego in Freud's model is clearly the product of 'nurture', while the id is the product of 'nature'. The ego has the job of balancing the competing demands of id and superego, and the demands of external reality. So in Freudian terms the ego is the mature, reality-based part of ourselves; very different, and confusingly so, from the way we tend to use the word in everyday language when we describe someone as 'having a big ego', meaning that they have a high opinion of themselves and like to have everything their own way. Freud wrote 'Where id was, there ego shall be' (1964 [1933]: 80). He was talking about the aims of psychoanalysis, but it also describes his view of human development, as the ego emerges over the course of childhood as a force that can control the impulses of the id and temper the demands of the superego.

The shaping of personality

We've seen that in Freud's model, the individual starts with certain basic instinctual needs. The id constantly demands the satisfaction that comes from meeting those needs. The ego has the job of mediating between the demands of the id, the demands of the external world and the demands of powerful others (the parents), who end up being internalised (or *introjected*) as the superego.

A person grows as a distinct and separate personality as the result of her ego performing its own unique balancing act. Each individual ego develops strategies for negotiating the competing pressures upon it and finds ways of resolving dilemmas, which in some cases will mean suppressing inconvenient things from consciousness.

If all goes well, the individual will progress to a stage where she can cope with adult life. But things can go wrong along the line, which may hamper growth. For example, traumatic events may be experienced beyond the capacity of the individual to properly cope with, or needs may go unmet. Difficulties can occur in any number of ways which, if not successfully resolved, will result in the individual being stuck to some degree.

Psychological defences

Freud saw the ego as employing a whole range of *defences* to protect itself against anxiety. One of the defences is *repression*, which works by shutting something out of consciousness altogether. But there are also a number of other defences, as we'll see. These defences are necessary at the time – the best that can be done under the circumstances – but they can sometimes subsequently become obstacles to development.

To consider this more closely, have a look at the following activity:

ACTIVITY 2.2

JENNY

This small child aged four lives alone with her mother (Mandy) who is highly volatile and unpredictable. Occasionally Mandy treats her kindly, but at other times Mandy erupts into frightening rage and violence, hitting her, depriving her of food, and threatening to abandon or kill her. Mandy also isolates her. Jenny doesn't know anyone else other than Mandy's friends. She does not know other children of her own age.

How would Jenny deal with this situation psychologically? How would she explain to herself what was going on? How would she comfort herself?

Please note: we are not asking you to guess what Freud might say about this. We are asking you to consider what you yourself think, based on your own experience and your own imagination.

COMMENTS ON ACTIVITY 2.2

The first thing that strikes us about this scenario is that a child cannot deal with it like an adult. An adult is aware of other possibilities, the possibility of escape, of sources of help (though, having said this, we need to acknowledge that choices and sources of help are limited for some adults too, for example vulnerable older people or women in abusive relationships). Her mother may abuse her, but to Jenny, Mandy is also the world, the source of her nourishment, the provider of her home.

A child also does not think like an adult in terms of logic, cause and effect and so on. (See Chapter 4 for a discussion of cognitive differences – differences in the structure of thought – between children and adults.)

The second thing that strikes us is just how intolerable it would be for a little child of this age to admit to herself that she was in real danger from the adult who cares for her, or that her mother was a bad person, or that her mother did not have her best interests at heart. The anxiety of this would be too much to bear and she needs to protect herself from it.

But Jenny is very little compared to Mandy. There is no way in reality that she can defend herself from what is going on. All she can resort to are psychological defences. She might tell herself, for example: 'This isn't really happening to me' or 'This isn't real', just as we do as adults, at least at first, when brought some terrible news such as news of a bereavement. This defence is known as 'denial' (another Freudian term that has entered everyday language).

Or she could tell herself that the Mandy who mistreats her is a different person from the Mandy who is kind to her. The kind Mandy is her real mum. This defence is known as splitting.

Or perhaps she could tell herself that she is bad, and that she deserves the treatment that Mandy gives her. This does not sound a very comfortable position to take, but it may well be less frightening to think of herself as bad, than to think of the large person who controls her life as being bad. This defence is known as turning against the self. In our experience, it is extremely common among children who have been seriously abused (as are denial and splitting). Even very little children – who from an outsider's perspective are quite obviously powerless – often blame themselves for abuse perpetrated against them.

(Continued)

(Continued)

The point about these defences is that they are necessary, the best that Jenny can do in the circumstances to protect her sanity. They are less damaging in the short run than facing the full reality of the situation. But in the long run, they may leave her with a seriously defective way of dealing with the world.

Jenny may grow up routinely blocking out painful feelings, or feeling of any kind. She may grow up with the habit of 'splitting' – holding in her mind contradictory stories at the same time. She may grow up with a view of herself as worthless and bad.

Defences are ways in which the ego tries to protect itself against anxiety – and anxiety may be caused by:

- increases in instinctual tension – tensions coming from the id: needs and desires demanding to be met
- a bad conscience – i.e. pressures from the superego
- reality – one of the defences is *denial*. Probably most of us have observed, at first or second hand, the way that people go initially into denial to protect themselves against the impact of some catastrophic event – a sudden bereavement for example – and will only gradually allow themselves to face the fact that this event has actually taken place.

Other defences are, for example, *projection* (where the individual avoids experiencing their own painful feelings by attributing them to some other person or object), *reaction-formation*, *introjection*, *'undoing'* and *repression*, which was discussed earlier. Freud's daughter Anna later developed the concept of defences in her book *The Ego and the Mechanisms of Defence* (Freud 1968 [1937]).

In *sublimation*, instinctual energies are discharged by non-instinctual behaviour (for example channelling sexual energies into creative work). This is a kind of defence, but is seen in Freudian theory as a healthy and adaptive one, in that energies are not bottled up but are redirected to some constructive purpose.

Most children do not have challenges as great as Jenny's in our example to contend with, but all children have to deal with an imperfect world, using whatever psychological resources are available to them at their particular stage of development. And the ways they find to deal with their experiences lay down a pattern for how they will approach experiences and relationships in later life.

Transference

The way in which feelings from past relationships affect present ones is known in Freudian terms as *transference*. We saw an instance of this in the example of Matthew in Chapter 1, where his mother described Matthew's behaviour to the visiting teacher as being 'just like his father', and saw herself as powerless to influence him in any way. We considered how she might now be transferring onto Matthew the feelings of angry and intimidated helplessness that she experienced in her earlier relationship with his violently abusive father. The transference effect will be even more powerful if her own father also behaved in this way, and this is quite likely. People do often seem to choose a partner who has something in common with a parent, and this can be understood in terms of the Oedipus complex, discussed below, or within the framework of attachment theory, which we will discuss in Chapter 3. There is also likely to be transference onto the teacher as an authority figure, particularly if he is also a man.

The Freudian term *countertransference* is used to describe the feelings experienced by the analyst in response to their patient, and it is a useful concept not just for psychoanalysts and therapists but for anyone in a professional helping relationship with another. These feelings come both from the worker's own past experience and from what is projected onto them by the person they are working with. For example, Matthew's teacher in Activity 1.3 might find himself feeling very angry at Matthew's mother's response to his concerns about her child. This could be to do with Matthew's mother's unexpressed anger being projected onto the teacher, or to do with something in his own past experience (perhaps his parents behaved in a similar way to Matthew's). Or it could be a combination of both.

Psychosexual Stages

If Jenny – in Activity 2.2 – had been 13 when the mistreatment started, the emotional and intellectual resources available to her would be different. They are different again for a baby subjected to abuse. Freud saw emotional development going through several stages (see Table 2.1), with each stage having its characteristic goals and its characteristic defensive strategies.

TABLE 2.1   Psychosexual stages

Stage	Age
Oral	*First Year*
Anal	*Roughly ages 2-3*
Phallic	*Roughly ages 4-6*
(Onset of Oedipus complex)	
Latency period	*Age 7 to adolescence*
Genital	*Adolescence onwards*

More controversially perhaps, Freud called these stages 'psychosexual' stages. And this is because he saw them as being based on the child's changing focus of *sexual gratification*.

(Many people find this a somewhat shocking concept, even nowadays, because we are accustomed to thinking of childhood as time that is free, or relatively free, of preoccupation with sex.)

During the *oral* stage the principle source of gratification is food and the comfort obtained from sucking, the latter being as important as the nourishment itself.

> The baby's obstinate persistence in sucking gives evidence at an early stage of a need for satisfaction which, though it originates from and is instigated by the taking of nourishment, nevertheless strives to obtain pleasure independently of nourishment and for that reason may be termed sexual. (Freud, 2003 [1949]: 24)

Freud's definition of 'sexual' in the above quote is worth noting. Many people might agree with most of this sentence but might use the word 'sensual'. Alternatively they might say that the gratification obtained from suckling was 'like sex' or 'analogous to sex', if they think that sex is primarily about reproduction, but acknowledge that it carries a whole range of other functions to do with pleasure, intimacy and so on. But a woman who enjoyed breast-feeding her baby might have no difficulty in recognising it as a sexual experience. Freud's reputation is that he says everything is to do with sex. He certainly *does* give sex a very central role but, as this quote shows, his definition of 'sex' is quite broad.

In Freud's model, people can get *fixated* at different stages for various reasons, which is to say they hang on to some aspects of behaviour characteristic of that stage – or *regress* (i.e. go backwards) to such behaviour at a time of stress. The orally fixated person has the mouth as their primary 'erotogenic zone', and tends 'to *identify* with others rather than to relate to them as others' (Rycroft, 1995: 122). This is because the oral stage is the most primitive stage, a time when a baby has not yet learnt that self and others are really separate things. (See Chapter 4 for further discussion on the growth of a child's sense of objects as separate to self.) Food and comfort come through sucking and taking in milk, and the mother who nurses him at the breast, or the carer who holds the bottle, are taken for granted as being there to serve his need. We often regress to an oral stage when we are ill and we find childhood foods comforting. And adolescence – a time of rapid advance towards independence – is also characterised by periodic regressions to dependence, as any parent will know. The teenager helplessly searching for a vital item in the chaotic bedroom from which parents have been banned for months while shouting, 'But you *must* know where it is!!' has regressed in that moment to the childhood stage when he was secure in the knowledge that if he signalled his distress loudly enough his parent would be able to make it better, whatever its cause.

During the *anal* stage, according to Freud, the anus and defecation are the major source of sensual pleasure. And at this stage of ego development, control of the body and socialisation of impulses are the child's major preoccupations. A basic but very important example of body control usually acquired during this stage is that of toilet training, when a child learns to resist the impulse to defecate whenever the urge takes her and to control and defer it.

So compulsive orderliness and excessive pleasure taken in power and control are, in the Freudian scheme of things, examples of anal fixation. The pleasure we take in orderliness and control was seen by Freud as akin to the pleasure taken by a child proudly looking into the potty after defecating and then presenting some particularly fine stools to his parent for admiration. Like other ideas of Freud's, this idea has entered everyday speech: the word 'anal' is sometimes used of someone who is very controlling and orderly ('I'm very anal about my CD collection'). Interestingly the phrase 'tight-arsed' is used of someone who is mean, though we do not know whether the latter term followed or preceded Freud. Taking pleasure in cruelty (sadism) – again to do with power and control – is also supposed to be characteristic of the anal stage (though sadism can also be oral – hurting through biting and devouring).

During the *phallic* stage the focus – for both boys *and* girls in conventional Freudian thinking – is the penis. (This is of course very controversial – and raises questions about how Freud viewed the sexes.) Fixation in the phallic phase might result in an adult who sees sexual activity as a test of potency, as opposed to an adult who has progressed to the *genital* stage, who would see it as the expression of a relationship.

It is during the phallic stage that the famous *Oedipus complex* is supposed to come into play. The name comes from the Greek myth of Oedipus as told in Sophocles' tragedy *Oedipus Rex*. As an infant Oedipus was left to die on a mountainside because it was prophesied that he would kill his father, the king, and marry his mother. But he was saved by a kindly shepherd, and went on unknowingly to fulfil the prophecy. He inherited his father's kingdom, brought down a curse upon his people and gouged out his own eyes in remorse when he discovered what he had done. The idea of the Oedipus complex is that, at the phallic stage, both boys and girls desire to have an exclusive sexual relationship with their opposite-sex parent, and become murderously jealous of their same-sex parent. This is countered however by, firstly, fear of the same-sex parent (in boys this is supposed to be a fear of actual castration by their father) and, secondly, contradictory feelings of love for the same-sex parent. At this stage girls are supposed to become aware of their own lack of a penis ('penis envy').

Resolution of the Oedipus complex is supposed to be achieved initially by identification with the same-sex parent, and suppression of desire for the opposite-sex parent. So, for example, by identifying with his father a boy can, as it were, vicariously have a sexual relationship with his mother – and no longer feel the need to kill his father. This then paves the way for a mature adult relationship which is not based on dependency or the need to control.

Control

Control is most obviously associated with the anal stage of development, but issues of control feature throughout the developmental process. Eating disorders are self-evidently oral in that they are concerned with food, and what is taken in (or not) by

(Continued)

(Continued)

way of the mouth. However, they are usually understood as being concerned with control. The anorexic, very often an adolescent, seeks to control her own appetite and body, and also ends up controlling those close to her; unable to make her eat, they can only watch helplessly as she starves herself. This can be seen as a denial of oral dependency, and very often features a conflicted relationship with her mother, and a battle for control which is played out over food. Anorexia can also be seen as an attempt to turn back the developmental clock and deny progression to adult sexuality – Freud's genital stage.

Phallic sexual behaviour, which places potency above relationship (seen in its most extreme form in rape and other manifestations of sexual violence) is also associated with control and power over others. Sexual desire and aggression are strongly linked, as they are in the myth of Oedipus.

The goal of a healthy developmental process is to establish a sense of autonomy and control over oneself which is secure enough not to need to use the defence of projection to exercise control over others.

Having accomplished the resolution of the Oedipus complex, the child then enters the *latency* phase until adolescence. This is viewed as a relatively quiet period, in psychosexual terms, between the struggles of the Oedipal phase and the struggles of adolescence.

The final phase of development (for Freud, that is: Erik Erikson, discussed below, suggested three further stages) and therefore not one which a person can be fixated in, is the *genital* phase, when the individual seeks a sexual partner as a substitute for the opposite sex parent, and as another and more permanent way of resolving the Oedipal conflict. (Sometimes, of course, the partner chosen is of the same sex. Freud wrote extensively about homosexuality in a way that transcended the taboos and prejudices of his time, and regarded it as part of the wide range of sexual expression encompassed within normal development.)

We are about to move on to discuss some developments of Freud's ideas. The following activity is to give you an opportunity to 'take stock' of what we have covered so far:

ACTIVITY 2.3

Can you think of examples – among people you know – of people who might be described as having oral fixations, anal fixations or fixations from the phallic stage, in Freud's sense?

Do you find that these concepts shed any light on behaviour (whether other people's or indeed your own)?

Thinking of the genital stage, can you think of examples of people who have chosen partners who remind you of one of their parents?

Can you think of instances, from your own experience of denial, splitting or projection?

At the beginning of this discussion, we asked you to consider your own pre-conceptions about what Freud was 'about'. Having considered this again, what do you think about Freud's ideas about sex – and its importance in human development?

What would you consider to be the major problems with Freud's theory, and what would you see as its strengths?

COMMENTS ON ACTIVITY 2.3

We can't comment on the people you know, of course, but it seems in our experience that certain characteristic patterns of behaviour are observable which could be described in Freudian terms as anal, oral and so on. It seems useful – and makes some sense to us – to think of these as patterns which come from different stages of childhood.

It seems quite common for people to choose as a partner someone who has something in common with a parent – e.g. appearance, character, role. For example, one of the authors had an aunt, oldest and favourite daughter of her bank manager father, who married a man who worked in a neighbouring bank and went on to become a bank manager himself.

Instances of denial, splitting or projection seem quite common in everyday life. An example of projection which one of us has encountered is projected anger as in: 'Of course I personally don't mind, but everyone else in the team is very angry with you.' In that instance the speaker may quite genuinely not be aware of being angry herself.

Although we've argued that Freud's definition of 'sexual' is broader than most people's, and in many instances the word 'sensual' could perhaps be substituted, Freud's preoccupation with the sexual drive over others is an issue for many people. It was one of the reasons that Carl Jung split with Freud.

Some other criticisms of Freud are discussed at the end of this chapter.

Developments of Freud's Ideas

Freud's ideas have proved to be very fertile ground for other thinkers and theorists, both in his own time and in the years since. It would be impossible here to give an account of all the different strands that have emerged, split off from, or been influenced by Freudian thought – they are so numerous and diverse. Alfred Adler, for example, split off from Freud in 1911. Carl Jung did likewise soon afterwards, falling out with Freud on a number of points after being a close colleague and disciple. This pattern of close personal and intellectual relationships followed by acrimonious splits was followed throughout Freud's life. It resembles the rivalry between father and son which he saw as part of the Oedipus complex, and perhaps helps to explain why he thought this idea so important.

The Freudian tradition threads its way through many aspects of the intellectual life of the twentieth century. It has influenced not only psychology but philosophy, literature, literary criticism and the creative arts. For example, surrealist artists such as Dali were much influenced by Freud, and the ideas of the French psychoanalyst Jacques Lacan about language have contributed to the development of postmodernist critical theory. Some of those who developed Freud's ideas would see themselves as remaining within his framework, others as moving on from it, branching off from it or making connections with other schools of thought. There have been feminist reworkings of Freud's and Lacan's ideas, for example in the work of Dorothy Dinnerstein, Nancy Chodorow, Julia Kristeva and Juliet Mitchell.

The development of psychoanalytic theory was deeply affected by historical events. Freud and many of his followers were Jewish and in the 1930s and 1940s, along with other intellectuals, found themselves forced to flee from Nazi persecution. Freud and his daughter Anna and Melanie Klein settled in England while other major figures, such as Erich Fromm, Karen Horney, Herbert Marcuse and Erik Erikson, emigrated to the United States. This geographical dispersal led to theoretical development taking rather different courses. In Britain, what is known as 'object relations theory' became the most important idea, while in the United States, 'ego psychology' became influential. Both developed thinking about the processes by which, as infants, we learn to relate to the outside world and develop a sense of who we are.

For the remainder of this chapter we will briefly look at the ideas of two members of the British object relations school, Donald Winnicott and Melanie Klein, and at the related ideas of Erik Erikson about ego development, to which we will be referring again later on in this book. Another member of the British object relations school, John Bowlby, and the Attachment Theory which he developed, will be discussed in more detail in the next chapter.

Object Relations and Ego Development

In early Freudian theory, people are seen as seeking to gratify primitive instinctual needs. An individual's relationship to others is seen in terms of 'drive reduction', the extent to which that relationship can be used to meet basic instinctual needs (e.g. for food and – of course – for sexual/sensual gratification). Later Freud began to focus more on relationship in his work on the Oedipus complex, and in his conception of the superego as an internalisation of a parental figure.

However, in the various developments of Freud's ideas described as object relations theories, the development of the *relationship* between an individual (the 'subject') and others (the 'object') takes centre stage. The word 'object' is used here not in the sense of a 'thing' but in the sense in which we refer to the object of a sentence. (In the sentence, 'I love my mother',

'I' is the subject and 'mother' is the object in grammatical terms.) In object relations theory, too, the focus shifts away from the Oedipal drama and the role of the father to the earliest stages of infancy and the child's relationship with its mother or primary carer.

The mirror

In object relations theory, human relationships are a prerequisite to a sense of selfhood. It is only through an intimate relationship with her primary carers that an individual can arrive at a sense of difference between self and others. Erikson wrote that our ability as adults to trust others stems in the first instance from learning as a child to trust that when our mother goes away, she will come back:

> The infant's first social achievement ... is his willingness to let the mother out of his sight without undue anxiety or rage, because she has become an inner certainty as well as an outer predictability. (Erikson, 1995 [1951]: 222)

This process of building up a sense of trust which will survive the process of separation is at the heart of attachment theory, which we will examine in the next chapter. Not all children ever do have this experience, of course. If you know anyone who experienced neglectful or very inconsistent parenting early in life (or if this applies to you yourself) you will probably agree that people with these experiences do indeed often find it very hard to trust others in adult relationships. So this basic sense of trust in infancy seems to be a precursor to satisfactory relationships later in life. Donald Winnicott (1896–1971) used the analogy of a mirror to describe how this works (Winnicott, 2005 [1971]: 111–18). All small children must rely on others to meet their basic physical and emotional needs. And Winnicott suggested that, if these needs are reliably met when they are expressed, then it is as if the carer is *mirroring* the child. A need seems to the child to bring a corresponding response, just as when we look into a mirror, our mirror-image produces actions that correspond to our own, and we see reflected back an image that we recognise as ourselves.

So, as a result of having her needs consistently met, the child would conclude (if not actually in words) that 'If I express my needs, they are met. If I express my feelings, they are recognised and acknowledged as valid. My carer knows who I am.' This, Winnicott suggested, gives her a sense of possessing power, an *illusion of omnipotence* (Winnicott, 2005 [1971]: 11). As a result of this experience, the child is freed up to be creative, to make demands of life and to spontaneously express needs and feelings. Through having her self mirrored and her needs recognised the child develops what Winnicott called a *true self*. People learn who they are by having their needs and feelings reflected back, just as we can only come to know what our own face looks like by seeing it reflected in a mirror.

But children are not necessarily mirrored. Needs can be ignored, feelings can be ignored, demands can be rejected or responded to negatively, for instance with anger, punishment or ridicule. And a child who does not have the experience of her needs being reliably met at this crucial early stage, or of her feelings being accepted as valid, will fail to develop a sense of trust and fail to properly develop a sense of herself as an autonomous being. In fact, Winnicott thought, for a child who has not been 'mirrored', human interaction in general becomes terrifying, and the child attempts to defend herself by developing a *false self* in which she denies her own feelings and needs and instead tries to anticipate the reactions of others. An extreme form of this would be the 'frozen watchfulness' of badly abused children, who do not play or explore but simply watch the adults around them, trying to guess what they are going to do next. But of course many of us have at least some difficulty in asserting our needs, and many of us feel more comfortable giving way to other people. (This seems to us to be particularly common among those, like many readers of this book, who are drawn to work in the caring professions.) Even in a very happy home environment, after all, a child's needs cannot always be mirrored. Winnicott was clear about this when he talked about the 'good enough' mother (Winnicott, 2005 [1971]: 10 and elsewhere). As Erikson said about early childhood:

> Even under the most favourable circumstances, this stage seems to introduce into psychic life ... a sense of inner division and universal nostalgia for a paradise forfeited. It is against this powerful combination of a sense of having been deprived ... and of having been abandoned that basic trust must maintain itself throughout life. (Erikson, 1995 [1951]: 224)

Winnicott described the process of weaning as one of disillusionment (Winnicott, 2005 [1971]: 13). He was talking about the difficult process of giving up the exclusivity of a physically and emotionally nourishing relationship with a mother figure and allowing in the wider world: other foods, other relationships, other experiences. He thought that one of the things that can help children across this bridge from mother to the outside world is the use of a *transitional object*: the favourite teddy or piece of grubby old blanket which is invested with huge emotional significance and which must never be lost until it is outgrown.

So it is an important part of a child's development that his needs should not always be met immediately and absolutely. Gradually the parent enables the child to allow that though the world can provide something like what is needed and desired, it will not do so automatically nor at the very moment the need arises or the desire is felt. The gap between wish and fulfilment stimulates the child to develop his own resources of creativity and resilience.

Good breast and bad breast

Melanie Klein (1882–1960) put less emphasis than the other object relations theorists on the external world and more on the child's internal fantasies. And she presented what many find a rather bleak and disturbing picture of what is going on in the mind of a small human being. Klein suggested that babies from an early stage simultaneously feel intense love and murderous, sadistic hatred towards the same object: the mother, and in particular the mother's breast. (If you don't believe that babies can have such violent feelings, look closely the next time you see a baby in a rage.)

The love felt by the baby for his mother relates to the comfort offered by the mother, while the hatred relates to the absolute power that the mother has to give and withhold this comfort. (Because, as we've just noted, no mother can hope to respond to *every* need.) To begin with, Klein thought, babies deal with these contradictory feelings by the classically Freudian mechanisms of *splitting* and *projection*. Instead of seeing the mother as one person, the baby splits her in his mind into two different people, or two different things – the 'good breast' and the 'bad breast' in Kleinian terminology. The rage which the hungry baby feels when food is not forthcoming is projected outwards onto the 'bad breast' which the baby then experiences as attacking and frightening. However, it is necessary for the child to move on from this position (the *paranoid-schizoid* position) because failure to do so could in her view lead to schizoid/paranoid disorders in later life, including (so Klein thought) schizophrenia.

The move from the paranoid-schizoid position takes the child to the depressive position, which starts to appear at about three months. At this stage she comes to see the mother as a whole person, so that:

> disappointment with the mother no longer turns her into something wholly bad and danger-ous: damage is no longer feared as total destruction. A good experience does not mean heaven forever; its loss is no longer the end of the world but is ... mitigated by the hope of good experiences in the future. (Segal, 2004: 38)

In the depressive position the child is able to experience and tolerate *ambivalence*; that is to have contradictory feelings of love and hate towards his mother at the same time. But guilt also appears at this stage when the child realises that his own feelings are ambivalent, and feels badly about the violent and negative feelings he has towards his mother. Inability to manage this guilt by finding a way of making *reparation*, that is, by expressing the love that he feels alongside the hate, could lead to depressive illness. However, contrary to what its name might suggest, this position is essentially a healthy one, based on reality rather than fantasy:

> The loved and hated aspects of the mother are no longer felt to be so widely separated, and the result is an increased fear of loss, states akin to mourning, and a strong feeling of guilt, because the aggressive impulses are felt to be directed against the loved object ... The very experience of depressive feelings in turn has the effect of further integrating the ego, because it makes for an increased understanding of psychic reality and better perception of the external world, as well as for a greater synthesis between inner and external situations. (Klein, 1986 [1946]: 189)

Klein talks about positions rather than stages, conveying the idea of an oscillation between positions rather than an orderly progression from one stage to the next:

Some fluctuations between the paranoid-schizoid and the depressive positions always occur and are part of normal development. (Klein, 1986 [1946]: 191)

We repeatedly revert to a schizoid position at times of difficulty and stress. For example, in a quarrel with a loved partner we may temporarily see them as wholly bad and malicious, and ourselves as wholly blameless and good. But Klein thought that real caring relationships require us to negotiate the difficulties of the depressive position, in which ambivalence has to be faced.

Klein described the integration of the ego as beginning with the depressive position, when the world begins to be experienced as a coherent whole, and the self which experiences it begins to feel coherent too. Erikson, whose work we will now discuss, saw the development of the ego as a lifelong process which begins in a similar way, with the baby learning to trust the world in which he finds himself.

Erikson's stages

Erik Erikson (1902–1994) saw the ego developing through a series of stages at each of which it faces a 'crisis', which must be resolved for the individual to move on to the next stage (see Erikson, 1995 [1951]: 222 ff). This is a classically Freudian model, both in its conception of stages, and in its suggestion that there are characteristic issues that have to be resolved at each stage before a person is fully capable of moving on. Indeed, the first five stages in Erikson's model do correspond to Freud's oral, anal, phallic, latency and genital stages. But a major difference is that Erikson's model spans the whole life cycle and not just childhood.

Also, while Freud referred to stages of *psychosexual* development, Erikson paid more attention to the social context of development and referred to *psychosocial* stages. Although there are many criticisms that can be levelled at his framework, it does provide a useful starting point for discussion of change across the human lifespan – and we will be returning to it in later chapters. His stages are summarised in Table 2.2.

As you can see each stage has a favourable outcome and an unfavourable outcome. The actual outcome for any individual would depend on how well the particular 'crisis', or challenge, of that stage had been successfully met. You'll also notice that an unfavourable outcome in one stage makes it more difficult to fully meet the challenge of the next stage. Thus, as we've already discussed, Erikson saw the task of the first stage (equivalent to Freud's oral stage) as being the establishment of a sense of trust. Clearly if it is not possible for an infant to establish a sense of trust in the environment because it is not a secure one, it would be more difficult to achieve the sense of autonomy which is the next stage (the anal stage, in Freudian terms). In turn it would be harder to develop the capacity for initiative which is the optimum outcome of the next (phallic) stage. This will then put the child at a disadvantage when she reaches the next stage and starts school, and make it difficult for her to apply herself to learning, so that she risks ending up with a sense of inferiority which she will carry into adolescence and adulthood, and which will affect her capacity to achieve the subsequent

TABLE 2.2   Stages of psychosocial development

Life Crisis	Favourable Outcome	Unfavourable Outcome
First Year *Trust v. Mistrust* The child needs consistent and stable care in order to develop feelings of security	Trust in the environment and hope for the future	Suspicion, insecurity, fear of the future
Second and Third Years *Autonomy v. Shame and Doubt* The child seeks a sense of independence from parents	A sense of autonomy and self-esteem	Feelings of shame and doubt about one's own capacity for self-control
Fourth and Fifth Years *Initiative v. Guilt* The child explores her environment and plans new activities	The ability to initiate activities and enjoy following them through	Fear of punishment and guilt about one's own personal feelings
Age Six to Eleven *Industry v. Inferiority* The child acquires important knowledge and skills relating to her culture	A sense of competence and achievement. Confidence in one's own ability to make and do things	Unfavourable reactions from others may cause feelings of inadequacy and inferiority
Adolescence *Identity v. Role Confusion* The young person searches for a coherent personal and vocational identity	Ability to see oneself as a consistent and integrated person	Confusion over who and what one is
Young Adulthood *Intimacy v. Isolation* The adult seeks deep and lasting relationships	The ability to experience love and commitment to others	Isolation; superficial relationships with others
Middle Adulthood *Generativity v. Stagnation* The individual seeks to be productive and creative and to make a contribution to society	The ability to be concerned and caring about others in the wider sense	Lack of growth; boredom and over-concern with oneself
Late Adulthood *Integrity v. Despair* The individual reviews and evaluates what has been accomplished in life	A sense of satisfaction with one's life and its accomplishments; acceptance of death	Regret over omissions and missed opportunities; fear of death

developmental tasks. Social factors will play their part too; in a context where it is hard to find secure and meaningful employment it will also be hard for her to develop a vocational identity and feel she is making a contribution to society.

Having said this, Erikson's model does not say that you have to have completed one stage before you go on to the next. In fact everyone is likely to have some unresolved issues from earlier stages (exactly as in the original Freudian model). But too much baggage from earlier stages will impede progress.

A new stage of life, according to Erikson, does however offer opportunities not only to tackle the new challenges that it presents, but also a chance to go back and deal with unresolved issues from earlier stages. Sometimes, for example, a person entering a 'midlife crisis', at the beginning of Erikson's sixth stage, may revisit unresolved issues from early adulthood and adolescence. (We'll discuss this further in Chapter 7.) And how the transition to adulthood is negotiated will in turn relate to earlier childhood experiences when the first steps were taken towards independence from parents. It is also common for new parents to find that the experience of parenthood reawakens their own unresolved early childhood feelings. This is often a contributory factor in postnatal depression. And in a family, of course, different members will be going through different stages at any given time. This creates a complex web of interactions which we will discuss further in Chapter 8, when we look at family systems.

As good a way as any of looking at Erikson's model is to test it against your own life:

ACTIVITY 2.4

What stage are you at in your life? Look through the stages you have already been through and see whether you agree with Erikson about the issues that were important at each stage.

Which stages do you think you negotiated most successfully? Which ones do you think you negotiated less successfully? (Everyone carries some 'baggage' from unresolved issues in earlier life – 'unfavourable outcomes' in Erikson's terminology.)

What do you see as the main drawbacks of Erikson's model?

COMMENTS ON ACTIVITY 2.4

One criticism of Erikson's model is that it is too linear and prescriptive. It may sketch out the issues we deal with, or try to deal with as we grow older, but it does not allow sufficiently for the many different routes that we may take.

You may also have felt that this model fits better with middle-class life in North America and Europe than it would in other cultures where decisions are made much more collectively and individuals have less choice (or no choice at all) about issues like marriage and career.

Criticisms of Freud and his Successors

We asked you earlier (in Activity 2.3) to consider what you saw as the main problems with Freud's model. We will conclude this chapter by discussing some of the criticisms that are commonly levelled at Freud and psychodynamic theory. Some of these apply primarily to Freud and some are more general criticisms of a wider range of psychodynamic approaches.

Originality

We have seen how later theorists built on the work of Freud, who is often seen as the founding father of psychoanalytic theory. But the claims that are made for Freud's ideas as original have also been challenged. Perhaps, for practical purposes, it makes little difference precisely who contributed to the development of these ideas, for they certainly do have their precedents. For example, if you look at the writings of the Greek philosopher Plato (who lived nearly two and a half millennia before Freud), you find a dynamic model of the human mind in which it is likened to a chariot in which the rider is the soul while the two horses pulling it are reason and desire (1973: 51).

Likewise in Sophocles' play *Oedipus Rex* (written nearly two and a half millennia ago), Jocasta, the wife and mother of Oedipus, says:

> Many a man before you
>
> In his dreams, has shared his mother's bed (Sophocles, translated by Fagles, 1984: 215)

Webster (2005) in particular argues that Freud's ideas are actually much less original than is usually thought.

Scientific method

Freud presented his theory of personality and human development as scientific, and sought acceptance from the scientific community of his day. However, it is questionable whether his methods were scientific in the way in which that term is usually understood. His methods, which relied on his clinical observations, could not eliminate his own subjective feelings and prejudices. That said, modern perspectives on scientific method accept that objectivity is never possible, and that the observer will always affect the outcome. In social research it is accepted that qualitative research, which looks in depth at the experience of a few people, has a different kind of validity from quantitative research, which may be more rigorous in terms of samples and control groups. In this respect Freud could be seen as a qualitative researcher par excellence.

Personal bias

Freud's use of self-analysis as part of the foundation for his theories is open to some criticism. As well as using material from the analysis of his patients, he subjected himself to the same process of analysis and used the results as the basis for his developmental theories. As his biographer Gay observes, 'Many of Freud's most unsettling ideas drew on acknowledged, or covert, autobiographical sources' (Gay, 1988: 90). The primacy which he gave to the Oedipus complex reflected the powerful relationship he had with his father; the theory was developed in the period immediately after his father's death. This bias made it difficult for him to look beyond the confines of his own cultural, social and gender position.

Patriarchy and feminism

Freud didn't understand women – he famously referred to female sexuality as a 'dark continent' (Freud, 1959 [1926]: 212). His concept of penis envy has attracted anger and scorn from feminists at the idea that women should be defined by their absence of a penis. But his case histories do show an understanding of how women were made ill by their social situation. Dorothy Dinnerstein has reframed penis envy in a way which is more consistent with feminism by talking about the little girl's envy of 'the social prerogatives which it (the penis) confers' (Dinnerstein, 1987: 52n). And there were plenty of women among Freud's intellectual and professional colleagues who played an important role in the development of psychoanalytic theory and practice. His daughter Anna was one of the most significant of these. He encouraged and supported her development as an analyst and was happy at the end of his life to see her as his intellectual heir who would carry on his work.

Seduction theory

Freud has been much criticised for changing his mind about believing what his patients told him about their experience of sexual abuse. As we have seen, Freud's theories were constantly evolving and changing throughout his life, and his position on seduction theory was part of this process. It is not the case, as his most vehement critics (e.g. Masson, 2003) maintain, that he abandoned a belief in the reality of sexual abuse altogether. For example, he wrote in one of his public lectures in 1916:

> You must not suppose, however, that the sexual abuse of a child by its nearest male relatives belongs entirely to the realm of fantasy. Most analysts will have treated cases in which such events were real and could be unimpeachably established. (Freud, 1963 [1916–17]: 370)

Much has been written on this issue, and you will have to read more in order to make up your own mind about it. Some suggestions for further reading are given at the end of this chapter.

Cultural specificity

It can be argued that the theories presented here were developed in relation to Western two-parent nuclear families in the first half of the twentieth century, and there is no reason to assume that they can be applied equally in different cultural contexts. And Western family life has itself changed: higher divorce rates have led to more complex family structures, and a child's parents may not remain a couple for very long. Most psychoanalytic theorists, from Freud onwards, pay little attention to sibling relationships (though see Mitchell, 2003), yet these can be of immense importance. For many families in southern Africa, where parents have died of AIDS, the bond between brothers and sisters is all that holds the family together.

Clearly you must make up your own mind about the strengths and weaknesses of Freud's ideas, and those of his successors. However, we would suggest that for all their shortcomings these ideas remain of value. Freud and other psychodynamic theorists have shed light on dimensions of human development which are not illuminated in the same way by any other body of theory. They give us a way of thinking about how we find our place in the world and of understanding the forces which drive us to seek relationships, and they explain why the quality of our earliest relationships is so fundamental to our well-being for the rest of our lives. In the next chapter we will look at attachment theory, which is concerned with how these relationships are established, and what happens when they go wrong.

Chapter Summary

- In this chapter, we looked at the development of Freud's ideas about the unconscious.
- We looked at Freud's conception of the structure of the personality (ego, id, superego) and his idea of psychological defences (such as denial, repression, projection and splitting).
- We then looked at his theory of psychosexual development (from oral, through anal and phallic stages, into the struggles of the Oedipus complex and the latency period and finally into the genital stage).
- We discussed the range of different developments that there have been from Freud's ideas.
- Finally we looked at the developments which (loosely) can be categorised as object relations theories and at some of the ideas of Winnicott (the mirror, the true and false selves, the transitional object), Klein (good breast and bad breast, the paranoid/schizoid and depressive positions) and Erikson (the concept of psychosocial development).
- We concluded by looking at criticisms of Freud and psychodynamic theory.

In the next chapter we will look at *attachment theory*, a body of theory that developed out of object relations theory.

Further Reading

On Freud and his ideas

Freud, S. (2003 [1949]) *An Outline of Psychoanalysis*. London: Penguin.
This is a short and perfectly readable summary of his ideas by Freud himself, not quite completed due to his death. Unlike some of his successors, Freud writes in a clear and lucid style.
Jacobs, M. (2003) *Sigmund Freud*. London: Sage.
Rycroft, C. (1995) *A Critical Dictionary of Psychoanalysis*, 2nd edn. London: Penguin.
Contains explanations of all the many terms and concepts.

On developments of Freudian theory

Elliot, A. (2002) *Psychoanalytic Theory: An Introduction*. Oxford: Oxford University Press.
An overview including Klein, Winnicott, Erikson, Lacan and others.
Erikson, E. (1995 [1951]) *Childhood and Society*. London: Vintage.
Segal, J. (2004) *Melanie Klein*, 2nd edn. London: Sage.
Winnicott, D.W. (2005 [1971]) *Playing and Reality*, 2nd edn. London: Tavistock/Routledge.

Criticism of Freud

Frosh, S. (1997) *For and Against Psychoanalysis*. London: Routledge.
Masson, J. (2003) *The Assault on Truth: Freud's Suppression of the Seduction Theory*. New York: Ballantine Books.
Webster, R. (2005) *Why Freud Was Wrong: Sin, Science and Psychoanalysis*, 3rd edn. Oxford: Orwell Press.

3 A SECURE BASE

THE IMPORTANCE OF ATTACHMENT

- John Bowlby and 'maternal deprivation'   47
- The biological origins of attachment   49
- The secure base and attachment behavioural systems   51
- The growth of attachment   54
- Internal working models   55
- Mary Ainsworth's attachment classification system   58
- Developments of attachment theory   61
- Criticisms of attachment theory   64

At the end of the previous chapter we looked at the development of Freud's ideas by object relations theorists. Attachment theory, the subject of this chapter, is an object relations theory par excellence. It is based on the proposition that the way we relate to others throughout our lives (subject–object relations, in other words) is shaped by our first relationship with our primary carer, who traditionally and still usually is the mother.

John Bowlby, who one might describe as the 'father' of attachment theory, was a psychoanalyst and a member of the British group of object relations theorists which also included Winnicott and Klein. His emphasis was very different from Klein's, however, and he was less interested in speculating about fantasies that go on in children's minds and more interested in developing a scientific approach that drew on verifiable, objective research on human and animal behaviour. Nevertheless, in modern attachment theory, which has developed from Bowlby's original ideas, you can still find ideas that owe a debt to Freud.

Attachment theory has been and continues to be very influential in the development of policy and professional practice. It has had its critics, but research in the rapidly developing field of neuroscience is now emphasising the crucial role that our early attachments play in the development of our brains and our cognitive and emotional functioning. It has been particularly important in fields where assessing parenting is a central issue. In Britain, for example, health visitors, social workers, teachers and others working with children and families are often involved in addressing questions such as the following. All of them are related to attachment:

- Are a child's needs being adequately met within this relationship?
- Can the relationship change?
- Would the damage done by disrupting this relationship be outweighed or not by the benefits of providing other more consistent carers?
- Could the child settle with new carers?
- If so, what therapeutic work would be needed to make that possible?
- Is the respite and support offered to a family by a shared care arrangement likely to be beneficial to relationships in that family?
- Does a child's rejection of their foster carers reflect a real problem with those particular carers, or is it the result of the child's difficulties with attachment that would be a problem in any relationship?

Writers such as Howe (1995, 2005), Berlin et al. (2005) and Juffer and Bakermans-Kranenberg (2008) use attachment theory as a reference point for developing and evaluating strategies for assessment and intervention in child care practice. And of course it is also vitally important in the field of fostering and adoption practice (Schofield and Beek, 2006; Golding, 2008).

In any of the caring professions – or indeed in life generally – you are certain to encounter many people who have problems with attachment. Attachment theorists argue that many other psychological problems actually have their roots in difficulties in early attachment relationships and that early attachment has strong links with mental health in adult life, the ability to form relationships, the ability to parent and the ability to deal with loss (see Chapter 7). And developments in neuroscience are shedding new light on the relationship between attachment and cognitive development (which we will discuss in Chapter 4).

The following activity may help you to gather your own thoughts on the subject:

ACTIVITY 3.1 ♩♩♩

(a) Think of a child you know who seems to have some problems in relating with his/her parent(s) or carer(s). What is it that makes you think there is a problem? How does it affect the child?

(b) Now think of an adult you know who seems to have difficulty with intimate relationships. What makes you think that there is a difficulty? What are your theories about what may have caused the difficulty in the first place?

COMMENTS ON ACTIVITY 3.1

(a) You may have mentioned that this child is reluctant to go to his/her carers, or seems anxious in their presence. Alternatively, you may have said that the child seems excessively clingy to his/her carers, and seems very anxious if separated from them at all. Or you may have said that the child appears to cling indiscriminately to any adult. Among the effects on the child, you may have noticed: poor concentration, difficulty in making friends, difficulty in judging social situations.

(b) You may have mentioned an adult who seems to have difficulty in committing themselves, and is always ending relationships because they feel trapped. Or an adult who is unable to talk about their feelings with their partner – or seems to talk about them compulsively. Or perhaps someone who always seems to let themselves be abused and dominated in relationships, and can't seem to end them, no matter how unhappy they feel ... If you know anything about this adult's childhood, you will probably notice that their relationship with parents/carers was problematic in some way. There may have been neglect or abuse, or abandonment of some sort. Or the parents may have been excessively controlling or excessively protective.

We'll now have a look at Bowlby's contribution to thinking about these matters.

John Bowlby and 'Maternal Deprivation'

Although a trained psychoanalyst, and a member of the British psychoanalytic community, John Bowlby (1907–1990) was critical of those psychoanalysts who focused (in his view) too much on fantasies and imaginary fears, such as a small boy's supposed fear of castration by his father, as if there were not enough real dangers in the world. He thought Klein and the Kleinians in particular were excessively interested in children's fantasies about their parents, and suggested (in the paper which he presented to qualify as a full member of the Institute of Psychoanalysis) that it would be much more fruitful to look at their parents' real characters (Bowlby, 1940). Bowlby was interested in the *external* factors that influence a child's development.

Bowlby was also interested in reconciling the insights of psychoanalytic theory with ethology (the study of animal behaviour) and with verifiable, empirical research in general. However, he was part of the psychoanalytic community, and though his ideas are expressed in much more down-to-earth 'common-sense' terms than those of some other writers in the psychoanalytic tradition, they recognisably follow the same pattern. As in classical Freudian theory, Bowlby's ideas included the concept of various unconscious strategies that come into play when needs can't be met at different stages, including strategies such as splitting or excluding things from consciousness (Bowlby, 1997 [1969]: 32). Like Freud, he saw these strategies being carried into later life.

Bowlby's particular interest was in the effects of separation of children from their parents. *Attachment*, *Separation* and *Loss* were the titles of the three volumes of his most famous work (Bowlby, 1997 [1969], 1998a[1973], 1998b[1980]). In 1950 he was asked by the World Health Organisation to carry out a study of children separated from their parents. (This was in the post-war context, when bereavement, evacuation, deportation and displacement had disrupted millions of families in Europe.) He looked at children separated from parents in various ways and interviewed disturbed adolescents and adults. He found a strong link between what he called 'maternal deprivation' and problems in adult life such as delinquency, mental illness and difficulties in parenting.

Bowlby's definition of 'maternal deprivation', in his original thinking, included loss of the mother or separation from the mother, as well as things like neglectful or abusive mothering. Both the word 'maternal' and the word 'deprivation' are targets of criticism, the former because of its exclusive emphasis on the mother, as opposed to the father and other carers, the latter because it conflates several very different things. As attachment theory has developed, it has taken on board some of the criticisms in both these areas.

In addition to these studies on the long-term effects of maternal deprivation, Bowlby and his colleague James Robertson also looked at the short-term effects on children of separation from their mothers (see Robertson and Bowlby, 1952). They made a series of films which graphically and painfully capture the process, and which have helped to educate generations of childcare professionals and to change childcare practices (*A Two Year Old Goes to Hospital* 1952; *Young Children in Brief Separation* 1967–71). What they observed was that children went through several stages:

1. A stage of *protest*, including crying, screaming, trying to find the mother and so on.
2. A stage of *despair*, when the child becomes listless and apathetic.
3. A stage of *detachment*, when the child seems to lose interest in the missing parent and starts to become involved again in other activities, though this involvement may be quite superficial and unengaged.

This last stage seemed to Bowlby to be the result of defensive mechanisms coming into play which meant that the child *repressed* (to use the Freudian term: Bowlby also used the phrase *defensively excluded*) feelings of grief and anger. If they were never resolved in any way, could these painful, angry, distressing feelings lead to the long-term problems which his other research seemed to indicate were associated with so-called maternal deprivation?

As you will see, attachment theory tries to bring these different observations together into a coherent whole.

Bowlby and social reform

Bowlby's interest in this topic was not, however, primarily academic. He was passionate about the need of children for love and security and he was influential in bringing about many changes that we now take for granted. For example, parents in the 1950s and 1960s were routinely told not to visit their children in hospital, because 'it only upsets them'. Bowlby decided that this was nonsense. Children did not get more upset when their parents visited, they just felt safe enough to *show* how upset they already were. Bowlby was a key figure in bringing about a change towards the modern approach of encouraging parental contact. Likewise, he challenged what he called 'the astonishing practice' of separating mothers and babies immediately after birth which was common in the 1950s. He described this practice as a 'madness of Western society' which he hoped would never be copied by 'the so-called less developed countries' (Bowlby, 1990 [1953]: 180). It is, of course, no longer normal in the West.

The Biological Origins of Attachment

A much-quoted comment of Bowlby's, made in 1951, was that '… mother love in infancy and childhood is as important for mental health as are vitamins and proteins for physical health' (Bowlby, 1951, cited by Rutter, 1981: 15). He saw the need for a close relationship – an attachment – between child and carer (and particularly *mother*) as being a basic biological need. And, like the rest of the object relations school, he didn't see this relationship as being important only insofar as it met basic primary needs: sexual needs and the need for food. He saw it as a need in its own right. We can easily observe, not only in humans, but also in other mammals, how strong the bond is between a mother and a child. Both mother and baby animals of many species become distressed and agitated if they are separated, and mother animals will often fight ferociously to prevent a baby being taken from them. Bowlby quoted, for example, the following vivid description from a piece of research in which baby monkeys were separated from their mothers for five-minute periods:

> Separation of mother and infant monkeys is an extremely stressful experience for both mother and infant as well as for the attendants and for all other monkeys within sight or earshot of the experience. The mother becomes ferocious … the infant's screams can be heard over almost the entire building. The mother struggles and attacks the separators. The baby clings tightly to the mother and to any object which it can grasp to avoid being held or removed by the attendant. With the baby gone the mother paces the cage continually … bites at it and makes continual attempts to escape. The infant emits high-pitched screams intermittently and almost continuously for the whole period of the separation. (Jensen and Tolman, 1962, cited by Bowlby, 1998a [1973]: 85)

So both mother and baby monkey called to each other and signalled their distress, and the mother made frantic efforts to get back to the baby. These are examples of what Bowlby termed *attachment behaviour*, but attachment behaviour also includes behaviour by the child that has the effect of attracting the mother's interest in a positive way, such as smiling, and indeed *any* behaviour that has the function of bringing mother and child together. And it is by observing the amount of attachment behaviour that we gain some sense of how strong an attachment exists. For instance, from the account just quoted of a baby monkey being separated from the mother, we conclude from the behaviour of both mother and baby that a strong attachment exists between the two. But it is important to note that a *strong* attachment is not necessarily the same thing as a *secure* attachment.

Attachment and Animal Experiments

Bowlby was interested in learning from animal experiments. But such experiments are controversial for two reasons: firstly, there is a question about *ethics.* Secondly, there is the question as to whether they are *valid.* Can information from animals tell us anything about human beings? The sociologist, Erica Burman, for example, emphatically rejects this (Burman, 1994: 87–9).

The most well-known animal experiments in the field of attachment were carried out by Harlow and his collaborators (Harlow, 1963). In one experiment, baby rhesus monkeys were separated from their mothers within 12 hours of birth and placed in cages with two types of surrogate mothers: one made of soft cloth and one made of wire. They found that the babies preferred the cloth mother, spending their time cuddled up to it, even if the experimenters arranged things so that it was the wire mother that actually provided milk. Babies raised with these surrogate mothers, or with no mothers at all, grew up incapable of normal sexual or social behaviour, and were neglectful and abusive mothers to their own babies.

There must be serious ethical questions about such experiments, but there *do* seem to be striking parallels here with human experience. (Indeed the striking parallels with humans could be argued to be one compelling reason why these experiments should be regarded as unethical.)

Bowlby believed that attachment behaviour is innate, part of our 'nature', and he theorised that this behaviour had evolved for a specific reason. A baby (human or animal) needs to explore to learn about the world. It cannot permanently be physically in contact with its mother. But it also needs to retain some proximity to the mother, on whom it depends for food and protection. The effect of attachment behaviour is to act as a kind of invisible elastic, maintaining a link between mother and child. Too much separation, whether in terms of distance (too far away), or in terms of time (too long), increases the anxiety levels of mother and child and increases the amount of attachment behaviour. When closeness is restored, attachment behaviour can go into abeyance and other behaviours can be resumed. Attachment behaviour is about *homeostasis* (a term we will come back to in Chapter 8), which means maintaining a steady state.

The effects of this can be observed quite readily. If you are a parent, for example, you will probably be familiar with the scenario in which you are sitting in a room with your children playing round you and you then decide to move to another room. After a period of time you find that your children have followed you. They may not necessarily want anything in particular from you, and they may well quietly resume their games when homeostasis has been re-established. For a more extreme example of attachment in action, you only need to consider the reactions of both parent and child when they accidentally lose one another in a busy street.

Parents, mothers, carers

You may have noticed that we sometimes use the word 'mother' to describe a child's primary attachment figure, which was also Bowlby's practice. In the case of some animals, there can be little doubt that the mother *is* the primary attachment figure (and indeed in some species, the males take no part in child rearing, and may not even have any way of knowing which are their own children). But, of course, children can and do have attachment figures other than the mother. And, even if the main attachment figure *is* the mother, they may well have other figures who are also important sources of protection and comfort. A criticism of attachment theory, as originally expounded by Bowlby, is that it makes the assumption that there has to be one single primary focus of attachment behaviour. In all cultures to some extent, and in some cultures to a great extent, childcare is of course a task that is *shared*, not only by mothers and fathers but also by grandparents, sisters, brothers, uncles, aunts and friends.

The Secure Base and Attachment Behavioural Systems

One way of looking at attachment is that the attachment figure is a kind of emotional anchor, a source of security, or, in the expressive phrase coined by Bowlby's collaborator Mary Ainsworth, a *secure base*. In the absence of the attachment figure, there is insecurity. Attachment behaviour is designed to restore the sense of security that comes from knowing that the secure base is there in case it is needed.

But on occasion the secure base will not be there. There will be unavoidable separations of one kind or another and there will also be occasions, more frequent and long-lasting for some children than others, when the mother or primary carer is physically there, but is not really available as a source of comfort, perhaps because she is preoccupied, or because she is angry with the child, or for some other reason, such as ill health, either physical or mental. Post-natal depression, for example, is estimated to affect 10–15 per cent of new mothers in the UK (Mind, 2013).

Children will adopt different behavioural strategies, depending on their circumstances, to obtain as much support as they can. Attachment behaviour is modified in the light of experience and each individual adopts a different repertoire of characteristic attachment behaviours. This repertoire, together with the response of the caregiver, Bowlby called an attachment *behavioural system* (Bowlby, 1997 [1969]: 304).

There are some children who grow up with no real sense of a secure base at all. Such children can be described as being in a state of *dissuagement*, a state of permanently having an unmet need (Heard and Lake 1986: 434). This is an extremely difficult situation to be in, and the child will resort to various defensive manoeuvres in order to minimise separation anxiety and/or to try to obtain support. The idea of defences is of course a concept derived directly from the Freudian model and, like Freud, Bowlby did not see these defensive patterns as merely temporary behaviours. He saw them being internalised by degrees into what he called an internal *working model* of the world, which an individual carries with him into later life (Bowlby, 1997 [1969]: 110–13).

We hope you can see how these ideas lead outwards from what begins as a relatively straightforward idea about the biological origins of attachment, into a theory about how human personality develops, and how relationships in early childhood shape and influence behaviour and relationships throughout life.

The following three propositions, extracted from Bowlby's book *Separation* (1998a [1973]: 235), may help to clarify what we have just been discussing:

1. '… when an individual is confident that an attachment figure will be available to him whenever he desires, that person will be much less prone to either intense or chronic fear than will an individual who has no such confidence.'
2. '… confidence in the availability of an attachment figure, or lack of it, is built up slowly during the years of immaturity – infancy, childhood and adolescence – and … whatever expectations are developed during those years tend to persist relatively unchanged throughout the rest of life.'
3. '… the varied expectations of the accessibility and responsiveness of attachment figures that different individuals develop during the years of immaturity are tolerably accurate reflections of the experiences those individuals have actually had.' (This last proposition, as Bowlby went on to say, was controversial in analytical circles because many psychoanalysts, such as Klein, put so much more stock on fantasy than on actual objective experience.)

We will return to these ideas later, in the discussion about *internal working models* and about *secure* and *insecure* attachment. The following activity is to give you an opportunity to think about how different patterns of relating to others can become established in childhood:

ACTIVITY 3.2

Think of three or four children, preferably of similar ages, from different families, and think about how they relate – or related – to their parents (or to their primary carers if these are not their parents).

Assuming that all children are seeking the reassurance that their carers are available to them for support, but that this is not equally available to all children all the time, what do you notice about the different ways in which these children gain their parents' attention? Can you see ways in which these children have adapted their attachment behaviour to meet the particular circumstances in which they find themselves?

COMMENTS ON ACTIVITY 3.2

The possibilities here are, of course, endless. The following are a few patterns which we have noticed:

- Some children learn that presenting symptoms of illness is a good way of attracting parental interest and attention. This is particularly so, of course, when parents are anxious about health. We have encountered children who have developed what seem like quite intractable health problems, which have consumed a good deal of their parents' time, yet which seem to disappear when the children are with other carers.
- Sometimes children of parents who are emotionally fragile can seem unusually 'grown-up', 'independent' and 'well-behaved'. Perhaps these are children who have learnt from experience not to make excessive demands on their parents, and they need to become like parents themselves in order to look after them?
- Some children, on the other hand, seem to subject their carers to an incessant barrage of demands as a way of reassuring themselves that their carers are available to them.
- Youngest children often continue to use 'cuteness' to attract positive attention at a much later stage than their older siblings did. ('Acting cute' is a form of attachment behaviour.) The older children in the family, faced with younger and 'cuter' rivals, have needed to develop other ways of getting parental attention.

We will return later to look in more detail at patterns established in childhood.

The Growth of Attachment

Unlike many animal species, human infants do not show obvious attachment behaviour from birth. But this does not mean that attachment is not developing from the very beginning of life. Attachment is a two-way process between baby and mother, and develops out of the interaction between them. Earlier, when we referred to Bowlby's description of research on monkey mothers and babies you will remember that the mothers' distress on separation was as great as that of the babies', and you may be able to draw on your own experience for examples of the close bond between parent and newborn baby.

We will now look at the stages in the development of attachment in childhood. If you look at the attachment literature, you will find some variation in the terms used and in the indicative ages given for each stage. One would expect, in any case, that there would be some differences between individuals in respect of the speed at which they develop. But, taking the ages as rough guidelines only, the following are the stages through which attachment is thought to develop. (The indicative ages which we have used here are from Howe et al., 1999: 19–21.)

1. **Pre-attachment (0–2 months)**

This stage is characterised by *undiscriminating social responsiveness*. At this stage babies enjoy social interaction. They are interested in human voices and human faces. But they can be left with different caregivers without seeming to be distressed. Experiments on monkeys carried out by Harlow (1963) and others in the 1960s and 1970s showed that very small baby monkeys could be separated from their mothers without causing any long-term difficulty, but that older babies separated from their mothers for the same period, showed long-term behavioural problems: this suggests that for monkeys too there is a pre-attachment stage. Also of relevance here are the findings of cognitive psychology, which we'll discuss in the next chapter. Piaget's model would suggest that at this very early age the baby would have no concept of the mother or carer as a separate individual with her own existence. At this stage the baby does not even know that objects exist when she is not looking at them. (According to Piaget the concept of 'object permanence' does not develop until about six months.) However, the newborn baby is most easily able to focus visually on objects which are at the same distance from him as the face of the person who is holding him and feeding him (Bowlby, 1997 [1969]: 327), so it is not surprising that this should quickly develop into a preference for this carer – usually the mother. If all goes well, her responses will be attuned to his cues – smiles, cries, babbling, arm and leg movements – and will set up the kind of mirroring process described in Chapter 2, which is the groundwork of a secure attachment.

2. **Attachment-in-the-making (3–6 months)**

We now see *discriminating* social responsiveness developing. Babies start to show different responses to different people. They respond more to familiar people than to strangers and they become increasingly focused on their main carer, smiling and babbling more when they are relating to her and being more easily comforted by her when distressed. The baby and his carer give each other feedback and become more attuned to each other, and the baby's mood, whether of pleasure or distress, is 'held' or regulated by the carer's response in the same way as she holds him physically in her arms.

3. **Clear-cut attachment (7 months to 3 years)**

During this stage a child will *actively seek proximity and contact* with his main carer whenever the distance between them becomes too great. And the child will display full-blown separation anxiety when the carer leaves the room. By this stage, of course, the child is learning to move independently, so he can take more control over the distance between himself and his carer. As well as becoming more active in seeking out the carer, the child will also become more active in maintaining contact. For example, the child will read the situation and alter his behaviour accordingly in order to optimise the response from the carer. (So we see *different* attachment behavioural systems developing, depending on circumstances, as discussed above in Activity 3.2.)

4. **Reciprocal relationship (from 3 years)**

As the child becomes more mobile and spends more time away from the carer, the pair enter a reciprocal state in which they share responsibility for maintaining equilibrium. Increasingly, a feeling of security can be maintained even during temporary separations – linked to cognitive developments which allow the child to think in more sophisticated terms about things like time and space, the reasons for a carer's absence and so on. (The child can feel that the carer is 'there for him', and hold her in mind even when she is not physically present.) Cognitive developments also allow the child to begin to be able to see things from the carer's point of view and to adjust behaviour accordingly, understanding that their carer also has goals and plans. The relationship becomes more of a partnership.

The description of the reciprocal relationship stage which we have just given does suppose that, by and large, the relationship between carer and child has gone well. Rather different patterns would otherwise emerge. Whatever pattern is established by this stage, though, will become the *internal working model* that the child will use as a standard to guide interactions with other people – and will carry on into the rest of his life. In adulthood, these attachment patterns have a profound effect on the way in which we choose and relate to our partners, and the attachments we make with our own children, and they with us.

Internal Working Models

What differences in behaviour are noticeable between children who have a secure relationship with their carers and those who don't? Have a look at the following activity:

ACTIVITY 3.3

What characteristic behaviours might lead you to think that there was a secure relationship between a child and her carer? What behaviours would lead you to feel that the relationship was problematic?

   The fact that children behave differently suggests that they have different ideas in their minds. What ideas might those be?

COMMENTS ON ACTIVITY 3.3

You may have described a secure relationship as being one in which a child goes easily to her carer, but seems confident enough of her carer's support to leave the carer's side and explore. A securely attached child has learnt the basic lesson of trust which you may remember Erikson saw as the first developmental task (see Chapter 2). The child has the belief that the carer can be depended upon. You may also have mentioned eye contact, mutually rewarding physical contact and mutually rewarding verbal communication.

   In the case of an insecure attachment, you may have thought either of clinginess or the opposite: the child avoiding or ignoring the carer (or perhaps you may have thought of children that exhibit a strange combination of both of these). Some children seem to have the idea in their minds that there is no point in going to their carers for support – or that to do so might actually do more harm than good. Other children seem to see it as their job to look after their carers rather than the other way round, or to feel guilty about the burden they are to their carers. Such children may seem over-preoccupied with the carer, constantly watching the carer for approval, or constantly checking that the carer is okay.

   You may have mentioned a lack of specificity about the relationship: the child treats other adults just the same way as she treats the carer. You may have mentioned a lack of mutuality: eye contact, touch or verbal communication do not seem to be pleasurable or rewarding to either party.

   Insecure children exhibit a number of different characteristic ways of behaving (different attachment behavioural systems). We will discuss different patterns of insecure attachment later on. For the purpose of the present discussion though, what we would like you to note is that children in different kinds of relationships (secure and insecure) appear to have different ideas in their minds about what they can expect from their carer, what is expected of them, and what is an appropriate way to behave.

We are thinking beings and our actions are based on ideas about the world that we carry in our minds, based on previous experience. We avoid fire and hot things, for example, because we have in our minds the idea that they can cause injury and pain. The same, Bowlby suggested, applied to attachment behaviour:

… each individual builds working models of the world, and of himself in it, with the aid of which he perceives events, forecasts the future, and constructs his plans. In the working model of the world that anyone builds, a key feature is his notion of who his attachment figures are, where they may be found, and how they may be expected to respond. Similarly, in the working model of the self that anyone builds, a key feature is his notion of how acceptable or unacceptable he himself is in the eyes of his attachment figures. (Bowlby, 1998a [1973]: 236)

A securely attached child (a child who has been 'mirrored' to use Winnicott's term) will have a working model of the world in which she herself is worthy of love and attention, others are expected to be responsive and reliable (at least in the absence of evidence to the contrary) and relationships with others are seen as rewarding and fun.

But what about a child whose caregiver is unpredictable or rejecting? In such circumstances, according to attachment theory, children develop a working model that is based, not on reality or on an accurate representation of self and others, but on *coping*. To achieve this working model, they will use *defensive exclusion* (or 'denial' as Freud would have called it) to shut out aspects of reality which do not fit the model, and to manage their anxiety. The resulting model is 'faulty'. It sacrifices many of the child's own needs, including the child's need for an accurate representation of reality, in order to accommodate the caregiver in some way, and to help the child to manage anxiety. Children with grossly neglectful parents, for example (like Jenny in Activity 2.2 in the last chapter), will think of all kinds of excuses for the neglect in order to protect themselves from concluding that their parents do not care about them. They may tell themselves that they deserve the neglect, or that they prefer things the way they are.

This concept of the *faulty working model* is very much in the psychodynamic tradition. As we've seen, Freud saw defences coming into play to protect an individual against the anxiety that comes with needs not being met. Winnicott's concept of a 'false self' (see Chapter 2) can also be seen as the result of a faulty working model. And, like Freudian theory, attachment theory maintains that, once established, defensive mechanisms become part of our makeup, so that as we move into adult life, and try to form new attachments, these will be informed by these faulty working models. In other words, adults who have internalised faulty working models as children try to form relationships *on the basis of a distorted view*. Thus, although faulty working models may be a necessary survival mechanism at the time they are established, a way of maintaining relationships which are the best currently available and keeping anxieties under control, there is a cost to pay in the long term.

These *costs* can be summed up as follows:

- Faulty models contain inaccurate information on which to base relationships, and therefore cause difficulties in forming new relationships successfully.
- 'Defensive exclusion' means that models can't be updated in the light of new experience. (Defensive exclusion is why faulty models tend to become 'set in stone'.)

- These systems tend to include *splitting* – the co-existence of incompatible ideas. (For example, 'My mum loves and cares for me very, very much' co-exists in the same mind as 'Unless I am very, very careful, my mother punishes me and tells me she never wanted me.' See Chapter 2 for more on splitting.) The habit of splitting prevents the development of a coherent sense of self. (People prone to splitting never know what they *really* think or who they *really* are.)
- Defensive exclusion removes the opportunity to process painful feelings, such as grief or anger. (If you can't admit to yourself you are angry, then you can never deal with it.) To put it in Kleinian terms (see Chapter 2 again), it becomes impossible to move from the paranoid-schizoid position to the depressive position.

Mary Ainsworth's Attachment Classification System

We've already noted that both clinginess and aloofness, though apparently opposite, can both be the consequences of poor attachment. When a child's attachment needs are not fully met, and the child develops a 'faulty working model', this may take one of several forms. Mary Ainsworth, a collaborator of Bowlby, developed the Strange Situation Test and proposed a classification, based on these studies of mother and baby interactions, which included three categories of attachment: *secure*, *anxious-avoidant* and *anxious-ambivalent* (Ainsworth et al., 1978). A fourth category, *disorganised* attachment, has since been recognised and there are also some individuals who have not experienced any type of attachment at all who can be termed *non-attached*. So we now have five categories, as follows:

Secure

The child shows a clear preference for the mother (or other primary carer) over others. The carer is sensitive to, and responds to, the child's attempts to communicate. The child is confident that the carer is available to give support and takes pleasure in the presence of the carer. The child shows distress on separation from the carer. On reunion they seek some reassurance, but then settle again.

Anxious-avoidant

This is also known as 'insecure-avoidant' (the word 'anxious' and the word 'insecure' are used interchangeably in this context) and one might describe it as the 'aloof' strategy. The child doesn't show much distress on separation from the carer and when she returns the child ignores or avoids her. The child does not seek out physical contact and is watchful and wary around the carer. Her play is inhibited and she shows little discrimination between her carer and others, including strangers. This pattern emerges when the parent is insensitive to, or rejecting of, the child's needs. The child has therefore learnt to minimise needs for attachment (through defensive exclusion) in order to avoid rebuff. It is as if the child is saying: 'Who cares? I didn't want it anyway.'

Anxious-ambivalent

Also called 'insecure-ambivalent' or 'resistant', this might be described as the 'clingy' strategy. The attachment is strong but not secure – a distinction that sometimes confuses people when parent–child relationships are being assessed. Here the child is distressed on separation but does not settle down on reunion. The return of the carer is longed for, but when it comes it is not reassuring: the separation anxiety continues. The anxious-ambivalent child is frightened to go off and explore the world, because she is uncertain about whether the carer will be there when needed. This pattern is the result of a parenting style that is not consistently hostile or rejecting, but is inconsistent, and where parents are lacking in empathy for the child's needs. Not surprisingly a history of separations from parents, and threats of abandonment, are also associated with this strategy. The child may adopt all kinds of strategies to keep the attention of the carer. Role reversal may take place, for example, where the child cares for the caregiver, paying more attention to the caregiver's needs than her own. But at the same time the child is angry about the unreliability of the carer, though this anger may be defensively excluded, so that the child is not consciously aware of it.

Disorganised

This occurs when the carer is viewed by the child as frightening (as in abusive situations) or as frightened. Either way, the carer is not available as a source of comfort or reassurance, though the child has nowhere else to go. In the case of abusive situations, the carer may simultaneously be the main *source* of danger or fear, while at the same time the only place to go for comfort. The relationship between Jenny and her mother Mandy described in Chapter 2 (Activity 2.2) is an example of this kind of situation, in which there is no 'right' response. Children exhibiting disorganised attachment may show a confused mixture of both ambivalent and avoidant responses (for example, seeking to be held, but then looking away and avoiding eye contact). Or they may simply 'freeze', showing neither positive nor negative reactions to separation and reunion. A great deal of research has recently been done to try to reach a better understanding of disorganised attachment, which of course is crucially relevant to professional child care practice, such that Green and Goldwyn (2002: 840) conclude that:

> There has been … a shift of emphasis in attachment literature away from the importance of the distinction between attachment security/insecurity to that between attachment organisation/disorganisation.

It is disorganised attachment that is most likely to produce long-term behaviour and mental health problems, so exploring this further has become the priority of research. Children whose attachment is disorganised will develop what Howe (2005) describes as 'brittle behavioural strategies' which seek to impose some control on their frighteningly out-of-control world. This control may take many different forms. Compulsive behaviour such as self-reliance, compliance or caregiving seek to impose control on the self, and minimise their dependence on caregivers, while controlling strategies such as aggression seek to coerce caregivers into meeting their needs. Addictive behaviours can also be seen as a way of meeting attachment needs; when no reliable caregiver is available a substance like food, drugs or alcohol can become a substitute for human relationships (Flores, 2004).

Research has shown that children who show disorganised attachment are likely to have carers who have themselves been unable to resolve childhood experiences of loss and trauma (Main and Hesse, 1990). Intolerable feelings arising from these experiences are then triggered by the stresses that arise when they become parents themselves, and they dissociate, going 'mentally offline' (Howe, 2011: 154) and no longer being able to respond appropriately to their children's needs.

The use of the term 'disorganised' to describe this kind of attachment had been questioned by Crittenden (2008) and other recent researchers. They see it as a highly functional and complex strategy for staying safe in circumstances where parenting is frequently chaotic and dangerous by adapting the attachment style to the demands and threats of the moment, alternating as necessary between compulsive anxious-avoidant and controlling anxious-ambivalent modes. For a summary of Crittenden's Dynamic Maturational Model of attachment, including her attachment 'wheel', see her website (Family Relations Institute 2011–2014).

Non-attached

This applies to children who have had no opportunity to form attachments of any kind. For example, it applies to children raised from an early age in some kind of institution, where, even if they are adequately fed and clothed and so on, they may have no opportunities to form personal relationships with carers. It may also apply in some cases to families where the carer is totally unavailable emotionally, as the result perhaps of mental illness. Non-attached children show serious problems in social relationships. They may show little preference for, or interest in, one person rather than another. They have difficulty in controlling their impulses. Their cognitive development may be impaired (Rutter, 1981).

ACTIVITY 3.4

(a) Thinking about adults that you know (perhaps the ones you thought of in Activity 3.1), can you think of some whose way of relating to others could be described as anxious-avoidant and of some whose way of relating to others could be described as anxious-ambivalent?

(b) If you would like to consider how your own childhood relationships affect your relationships now, one way to look at it would be to write down a list of messages that you characteristically received from your parents – positive ('You are special'), negative ('I'm too busy to attend to you') or neutral. You can then consider how these messages have affected your characteristic stance in relation to other people. *Please note though that this can be surprisingly distressing. It may be best done as a structured and facilitated small group discussion with people you trust, when you can compare and contrast your responses with those of others.*

COMMENTS ON ACTIVITY 3.4

(a) Most of us probably know people who are avoidant or ambivalent in relationships, sometimes to surprising extremes. If you are familiar with the childhood history of these people, you may well see, we suspect, that the parents were either rejecting or unresponsive (in the avoidant case) or inconsistent (in the ambivalent case).

(b) If you decided to do the second part of the exercise, you will probably have noticed how powerful some of those parental messages are in terms of the emotional response they produce – and it may have struck you that these messages from your childhood do indeed affect the way you deal with the world now. One could argue that this is a demonstration of internal working models in action. (Parent message cards, incidentally, on which a large number of such messages are written out, one per card, can be used as a therapeutic tool: the idea being to sort them into two piles, those that apply and those that don't – or those that you would wish to pass on to your children – and those you would not.)

Developments of Attachment Theory

Privation and deprivation

Research by Michael Rutter and others confirms Bowlby's original insistence on the importance of early life experiences on children's long-term psychological development. In a study published in 1998, Rutter and his collaborators in the English and Romanian Adoptees Study Team, found that gross early privation was a major cause of cognitive deficits among Romanian orphans adopted in the UK and concluded that 'psychological privation was probably a more important factor in this than nutritional deprivation' (Rutter et al., 1998: 465). But Rutter has pointed out that Bowlby's concept of 'maternal deprivation', as originally formulated, was a confusing one because it lumps together many different factors, and because the words 'maternal' and 'deprivation' are both somewhat misleading.

He argues that things such as cognitive delay and language delay in children from deprived backgrounds, may be due to lack of *stimulation* in those environments. This is a different thing from the lack of emotional warmth, which research by Rutter and others confirms is linked to deviant and anti-social behaviour in later life. Emotional warmth and cognitive stimulation are different factors, and the lack of each of them has different effects, though in certain environments, both may be lacking.

Importantly Rutter also argues that *privation* (that is to say, a chronic *lack*) rather than deprivation (that is, a specific *loss*) is what causes long-term psychological problems.

> Loss of an attachment figure, although a major factor in the causation of short-term effects, seems of only minor importance with respect to long-term consequences … Indeed the evidence strongly suggests that most of the long-term consequences are due to privation or lack of some kind, rather than to any kind of loss. (Rutter, 1981: 121)

The 'maternal' part of 'maternal deprivation' is also questioned because it implies a unique importance to the mother. Rutter does not think this is substantiated by research evidence and writes:

> most children develop bonds with several people and it appears likely that these bonds are basically similar … the chief bond need not be with a biological parent, it need not be the chief caretaker and it need not be with a female. (Rutter, 1981: 127)

Recent developments in neuroscience

Rutter's work linked emotional and cognitive development, and the fast-developing area of neuroscience research is shedding more light on how the two areas are linked. Neuroscience is the study of the development of the brain, and how it operates with the rest of the nervous system to shape emotion, cognition and human behaviour. Technical developments such as brain scans have made new areas of information available, and work in this field of research is still progressing rapidly.

Findings from neuroscience research give strong support to the principles of attachment theory developed by Bowlby and his successors. A picture emerges of the critical importance of the first three years of life, when the right hemisphere of the brain is undergoing an explosion of development. The right brain operates in an intuitive, holistic fashion and is associated with unconscious processes, as opposed to the left brain, which develops later and is involved in the logical and linear functions that are necessary for the acquisition of language and the development of reasoning powers (Gerhardt, 2004: 36, 51). So it is the right brain that is involved in the processes of attachment, and dominates the first years of life, while the left brain becomes more important later.

The biology of the brain is too complicated to describe in detail here, but, briefly, what happens in the early period of rapid growth is that new pathways and connections (known as 'synapses') are made between different cells in the brain (neurons) and the nervous system. The speed at which the brain develops at the beginning of life is phenomenal – 'equivalent to a rate of 1.8 million new synapses *per second* between two months' gestation and two years after birth' (Eliot, 2001: 27, quoted by Balbernie, 2001: 240). However, only those connections which are reinforced by regular use will survive and develop, producing a system of established or 'hard-wired' neural pathways. And it would seem that attachment patterns are among the pathways that are established and reinforced in this way. Ainsworth argued that attachment is 'built into the nervous system in the course and as a result of the infant's experience with the mother' (Ainsworth, 1967: 429, quoted by Schore, 2000). The work of Schore and other neuroscientists has confirmed Ainsworth's view, and begun to explain, and continues to explore, the processes through which this takes place.

One area where neuroscience has given support to previous thinking about human development is the importance of eye contact and visual perception. Both attachment theory and Winnicott's concept of mirroring in object relations theory (see Chapter 2) recognise the importance of this in early infancy, and research evidence shows rapid change and development at about eight weeks in the part of the brain that processes visual information (Schore, 2001: 17). This sets the stage for a period of development characterised by rich visual communication and exchange, when an unconscious synchronisation takes place between carer and infant, and the infant learns to feel connected, held and secure. Genetics research is shedding more light on 'critical periods' like this in brain development. More is being discovered about the way in which certain genes throw switches in the brain to enable it to respond to environmental stimuli, which then makes possible the rapid neurological development which must take place in a very specific window of opportunity, as is the case with visual perception, which may not develop at all if this window is missed (Ridley, 2004: 163–7).

Schore (2000; Schore and Schore, 2008) describes attachment theory as a *regulatory* theory: the unconscious exchanges between the infant and his carers give him the means to begin to regulate the power of his feelings. If his carer is attuned to him, she will reflect back and amplify his pleasurable feelings (for instance by responding to his babbling with her own affectionate baby-talk) and soothe his unpleasurable feelings (for instance by cuddling and rocking him and making reassuring noises to him when he is crying and distressed). This is the very first step towards having another view of himself and his experience of the world, which will eventually enable him to 'mentalise' – a term coined by Peter Fonagy et al. (2002) and associated with the acquisition of a theory of mind (something we will discuss more fully in our next chapter).

Neuroscience points to a close connection between emotional and cognitive development: 'Research suggests that emotion operates as a central organising process within the brain' (Seigal, 1999: 4, quoted by Balbernie, 2001: 237). It also demonstrates just how complex the relationship between nature and nurture is, as a consensus emerges that the physical development of the human brain is designed to be moulded by the environment it encounters, particularly in the early years of life (Schore, 2001: 14).

Bowlby broke new ground by bringing together two previously separate disciplines: psychoanalysis and the study of animal behaviour. Present-day neuroscience continues in this multi-disciplinary tradition as it develops its psychoneurobiological model of human development.

Attachment in later life

Bowlby's work focused on babies and young children, but present-day attachment theory takes a much longer view, and presents a case for the importance of an understanding of attachment across the whole lifecourse (Howe, 2011). We will find ourselves revisiting attachment theory in the later chapters of this book which deal with adolescence, adulthood, old age, bereavement and disability.

Increasingly, links are being made between disorganised attachment in children and the kinds of mental health problems which can occur in adulthood when these attachment issues are unresolved. These include personality disorders (Crittenden and Newman, 2010), eating disorders (Barone and Guiducci, 2009), drug and alcohol abuse (Schindler et al., 2005) and also post-traumatic stress disorder (Kobak et al., 2004). And the effect of these problems extends way beyond the individuals concerned, and poses questions of social and economic policy for the whole of society:

> The behavioural and mental problems shown by the majority of those who have suffered early trauma and maltreatment point to the heavy cost, both social and material, that societies pay when children are raised in environments where stress, disadvantage, poverty, violence and neglect are endemic. (Howe, 2011: 196)

Criticisms of Attachment Theory

As we have noted, Rutter took issue with some of the earlier formulations of attachment theory, and their emphasis on mothers and their claim that children were essentially 'monotropic' (forming a primary attachment to just one person) can be criticised from both a feminist and from a multicultural point of view.

We would suggest that not only mothers but also many fathers would object to the restricted roles to which Bowlby sometimes seems to consign them. However, those roles were seen as the norm in the immediate post-war period in which Bowlby was writing.

A number of feminist writers (for example, Burman, 1994) have criticised Bowlby for 'tying women to the home', by implying that if the mother leaves her child at all, this will result in long-term harm. In fact, it has been argued that one reason that Bowlby's ideas became popular when they did is that they provided a rationale for taking women out of paid work following the war years when so many women had joined the industrial workforce, and expecting them to stay at home rather than compete for jobs with men returning from the war. Attachment theory could be used as a pretext for not providing good day-care facilities, for example, or for denying women an equal role with men in the workplace.

From a multicultural point of view, one could also argue that the insistence on the monotropic mother–child bond has the effect of setting up the European/North American 'nuclear family' as the model for childrearing, ignoring the more communal approaches that are the norm in other parts of the world. In other words: attachment theory, in its original formulation, is distinctly 'Eurocentric'. Even within the terms of Western culture, overemphasis on the monotropic mother–child bond seems to undervalue other relationships, such as those with the father, grandparents and siblings.

It can even be argued that if a child relies too exclusively on care from one person, her mother, this may in the long run itself be damaging, placing undue pressure on the mother which will itself harm the relationship if she is worn out, or bored, or becomes resentful of the child. And these days, unlike in the 50s, it is very common, and frequently an economic necessity, for a mother to return to work in the first year after her baby's birth.

However, although there are criticisms that can be made about attachment theory as originally formulated by Bowlby, it would be a mistake to discard Bowlby's ideas about the importance of attachment and a secure base in childhood, or his ideas about the influence of childhood experience on adult life, merely because his conception of what this might consist of was limited by the particular perspective of his own times.

Bowlby's ideas were related to the ideas of other object relations theorists such as Winnicott, and also to the ideas of Freud himself. One lasting legacy of Freud seems to be an increased recognition of the deep emotional needs of young children and of the profound damage that can be done if these needs are ignored. Bowlby translated this insight into a theory which has proved to be something that can grow and develop in the light of new evidence, and into a practical concern which has been a major influence on public policy, and on the way we think about children and their needs.

Chapter Summary

- In this chapter, we looked at John Bowlby's ideas about the importance of early attachment for long-term psychological health.
- We considered his ideas about the biological origins of attachment and attachment behaviour.
- We looked at the stages in the development of attachment.
- We considered the idea of 'internal working models' – of self and others – learnt in early relationships and carried into later life.

(Continued)

(Continued)

- We looked at Mary Ainsworth's classification system for secure and insecure attachment (the latter being divided into anxious-avoidant and anxious-ambivalent – disorganised attachment and non-attachment are two additional categories).
- We considered developments of Bowlby's theory in work by Rutter and recent research in neuroscience.
- We looked at criticisms of attachment theory from feminist and multicultural points of view.

In this and the previous chapter we have been looking primarily at emotional development. In the next chapter we will move on to look at cognitive development: the development of thinking.

Further Reading

Foundations of attachment theory

Ainsworth, M., Blehar, M., Aters, E. and Wall, S. (1978) *Patterns of Attachment: A Psychological Study of the Strange Situation.* Hillside, NJ: Lawrence Erlbaum.

Bowlby, J. (1990 [1953]) *Childcare and the Growth of Love.* Harmondsworth: Penguin.

Bowlby, J. (1997 [1969]) *Attachment.* London: Pimlico.

Bowlby, J. (1998 [1973]) *Separation.* London: Pimlico.

Bowlby, J. (1998 [1980]) *Loss.* London: Pimlico.

Holmes, J. (1993) *John Bowlby and Attachment Theory.* London: Routledge.

General introductions to attachment theory and its application

Howe, D. (1995) *Attachment Theory for Social Work Practice.* Basingstoke: Macmillan.

Howe, D. (2005) *Child Abuse and Neglect: Attachment, Development and Intervention.* Basingstoke: Palgrave.

Howe, D. (2011) *Attachment across the Lifecourse.* Basingstoke: Palgrave Macmillan.

Neuroscience and attachment

Gerhardt, S. (2004) *Why Love Matters: How Affection Shapes a Baby's Brain.* Hove: Routledge.

4 THE EMERGENCE OF REASON

THE DEVELOPING ABILITY TO UNDERSTAND

- Cognitive psychology and cognitive development   68
- Learning to make sense of the world   70
- Assimilation, accommodation and equilibration   71
- Stages of cognitive development   73
- Piaget's model: challenges and developments   79

Suppose you are a teacher in a nursery school. In your class is a 4-year-old boy whose mother has to go to hospital for an operation. She is a lone parent with no relatives in the area, and it is going to be necessary for the little boy to go to a foster home for seven nights. How do you help a 4-year-old make sense of the fact that he must go and live with strangers for a week? It's not just a matter of making him feel cared for, or of helping him cope emotionally, and giving him an opportunity to express his feelings (as Bowlby advocated), vitally important though that is. It is also a matter of making the facts intelligible to him. What is a hospital? What is an operation? What is a foster home? What, for that matter, is a *week*? All these concepts need explaining.

This chapter represents something of a change of gear from the two previous chapters. We have been considering how childhood experience influences emotional development. We are now going to look at how a child learns to make sense of the world. We are moving into what is known as cognitive psychology – or, more specifically, into developmental cognitive psychology.

In particular, we are going to focus on the work of Jean Piaget. If Bowlby is the father of attachment theory, Piaget could perhaps be described as the father of developmental cognitive psychology. Just as with Bowlby, many of Piaget's ideas have been challenged by subsequent research, and we are not offering them here as the 'last word'. Nevertheless, because of Piaget's importance in the development of thinking in this field, the easiest way to introduce this topic is to begin with Piaget and then discuss some of the problems with his ideas that subsequent research has identified and look at some of the other theories and theorists who can contribute to our understanding of cognitive development.

We began this discussion by making a distinction between cognitive development and emotional development. But in reality the two are closely interlinked. If you look back after reading this chapter at the developmental ideas of Freud or Bowlby, or those of Klein or Erikson, you will see that each stage presupposes a level of cognitive development also. Children cannot reach an understanding about their relationship with others, for example, until they are able to grasp that others do actually have a separate existence.

As discussed in the previous chapter, a secure emotional base allows exploration and learning to take place. The insecure baby monkey puts all its energies into attempting to find comfort, and does not explore as much as does a monkey that is confident that its mother is available when needed – and any teacher will confirm how difficult it is to get troubled children to settle and concentrate in class. So a solid emotional base gives the security that supports learning. But the reverse is also true. Learning about how the world works helps us to make sense of troubling events. Moves and losses, for example, are particularly difficult for children at an age when they are old enough to know what is happening but not old enough to make sense of it. It is easier for a child to spend a week away from home when that child is capable of grasping the concept of 'a week'.

For those who work with children, it is important to have some understanding of cognitive development as well as emotional development because the two go hand in hand.

Cognitive Psychology and Cognitive Development

To us as adults, most of the time, it seems as if the outside world – the world of people, objects and events – is just self-evidently *there*. But in fact all that we can ever know about that outside world comes to us in the form of millions of electrical impulses that reach our brains from our various sense organs: light-sensitive cells in our eyes, cells in our ears that are sensitive to vibrations in the air, pressure sensors in our skin. The 'world' that we feel ourselves to inhabit is not 'just there' at all, but is something which we have somehow reconstructed from these countless signals. Once in a while we may get a sense of this. You have probably had the experience of seeing someone out of the corner of your eye and noticing all kinds of details: a beard, glasses, a slight stoop. But then you look round and see it was only a coat hanging on the back of a door. All those details were just intelligent guesses made by your brain on the basis of the limited information available.

Cognitive psychology is the branch of psychology that deals with the interpretation of sensory events: how they *register* (perception), how we store them in memory and retrieve them, how we learn from experience and make use of images, symbols, concepts and rules in thinking, reasoning and problem solving. In short it is about how we process and interpret *information* (in contrast to psychodynamic theory which is more about how we process *feelings*).

And this business of processing and interpreting information is a skill. Some skills are innate and present at birth (horses are born with the ability to walk) but some skills have to be learnt. The study of human development suggests that most of these cognitive skills are not present at birth, not even very basic ones such as the ability to understand that the patterns of colours in front of our eyes represent objects out there in the world. Although the skills have to be learnt, the process of learning follows pathways that may in themselves be innate (as with the growth of the body), influenced by a complex interaction of genes and environmental triggers, as we saw in Chapter 1.

The following activity may help you to start to think about the different ways in which children function cognitively at different ages.

ACTIVITY 4.1

Think of a child of 4 or 5 years old that you know or have worked with. What is different about the way this child thinks and understands the world, from the way adults think about the world? What kinds of ideas does this child – and others of this child's age – characteristically find difficult to grasp?

COMMENTS ON ACTIVITY 4.1

Some things you may have thought of:

1. Geography – small children have little grasp of geography, not only in the sense of not knowing so many facts, but in being unable to grasp ideas such as distance (if you go on a journey with a small child, she may repeatedly ask, 'Are we nearly there?'), or the idea that, say, a different town may still be in the same country.
2. Time – you may have thought of examples where small children have similar difficulties with adult ideas of time as they do with space. 'Next month' does not mean much to a 5-year-old.
3. Money – small children have difficulty with the concept of money. When you go to a shop and receive change, they have difficulty understanding what change is, however carefully it is explained to them. Small children may think that change is simply a gift.

Learning to Make Sense of the World

When dealing with children, adults (including many adults whose job involves working with children) are prone to make one of two incorrect assumptions:

- *That children think and understand just like we do.* For example, if you are a parent, you might possibly have had an experience like the following, which once happened to one of the authors. A family is setting off in the car on the annual holiday which has been discussed for months. Twenty miles down the road, the youngest child suddenly asks: 'By the way, where are we going?' The holiday *may* have been discussed for months, but unfortunately the adults had never done so in terms which were comprehensible to this child.
- *That children don't think at all about the world about them.* Some parents discuss all kinds of adult matters in front of their small children, and, if the wisdom of this is queried, simply say: 'Oh, don't worry about him, he's not listening to us and anyway he doesn't understand …'

The big insight of the Swiss psychologist Jean Piaget was that *both* those assumptions about children are untrue: children do think, as adults do, but they don't think in the same way as adults. This insight came to him early in his career when he was working on intelligence tests and realised that children regularly made the *same kinds of mistakes*. There was a pattern to their mistakes, in other words, which suggested that they were thinking in a consistent way that had a logic of its own, even though this was not consistent with adult logic.

Jean Piaget, who died in 1980, was born in 1896 in Switzerland. Although one of the most famous names in developmental psychology, he in fact did not see himself as primarily a psychologist at all, but as a biologist and a philosopher. He described himself as a 'genetic epistemologist'. Epistemology is the philosophy of knowledge, so what he meant by this was that he was interested in the origins of knowledge.

Piaget believed that a child is actively involved in the development of her own thinking and he saw the active search for knowledge as being something that children do, and want to do, for its own sake, and not just as a means to other ends. In Piaget's view a child finds her way through successive stages of cognitive development rather like a scientist, experimenting and developing evermore sophisticated models to explain the world, until eventually a level is reached where she is able to reason abstractly, think about hypothetical situations and organise rules about the world in her mind. Piaget saw cognitive development moving – in all children – through several stages, each one of which is characterised by a different way of thinking about and understanding the world. And he identified four factors that might be involved in this developmental process:

- physical maturation (that is, actual physical changes in the brain during childhood, resulting in the emergence of new abilities)
- experience

- social transmission (what we learn from other people)
- equilibration (a concept which we will explain and discuss a little later on).

Given that Piaget saw all children, regardless of culture, as going through the same basic stages, one might think that he would see physical maturation as being a major factor. But Piaget did not think that physical maturation could explain much of the change. His reasoning was that although children in different cultures go through the same stages of cognitive development, they reach different stages at different speeds, whereas if it was purely a matter of brain growth, one would expect the speed to be constant across cultures.

Experience and social transmission are (of course) factors in a child's learning, but Piaget did not take the view that our knowledge and understanding are simply the sum of what we have experienced or been taught. His view was more that children would use the information presented to them by experience as experimental data with which to develop their thinking about the basic rules that operate in the world. So children with very diverse experiences would nevertheless come to the same basic conclusions and develop their thinking along essentially the same paths because basic properties of the universe, like time and space and number, work in the same way everywhere. You could learn the concept of number, for example, in any environment, though some children may begin by counting marbles, others by counting stones.

As far as social transmission is concerned, teaching could be used to speed up a child's progress, provided that it was pitched at an appropriate level. There are some things that a child simply cannot be taught below a certain age. Certain ideas cannot be grasped until other more basic ideas are in place, just as one cannot place a building block one metre above the floor until there is a pile of other building blocks beneath it to hold it in place. Outside factors make a difference, but the essential driving force of cognitive development is something from *within* the child.

Assimilation, Accommodation and Equilibration

The basic building block of learning, according to Piaget, is what he called a *schema*. 'Schemas' are basic patterns of coordination between perceptions and actions. Grasping at a colourful object, for instance, could be described as a 'schema'. When a child encounters a new object or situation, she will try to deal with it in the first place by applying ideas and habits learnt from dealing with other objects and other situations. For example, if she is familiar with eating Smarties, she may try to eat other round, brightly coloured objects like beads or small parts of toys like Lego. This process Piaget called *assimilation*.

However, when a new object turns out not to fit into an old schema, schemas then have to be changed to fit the new object. In the example above, when the child finds that the object doesn't taste like a Smartie she will probably stop trying to eat it and explore other ways of playing with it. She will also revise her ideas about small round coloured objects, recognising that they don't always have the same properties. This process Piaget called *accommodation*.

Mental growth involves both assimilation and accommodation. The only way we can deal initially with a new situation is to try to apply ideas learnt from other situations (assimilation), but no one would progress with learning about the world if they did not modify their ideas in the light of experience (accommodation). This process of combining assimilation and accommodation he called *equilibration*.

So more complex ideas develop from simpler ones through an alternating process of accommodation and assimilation. And Piaget argued that this process could only take place in a certain sequence. More complex blocks could only be put in place when simpler ones have already been laid. This is why Piaget (unlike Vygotsky, whom we will discuss later) saw experience and social transmission as being of secondary importance in learning. No amount of information or stimulation could impart a new idea to a child unless she was at a stage where she was able to grasp it.

We have now used the analogy of building blocks twice, because this seems to sum up the assumption behind Piaget's theory, which is known as constructivism. Before going on to look at Piaget's stages of development, the following activity is an opportunity to consider this analogy:

ACTIVITY 4.2

Piling up building blocks is one metaphor for human development. Another might, for example, be going on a journey. Are there any other metaphors that could be used for human development? Do different metaphors make us look at the process in a different way?

COMMENTS ON ACTIVITY 4.2

The metaphor of building blocks may seem to be a reasonable way of describing human learning – and it may be – but one should always be careful about the power of metaphors. For example, you might have described learning as being like colouring in a picture, or of accumulating useful objects in a sack. If so, you may have noticed that the implications of these analogies are different. With building blocks, you have to start at the floor and work upwards. But with colouring books and filling sacks, you don't have to start in any particular place, or perform tasks in any particular order.

In thinking critically about Piaget's ideas, one question you could ask is whether building blocks are the best metaphor. Does colouring fit better? Or are some aspects of learning like building and others like colouring?

Critics of Piaget often point out that development doesn't follow quite such a neatly ordered sequence as the model suggests. The same criticism could be made of other kinds of 'stage' models of human life (for example, Erikson's model discussed in Chapter 2): often we don't move neatly through different stages so much as go back and forth between different states or levels.

TABLE 4.1   Piaget's stages of cognitive development

Stage	Approximate Age
Sensori-motor	0–18 months
Pre-operational	18 months to 7 years
Concrete operations	7–12 years
Formal operations	12 + years

Stages of Cognitive Development

Piaget identified four basic stages in the development of a child's thinking, illustrated in Table 4.1. It should be emphasised that the approximate ages are a rough guide only: the stages are defined by the level of abstraction that the individual is capable of.

We'll now look at the stages one by one:

The sensori-motor stage (0–18 months)

Piaget proposed that babies start with basic physical reflexes, learn to modify these and then extend them by a process of assimilation and accommodation until – at the end of this stage – they are able to hold representations of things in their minds and plan out what they do. He thought that development in different areas – the understanding of space, say, or of number, or of cause and effect – proceeds in parallel. They all require the same basic underlying structures of reasoning. For example, sensori-motor development occurred alongside development of the idea of *object permanence*: the idea that objects still exist, even when you can't see them. Thus, a child starts out with little or no idea that objects really exist at all. (Why, after all, should a baby be able to know that the colours and shapes that she sees are anything more than just colours and shapes?) The child then progresses to a point where she doesn't just see objects but actively looks for them. Alongside this development, the child is similarly progressing in terms of sensori-motor control from movements which exist for their own sake and have no other purpose, to movements which are not only purposeful but planned in advance.

The pre-operational stage (18 months to 7 years)

At the conclusion of the previous stage, the child was beginning to hold representations of things in her mind. This ability develops in the pre-operational stage when representations of many kinds are used with increasing sophistication. The child acquires language, learns to make and interpret pictures and uses one object to represent another in imaginative play (a box is a car, a doll is a baby). So the *meanings* of objects and events are now being manipulated as well as the actual objects which the child learnt to manipulate in the previous stage. This is a major advance in the ability to think. But, as you probably concluded in Activity 4.1, a child during this stage still thinks in a very different way from an adult.

The following are some of the ways in which, Piaget suggested, the thinking of a child is different during this stage:

- The child tends to be *egocentric*. This is not necessarily to say that the child is *selfish* but that the child finds it difficult to see things from a point of view other than her own. For example, a child talking on the telephone may point to something in the room and refer to 'that thing over there', seemingly unaware that the person on the other end of the phone cannot possibly know what she means. Or a child playing hide-and-seek may hide her face, without realising that the rest of her body is just as visible to others as it was before, even though invisible to her.
- The child is prone to *centration*. She tends to fix her attention on one aspect of a situation and ignore other aspects. She has difficulty in recognising that a situation may have a number of dimensions. To give an instance encountered by one of the authors: a child of 4 is talking with his mother about how everyone he knows goes to the same school. This is an interesting idea which hasn't struck him before. 'But how come I know granny then?' he asks. 'She doesn't even *go* to my school!' Struck with the idea of school as the place where you get to know people, he has failed to hang on to the idea that there might be other contexts too in which you can meet people.
- There is a *lack of reversibility* in the child's thinking. This means that the child is unable to mentally reverse a series of events or steps of reasoning. To us as adults it follows that if we take three Smarties away from a pile of twenty, there will be twenty Smarties there again if we add another three. Or, if some water half fills a glass and we pour it into a mug, it will still half fill the glass when we pour it back again. There is a whole

range of actions which we understand to be reversible. But these things are not self-evident to a pre-operational child. The word *operation* in Piaget's terminology refers to these reversible logical processes. The term *pre-operational* thus refers to the stage when the child has not learnt to use 'operations'. We mentioned earlier the inability of small children to grasp the concept of giving change in shops. Buying something, paying for it and receiving change is a good example of an operation in Piaget's sense. The price of the item bought and the change, we as adults understand, add up to the amount handed over to the shopkeeper. If we change our minds about the purchase and return the item, we will get back the price of the item which, with the change, adds up to precisely the same as the money we first handed over. But this is very difficult to explain to a 5-year-old.

So a child at this stage has a 'pre-logical' understanding of the world, based on subjective impressions and hunches, rather than on logical thinking, and based on a view of the world that has themselves at its centre. That is, after all, how it subjectively *appears* to all of us, but as we grow older we learn that this is not really the case. One aspect of this is that children at this age in particular are prone to 'magical thinking'. The following conversation is reported by Piaget with an 8-year-old child (child's words in italics).

> You have already seen the clouds moving along? What makes them move? – *When we move along, they move along too.* – Can you make them move? – *Everybody can, when they walk.* – When I walk and you are still, do they move? – *Yes.* – And at night, when everyone is asleep do they move? – *Yes.* – But you tell me that they only move when somebody walks. – *They always move. The cats, when they walk, and then the dogs, they make the clouds move.* (Piaget, 1930: 62)

Those who work with children have to watch out for the combination of magical thinking and egocentrism which can make pre-operational children in particular feel that they are responsible for events which in reality have nothing to do with them: a traffic accident in which a relative was injured, perhaps, or their parents' divorce.

The following activity is a further look at the practical implication of pre-operational thinking.

ACTIVITY 4.3

Suppose you are a doctor or nurse, explaining to a child of 6 why he needs to have an operation – and what will be entailed.

Bearing in mind that a child of 6 thinks in a different way from adults, how should you go about this?

COMMENTS ON ACTIVITY 4.3

- Many people, when talking to children, are careful to adopt a kind and reassuring tone of voice, to talk about things familiar to the child and to use words which the child is likely to know – and all these things are of course important. But it is also important to ensure that the ideas presented to the child are comprehensible at his age.
- Because children at this age tend to centration, a complex discussion of the kind 'on the one hand, on the other hand' is likely to mean nothing to the child.
- The child's concerns may be focused on particular aspects of the situation which can be quite different from an adult's. To give an example: it may be that the thing that most worries the child is not the operation at all but having the bandages removed later, because he is terrified of pulling off sticky plasters.
- The child may come with powerful preconceptions which are quite irrational ('People who have surgery always have their legs removed', 'My illness is a punishment because I hit my little brother'). It might be a good idea to ask the child to describe his understanding of the situation – though of course the child may not want or feel able to tell you all his thoughts.

Being aware of children's very different ways of thinking is of course only part of successful communication with children. There are a lot of other issues too: awareness of a child's emotional needs and of his relationships, for example. And any adult trying to communicate with a child, such as a doctor or nurse in the above example, needs to be aware of the huge power difference between an adult and a child. But being aware of children's levels of cognitive understanding remains very important.

Theory of Mind

Closely related to 'egocentrism' in Piaget's sense is the concept in cognitive psychology that is known as a 'theory of mind'. What is meant by this is an 'ability to explain and predict the behaviour of others by attributing to them mental states, such as beliefs, desires, emotions or intentions' (Gallagher and Frith, 2003: 77). In other words, having a 'theory of mind' means that we try to understand other people's actions by forming theories about what is going on in their heads.

Having a 'theory of mind' is necessary in order *not* to be egocentric, because it is about recognising that 'other people have a different perspective from ours' and that 'to understand their behaviour we have to take account of their perspective as well as the state of the world from our own perspective' (Gallagher and Frith, 2003: 77). Research into brain development is increasingly recognising the link between attachment (which we discussed in Chapter 3) and the development of a theory of mind, or mentalisation; 'understanding of minds is hard without the experience of having been understood as a person with a mind' (Fonagy and Target, 2005: 334).

The development of a 'theory of mind' in children can be tested in experiments such as a 'change of location' task in which children 'witness a character placing an object in one location and then leaving the room. In the character's absence, children witness the object being moved to a new location. Children are then asked where the character will look for his object upon his return' (Bernstein et al., 2007: 1375). If children understand that the character has a different perspective from their own, then they will suggest that the character will look in the place where he left it. If they have difficulty with understanding that the character has a different perspective, then they suggest that he will look in the place where *they* know it to be. Bernstein et al. note that 'children younger than about 4 years of age typically state the latter option' (2007: 1375).

Simon Baron-Cohen (1989, 1997) proposes that difficulty in developing a theory of mind is a specific developmental problem characteristic of autistic children, and uses the term 'mindblindness' to describe this.

The concrete operations stage (7–12 years)

In this stage the child is now able to grasp what Piaget called 'operations'. A child at this stage will have no difficulty grasping that when water is poured from a tall container to a broad one, it is the same amount of water and will come back to the original level when poured back into the first container. But, although the child becomes at home with external, *concrete* operations of this kind, she is still less at home with more abstract kinds of operations.

During the concrete operations stage, Piaget thought, there is a gradual waning of egocentric thinking (to repeat: this word is meant here in a cognitive sense and not a moral one). There is an increasing ability to *decentre*: to recognise and take into account the fact that many phenomena have several dimensions to them.

The child now grasps the idea of *reversibility* and growing logical insights lead to the development of concrete operational structures such as *classification* (sorting things out into categories), *seriation* (placing things in a logical order: of size, for example) and *conservation* of size and number (for example, water poured into a different shaped container is still the same amount of water).

The reason that a pre-operational child has difficulty with conservation of size and number is that she understands them in a *perceptual* way, as a description of the way things look, whereas the concrete operations child has got hold of the idea that number is not just about appearances. Likewise, a child at the pre-operational stage can find the way from A to B if it is a familiar route but she does so on the basis of remembering things on the way, and could not make a map of the route, while a child at the concrete operations stage could do so.

Another example of this shift is in the understanding of what are called *relational* terms (for example: 'This colour is *darker* than that one'). It can be shown that a concrete operations child understands that such terms describe a *relationship* between two things (between two colours in our example). But a pre-operational child sees words such as darker, bigger and so on, more as synonyms for 'very dark' or 'very big'. Once again, the concrete operations child is using logical concepts to organise experience, while the pre-operational child is relying on perception.

The contrast is apparent again in *classification*. Small children have difficulty with the idea of categories within other categories. We mentioned, for example, when discussing Activity 4.1 that small children have difficulty with the idea that a different town may still be in the same country. A statement such as 'We're driving from London to Bristol, but we'll still be in England', may be baffling to a pre-operational child. The concrete operations child is at home with such concepts.

But while able to use these sorts of rules and structures, a child at the concrete operations stage still finds it difficult to think in a self-conscious way about the rules she is using.

Comparisons with Psychodynamic Stages

If you compare Piaget's concrete operations stage with Freud's psychosexual stages, or Erikson's psychosocial ones, you'll find that it corresponds roughly to what Freud called the latency period (a period when the turmoils of the Oedipus complex were set aside while the child pursued more outward and practical concerns). Erikson saw this as a stage whose successful outcome was a sense of competence and achievement, and confidence in one's own ability to make and do things. These seem broadly consistent with Piaget's view of this stage as one in which concrete operations are mastered. While Piaget's model is not a psychodynamic theory, and does not even purport to address the same kinds of questions, Piaget did have a psychoanalytic training.

The formal operations stage (12+ years)

According to Piaget the stage of formal operations is normally reached at the beginning of adolescence and it is the final stage. This does not mean, of course, that Piaget was suggesting that a 12- or 13-year-old functions in exactly the same way as an adult in every respect (the ways in which this stage is different will be the subject of Chapter 6). But he thought that, when it comes to using rules and solving problems, a young person at this stage does indeed operate in much the same way as an adult. Piaget's theory would suggest that 11-year-olds, though very proficient in all kinds of ways, are less flexible in the way they think about problems and new situations than 14-year-olds – who, on the other hand, operate with much the same degree of flexibility as adults.

At the formal operations stage we are able not only to master basic, concrete operations, but also to perform operations *with* operations. Faced with a problem, we are able to:

- be self-consciously deductive (consciously going into problem-solving mode, so to speak) and consider all the possible ways a problem might be solved
- use abstract rules to solve a class of problems
- reflect on the rules we are using and be aware of our thought process
- use 'higher order' or analogical reasoning, for example making connections between problems that at a surface level seem quite different, but which have some likeness in terms of their logical structure.

The following experiment (Piaget et al., 1977, described in Goswami, 2011: 405) may make this slightly clearer. Piaget and his colleagues gave children a set of jumbled pictures and asked them to sort them into pairs. So, for example, given pictures including: *dog, feather, vacuum cleaner, car, dog hair, ship, bird* … etc., they might pair *bird* and *feather*, and *dog* and *dog hair*. Children at the concrete operations and formal operations stage do not find this difficult. Children at the pre-operational stage will tend to pair pictures in idiosyncratic ways of their own.

Children were then asked to *pair up the pairs*. Thus, for example, the pairs *dog* and *dog hair*, and *bird* and *feather* might go together as they both describe a similar relationship (as might the pairs *pilot* and *aeroplane*, and *driver* and *car*, for instance). This is an example of 'higher order' analogical thinking, because the participants were being asked to make connections not on the basis of anything visible on the cards, but on the basis of types of relationships. They were being asked to consider the rules that they used to form the pairs in the first part of the experiment, and then to find a second level of rules which could be used to pair up the rules themselves. In other words, they were being asked to make rules about rules, or to categorise categories. This was possible for young people in the formal operations stage, but it was too abstract for concrete operations stage children.

Piaget's Model: Challenges and Developments

As we said at the beginning of this chapter, Piaget's model cannot be taken as a definitive account of cognitive development. Criticisms of Piaget's theory come from many different quarters, and other theorists have made important contributions to the field.

Vygotsky and the role of language and culture

One notable aspect of Piaget's thinking is the surprisingly secondary importance he assigns to language and social interaction. The Russian psychologist Lev Vygotsy (1896–1934) put much more emphasis on language and saw the capacity to learn through instruction as a basic feature of human intelligence.

Vygotsky was born in the same year as Piaget, but the context of his work and the history of its influence on Western psychology was very different. He died while still in his thirties, having produced a considerable body of work, but this did not become widely known in the West until much later, until the sixties and seventies when the cultural divide between East and West was beginning to break down. Vygotsky was active in the early, idealistic days of the Russian communist revolution, and his thinking is strongly influenced by the Marxist view of social, cultural and historical processes as driving the development of individual and collective consciousness.

One of Vygotsky's most influential concepts is that of the *zone of proximal development*. This describes the gap between what a child can accomplish unaided and what she can do with help from adults or more capable peers (Vygotsky 1978: 86). His view that 'the only good learning is that which is in advance of development' (1978: 89) differs from Piaget's view that a developmental stage must be reached internally before advances in learning can take place, and it shows how Vygotsky conceptualises development as an interactive process between the individual and society.

Language is one of the most important mediums through which this interaction takes place, and consequently Vygotsky attached much more importance to the role of language than Piaget did. He suggested that the role of language and instruction is so crucial in guiding action that, when it is not provided externally, we learn to provide it for ourselves. Piaget saw the fact that small children chatter to themselves as an example of egocentrism, because the child chatters away and it doesn't occur to her that what she is saying means nothing to anyone else, and because private speech disappears as the child grows older. But Vygotksy saw language as basic to thought and suggested that a child using private speech was giving instructions to herself as a strategy to keep her focused on a task. Private speech, in Vygotsky's view, did not disappear, but simply became internalised as the interior monologue which goes on in our heads even as adults (Vygotsky, 1962).

In fact Piaget's exploration of the underlying conceptual structures which children use when solving problems could have been flawed by the fact that he did not address issues to do with language. It is possible, for instance, that children may actually possess concepts such as object permanence but may not demonstrate this if adults put questions to them in a way that they cannot grasp. To complicate this, the opposite can also be true. Children may be taught to repeat a rule, but without understanding the underlying concept. One of the authors once poured water from a tall glass into a wide one and asked a 7-year-old whether the amount was the same or not. 'The same', she said, but then added: 'I know because my teacher told me.'

The contradictions in these examples make more sense if we understand them as examples of learning in the zone of proximal development, where the interactions with adults are a part of the learning process. Followers of Vygotsky use the term 'scaffolding' to describe the educational methods that adults can use to help children move from one stage of understanding to the next (Wood et al., 1976: 90). Vygotsky's model of development is rather different from the 'building block' model of Piaget and others. It is a relational one, which arises out of the Marxist concept of a dialectical process, a back and forth interaction between two different perspectives which leads to the emergence of a new understanding.

Building blocks and stages

Some research seems to confirm Piaget's ideas about different kinds of thinking at different stages. But a lot of experimental evidence now suggests the various cognitive milestones are reached much earlier than Piaget envisaged. There is experimental evidence, for example, that the concept of object permanence is present at least as early as three months. Renée Baillargeon (1987) devised an elaborate apparatus whereby a toy car rolled down a track. A screen could be placed in front of part of the track and a box could be placed behind that screen either *next* to the track or *on* it, so that it looked as if the car could not get past it. In both cases the car could in fact pass the box. She compared babies' responses to the apparently 'possible' event of the car reappearing from behind the screen when the box had been seen to not be in its way and the apparently 'impossible' event of the car seeming to have passed through the box. She found that babies stared for much longer at the apparatus in the 'impossible' case. If they had no concept of object permanence, Baillargeon argued, why would the 'impossible case' be any more interesting than the other case? Later work by Baillargeon and colleagues, using similar experiments, has continued to explore the way in which infants perceive and interpret objects, and is showing that there are several different cognitive systems involved in interaction with each other (Baillargeon et al., 2011: 41). They have also carried out experiments which show that these very young children can be 'taught' to perceive confusing objects and events correctly even though this would normally be beyond what would be expected at their developmental stage (2011: 30). In Vygotsky's terms this could be seen as an example of learning in the zone of proximal development, with the researchers providing 'scaffolding'.

Other researchers have challenged what Piaget said about 'egocentricity' and demonstrated that small children *are* able to view many types of problem from points of view other than their own (for example, Cox, 1991). It can also be demonstrated that children as young as 2 can make deductions by analogy. This is done by showing children how to do one task with one set of materials, and then giving them another analogous but different task with a different set of materials. They do better at the new task than children not previously shown the analogy. Chen et al. (1997) even claim to have demonstrated analogical reasoning in children less than a year old.

One challenge to Piaget's theory comes from the simple observation that babies at only three days old will imitate an adult sticking out her tongue. How can a baby know that the tongue of another person is in some way equivalent to her own, if she has not yet learnt to interpret the signals in her optic nerves as objects at all? It seems that Piaget's 'building block' model, in which each block can only be put in place when the previous block is already there, may be too rigid. Or, at least, it does not apply to every aspect of cognitive development. Perhaps a more complicated analogy needs to be found which allows for the fact that some aspects of the structure are already in place at the outset, and that others can emerge at different speeds?

It is also the case that forms of thinking characteristic of children do not simply disappear in adulthood. Adults can be prone to magical thinking of various kinds. In particular, when facing trauma or bereavement or acute stress, adults can regress to childlike ways of thinking, demonstrating how cognitive and emotional functioning can often be interlinked and interdependent.

Modularity

There are also challenges to Piaget's idea that cognitive development necessarily unfolds 'across the board' as newer and more powerful thinking skills are acquired and applied to different areas. Jerry Fodor (1983) is associated with the idea that the mind consists of a number of separate systems ('modules') which have evolved to deal with particular functions. A number of different modules have been suggested including language acquisition, 'visual analysis of objects and space', 'theory of mind' and face perception (Kail, 2004: 446). One would predict from a modular model that development could occur unevenly rather than 'across the board', and certainly it is not hard to find evidence that this can be the case. For example, there are high-functioning autistic children who have remarkable mathematical abilities but who have difficulty with 'theory of mind', and dyslexic people who are very intelligent in other respects but who have difficulty in writing. (For those interested in these debates, Annette Karmiloff-Smith (1995) proposes a model somewhere between that of Fodor and that of Piaget.)

Brain development

Finally, although Piaget did not emphasise physical maturation as a major factor in the development of our thinking, it is known that the brain continues to grow and develop throughout childhood and adolescence and into adulthood. It is almost certainly the case that some of the cognitive changes that occur in the course of childhood can be explained, not in terms of 'equilibration' producing a gradually more sophisticated model of the world, but in terms of the changing capacities of the brain itself (that is, to use computer terminology, in terms of 'hardware', rather than simply 'software'). As we have already seen in previous chapters, neuroscience is currently an area of intense research activity which continues to produce new knowledge about cognition and how it relates to the development and functioning of different areas of the brain. So, for instance, Casey et al., describing the structure of the brain at different ages, conclude that 'brain regions subserving primary functions such as motor and sensory systems mature before higher-order association areas that integrate these primary functions (e.g. prefrontal cortex)' (2005: 242), which would suggest a physical basis for some of the increasing mental sophistication which Piaget described. So would the evidence (discussed by Spear, 2000: 422, in a review of literature on the effects of brain development in adolescence) that adolescents who physically mature early do slightly better in IQ tests than adolescents who are late to mature.

Increased understanding of brain function is producing new developmental models. Information processing models, which have their origins in Piaget's work, show in detail how the brain's neural network develops, and how and where in the brain different kinds of information are processed, and therefore which processes will occur later rather than earlier. These later developing areas are those that enable the processing of complex information through logic and reasoning (Halford and Andrews, 2011: 715). Neuroconstructivism (Mareschal et al., 2007) is another recent model which takes account of the emerging understanding of how biological and environmental factors interact in the development of the brain (we described this briefly in Chapter 1). Indeed, it challenges the computer analogy of the brain that we used above, which separates experience-dependent 'software' from biological 'hardware', proposing that they cannot be studied and understood independently of each other, and that the 'software' of experience changes the underlying 'hardware' (Westermann et al., 2011: 725).

Concluding comments

Although we have concentrated on Piaget's model of cognitive development in this chapter, we hope we have made it clear that there are alternative models, and also many things that are still not fully understood about cognitive development. It is important to recognise that cognitive development does not simply take place in the individual brain, but in relationships and interaction with others in a social and cultural context. It cannot be rigidly separated from emotional and moral development, and the processes by which we learn to take our place in society, which we will consider further in later chapters. Nevertheless, Piaget's insight that children do think in *systematically* different ways from adults does, we suggest, remain valuable, and his account of the *qualitative* differences in the ways in which people think at different stages seems to us to remain valid and relevant (even if reality is rather more complex than the model allows). As we said earlier, many people make the mistake of assuming, on the one hand, that children don't think at all or, on the other, that they think in exactly the same way as adults. Piaget helped us to recognise that children's minds are just as full of thoughts as the minds of adults, but that those thoughts may work in very different ways at different ages.

Chapter Summary

- In this chapter we looked at the concept of cognitive psychology and at cognitive development, including its relationship to emotional development as discussed in the previous chapters.
- We then looked at the work of Jean Piaget and his ideas about the nature of human cognitive development. His key insight was that children's thinking differs from adult thinking in consistent, systematic ways.
- We introduced some of Piaget's basic concepts including *accommodation*, *assimilation* and *equilibration*, as well as specific uses of the terms *schema* and *operation*.
- We then described Piaget's stages of cognitive development: the *sensori-motor* stage, the *pre-operational* stage, the *concrete operations* stage and the *formal operations* stage, looking at the characteristic thinking that Piaget suggested occurred at each stage.
- We looked at challenges to Piaget's model and Vygotsky's emphasis on the importance of language and learning through instruction, and at more recent developments in cognitive theory.
- We concluded that while Piaget's original insights remained useful, they should not be seen as the 'last word' on cognitive development, a subject which is still being explored, debated and argued about in the scientific community.

We have now looked at Piaget's theory of cognitive development and at psychodynamic theories. Though they may seem worlds apart, they do have in common that they are attempts to map out what goes on in people's heads. This is in stark contrast to the behaviourists, whom we will consider in the next chapter.

Further Reading

On Piaget

Boden, M. (1994) *Piaget*. London: Fontana.

On Vygotsky

Daniels, H. (ed.) (2005) *An Introduction to Vygotsky*. Hove: Routledge.

On cognitive development

Goswami, U. (ed.) (2011) *The Wiley–Blackwell Handbook of Cognitive Development*, 2nd edn. Oxford: Blackwell.

Taylor, L. (2005) *Introducing Cognitive Development*. Hove: Psychology Press.

5 MAKING CONNECTIONS

IDEAS FROM BEHAVIOURISM

- Classical conditioning — 88
- Behaviourism — 89
- Operant conditioning — 90
- Cognition and behaviour — 96
- Observation and social learning theory — 97
- Learning and the acquisition of gender roles — 99
- Learning theory and human development — 102

Every day, when John comes home from work, he opens the fridge and eats some cheese. If he stopped to think about it, he'd say this wasn't a good idea because he has a bit of a weight problem, but, for some reason, he just keeps doing it. Jenny invariably lights up a cigarette after a meal, and, when she's very anxious, she will often smoke one cigarette after another. Malik is ten years old and, whenever he finds something difficult in his class at school, he will start to run around shouting, and distracting the other children.

These are habits, characteristic patterns of behaviour. We all have them. Often they are harmless, or even beneficial, but sometimes they can be destructive either to ourselves or to others – in Malik's case, for instance, his behaviour gets in the way both of his own learning and that of the other children too – and people in the helping professions, whether social workers or nurses, teachers or doctors, often have to try to think of ways of managing destructive patterns of behaviour that adults or children have somehow got into. But where do these habits come from? Since we are not born opening fridges, or smoking cigarettes, or shouting in classrooms, we must have learned these behaviours somehow, but it's a very different kind of learning than the one we talked about in the last chapter. Jenny doesn't smoke as a result of some logical process of reasoning. John would probably be hard pressed to explain why and when he got into his comfort eating habit. Malik almost certainly doesn't know why he feels the need to disrupt his class on such a regular basis.

So what is the reason for his behaviour? If you think about it for a moment, you may well conclude that a part of the reason for his behaviour is because it has some sort of consequence which feels good. Perhaps he likes the fact that it gets him a lot of attention? Or perhaps it provides a welcome distraction from the uncomfortable feelings he gets, when something seems difficult to understand? What we are talking about now is a kind of learning that's simply about making connections: connections between a situation, a behaviour and a consequence. And this kind of learning can take place without any kind of reasoning process, or even without conscious thought. Animals learn in this way, and animal trainers typically operate by rewarding behaviours they want to encourage, building connections between a command, a particular behaviour and a pleasurable reward.

A whole branch of experimental psychology is based on this idea of learning by association. Once called *connectionism*, then *behaviourism*, this body of ideas is also referred to as *learning theory*. The methodology associated with it is often called *behaviour analysis*. The characteristic style of this school of psychology is an experimental method, based on the physical sciences, in which guesswork and intuitive hunches are avoided, and connections are only asserted to exist when this can be proved statistically in a controlled experiment. So behaviourists typically try to avoid speculating about what is going on inside the heads of their subjects, and even to avoid words like 'feelings' and 'thoughts'. In the heyday of behaviourism, in the mid-twentieth century, some of its practitioners argued that all learning and all behaviour could be explained in terms of these connections between situations, actions and consequences. This is no longer a widespread view, and we certainly don't subscribe to it, but we do think that this is an important aspect of learning.

Unlike the other ideas we have discussed in the last three chapters, learning theory does not offer a model of development. It is not a stage theory, for instance, in any shape or form. It is simply a series of generalisations about how new behaviour is learnt, and much of the material we will now discuss comes from animal experiments and not from the study of human beings at all. So why have we included it in a book on human development?

There are a number of reasons. Firstly, this way of looking at things provides an important contrast to the theories discussed so far, a reminder that development doesn't have to be looked at as a stage process, or as an 'innate phenomenon which leads to an inevitable sequence of behaviours' (Dillenburger and Keenan, 1997: 14). Secondly, it describes a mechanism of learning which can be very helpful for thinking about many aspects of social development, including the learning of gender roles, which we'll discuss at the end of this chapter. (How do boys learn to behave in stereotypically 'boyish' ways? There's a good case for thinking that, in large part, it's because they're rewarded for doing so, and rewarded for avoiding behaviour that is stereotypically 'girlish').

Thirdly and finally, learning theory looks at patterns of behaviour and asks a very simple question, not 'what is the origin of this behaviour?' but 'what is it that keeps that behaviour going?' This has been a fruitful source of ideas for schools of therapy that avoid the psychoanalytic emphasis on delving into the past, and look instead at the here and now. So learning theory has had important practical applications – and has been an important influence – in the caring professions. Many parenting programmes, for instance, teach parents to look at the way they inadvertently reward their children's problem behaviour. Cognitive behaviour therapy (which we'll also come back to) works by getting people to look at their own behaviour in the same kind of way.

And so, though we don't subscribe to the view that this way of looking at behaviour can be used to answer all the questions we might want to ask about human development, we do think that, in conjunction with other ideas, it makes an important contribution to our understanding of how we are shaped by circumstances into the people we become.

Before going any further, though, you might like to use the following activity to review your own experiences of learning by association:

ACTIVITY 5.1

Can you think of examples in your own experience where a particular sensation (sight, sound, taste, smell) regularly evokes a particular response? Can you think of an instance where a particular set of circumstances seems to bring about an automatic response in you?

COMMENTS ON ACTIVITY 5.1

Most people can probably think of particular smells, or pieces of music that set off associations. Certain pop songs, for example, are often evocative, calling to mind a whole string of memories of the time when that particular song was commonly being played, and of feelings associated with that time. The smells of certain kinds of disinfectant immediately call to mind for some people childhood fears about hospitals and operations. These are instances of connections which are learnt when things come together at the same time.

An example of a certain situation seeming to bring about an automatic response is this: if you are a driver, you will probably have had the experience of getting in your car and being on the way to work before you realise that in fact it is the weekend, and you were not intending to go to work but to drive in the opposite direction. Being in the car set you off on a chain of actions so familiar that you didn't even think about it. Smokers trying to give up often report that certain situations – the end of a meal, for example – trigger an intensely strong desire to light a cigarette.

Classical Conditioning

Ivan Pavlov (1849–1936) was a physiologist, not a psychologist, and his primary interest was in the digestive system: he received a Nobel Prize for his work in this area. As part of this work, however, he became interested in finding out what stimuli set the digestive juices flowing. He demonstrated that dogs start to salivate at the sight or smell of food and that this appeared to be an innate, involuntary *reflex*, like the automatic knee-jerk reaction when one is struck above the knee. Pavlov then tried sounding a buzzer every time food was given to the dogs. He found that after a while the dogs started to salivate as soon as they heard the buzzer. An innate reflex had been 'conditioned' so that it occurred in response to a new stimulus. This is what he termed a 'conditioned reflex' and this particular type of conditioning is known as 'classical conditioning'.

Pavlov then went on to explore exactly how this kind of connection worked, by experimenting with different possibilities. Some of his key concepts can be summarised as follows:

- **Extinction** – Pavlov found that if a dog had been conditioned to salivate in response to a buzzer that preceded food, it would then continue to salivate in response to the buzzer alone. However, this effect did not last forever. If the buzzer ceased to be followed by food, then after a while the conditioned reflex would wear off and the sound of the buzzer would no longer result in salivation. In Pavlovian terms, the conditioned reflex had become 'extinct'. To give a human example: a quitting smoker may for a long time feel a strong craving for a cigarette after a meal. But after some time that craving fades, until a point is reached where the end of a meal does not trigger a desire to smoke.
- **Spontaneous recovery** – but Pavlov also found that, if a conditioned reflex has been allowed to become extinct, it can very quickly be re-established. So a dog may have been conditioned to salivate at the sound of a buzzer, and this conditioned reflex may then have been allowed to become completely extinct, so that the dog does not salivate at all in response to food. But if the buzzer now starts to be sounded at feeding time again, the original conditioned link will reappear rapidly at full strength, much more quickly than it would appear in a dog which had never previously been conditioned. In other words, even though the link has been extinguished in terms of behaviour, some record of it clearly remains in the dog's brain. Again, we can use the comparison of a quitting smoker. After a sufficient time has elapsed, this person may no longer feel a craving for a cigarette at the end of a meal. But if that person takes up smoking again, all those conditioned connections seem to reappear very rapidly at full strength.
- **Generalisation** – if a dog has learnt to salivate to a buzzer, this response will tend to generalize to other sounds also. For example, the dog will salivate not only if it hears a buzzer but also if it hears an electric bell. (This concept has some similarities with Piaget's assimilation, discussed in the previous chapter.)

- **Discrimination** – however, while generalisation occurs by default, dogs can be trained to finely discriminate between different stimuli. If you are the owner of a cat or dog you may have observed how animals can learn to distinguish the particular engine sound of the family car, and respond to this one sound, while ignoring all others.

These basic concepts are central to learning theory. What you may notice about them is that, unlike either psychodynamic theories or Piaget's theory of cognitive development, these concepts of conditioning, extinction, spontaneous recovery, generalisation and discrimination do not purport to describe anything that might go on in the dogs' minds. They are purely and simply descriptions of relationships between different types of stimulus and observed and measurable responses.

The insistence of behaviourists that only observable behaviour should be studied can seem perverse. But of course we cannot know directly what goes on in the mind of another person, let alone an animal. It is possible to train a pigeon to discriminate, say, between red and other colours but it is impossible to know what red actually looks like to a pigeon. Indeed, two *people* cannot know whether the colour red looks the same to each of them.

Therapeutic approaches derived from behaviourism do not try to get inside the patient's mind to the extent that psychoanalysis does. Instead, they are aimed at finding practical ways of unlearning behaviour that is causing problems, or learning new behaviour.

Behaviourism

A very influential figure in psychology in the middle of the twentieth century, J.B. Watson (1878–1958) was the one who actually coined the term 'behaviourism'. He was an enthusiastic advocate of the use of conditioning techniques to make people conform to the needs of society, and was extremely confident in their ability to actually do so, as the following quote illustrates:

> Give me a dozen healthy infants … and my own specified world to bring them up in and I'll guarantee to take any one at random and train him to become any kind of specialist I might select. … (Watson, 1931: 104)

He was also a pioneer of the use of sexual imagery as an advertising tool, believing that if people could be taught to make a connection (even if an unconscious one) between a brand of cigarettes, for example, and sex, it would make them buy more. His views were parodied in Aldous Huxley's famous futuristic novel *Brave New World:*

> Patiently the D.H.C. [Director of Hatcheries and Conditioning] explained. If the children were made to scream at the sight of a rose, that was on grounds of high economic policy. …

'A love of nature keeps no factories busy. It was decided to abolish the love of nature, at any rate among the lower classes. ... Hence those electric shocks.' (1955 [1932]: 29)

In Huxley's novel children were shown flowers and given an electric shock. An electric shock causes an involuntary response of pulling back. A flower does not normally provoke this response, but could be made to do so by associating flowers with shocks. This is an example of classical conditioning, which, as we've seen, is about connecting a new stimulus to an existing basic reflex. The new stimulus is connected to something that provokes an automatic response – and, incidentally, also gives pleasure or pain, though Pavlov did not concern himself with these subjective experiences.

But Watson argued that rewards or punishments were not necessary to make a connection between two things. Simply the fact that two things occurred together was enough. The connection would be stronger if the two things occurred together *frequently* or if they had occurred together *recently*. Thus an animal placed in a maze might wander around until it found its way out. If placed back into the maze it would find its way out more quickly, not necessarily because it had been rewarded for finding its way out, but simply because finding its way out was the last thing it did in the maze. A human parallel here might be our example of getting in a car and driving without thinking along a familiar route. It is not as if this is particularly rewarding: it is just that this is what you did last time you got into the car. You might also notice that if you use a certain word in conversation that you don't often use, you will often find yourself repeating the same word in later conversations.

Operant Conditioning

Animal trainers have known for centuries that animals can be taught to behave in certain ways when this behaviour is followed by a reward – and discouraged from behaving in other ways with punishments. Parents, of course, have also applied this principle to children. This kind of learning is different from that studied by Pavlov because it is not just about conditioning innate reflexes to new stimuli but about connecting voluntary behaviours to stimuli. It has become known as *operant* conditioning, for reasons which we will explain, as opposed to Pavlov's *classical conditioning* (also known as *respondent conditioning*).

Concepts such as extinction, generalisation and spontaneous recovery apply to operant conditioning also. And the original researchers into operant learning, no less than Pavlov, avoided speculating about insight or thought on the part of animals. Animals are simply seen as trying various behaviours more or less randomly at first. Those that are rewarded become part of the animal's repertoire, while those that are not rewarded do not. It is a process analogous to Darwin's theory of natural selection, but applied to behaviours rather than to genetic variations: those that prove successful survive, while those that don't, die out.

> In both operant conditioning and the evolutionary selection of behavioural characteristics, consequences alter future probability. Reflexes and other innate patterns of behaviour evolve because they increase the chances of survival of the species. Operants grow strong because they are followed by important consequences in the life of the individual. (Skinner, 1953: 90)

Skinner (1903–90) was the inventor of the term 'operant conditioning' (although he was not the first to explore this kind of learning) and he was a dominant figure in post-war behaviourist research. His classic experimental tool was the so-called Skinner Box, consisting of a cage in which there was a food dispenser with a lever above it. In the most basic version of this experiment, a rat presses the lever and the food dispenser drops a pellet of food into the tray beneath it. Not surprisingly, when this happens on a regular basis, the rat goes on pressing the lever in order to get the food.

In Skinner's terminology, the rat's original pressing of the lever is termed *operant behaviour*, meaning a behaviour that occurs with no obvious stimulus, as opposed to *respondent behaviour*, an example of which would be pulling your hand away from a hot stove, or Pavlov's dogs involuntarily salivating at the smell of food (hence 'operant conditioning', as opposed to 'respondent conditioning').

Reinforcement

In Skinner's experiment above, the rat was rewarded with a pellet of food when it pressed the lever, and this increased the frequency of the lever-pushing behaviour. This is known as *positive reinforcement*. *Negative reinforcement* of behaviour means that something unpleasant is *removed* as a consequence of it. In the context of Skinner's experiment, negative reinforcement would be something like an electric shock which the rat can only stop by pressing a lever. Think back to the example of Malik which we gave at the beginning of the chapter. If we think that he disrupts the class because he likes the attention it brings him, that would be *positive reinforcement*, while if we think that he does it mainly because it stops him having to concentrate on work he finds too difficult, that would be *negative reinforcement*.

Punishment, which reduces a behaviour rather than increasing it, can also be positive or negative. In Skinner's experiment a positive punishment would have been giving the rat an electric shock as opposed to the positive reward of a pellet of food when it pushed the lever; clearly this would not have reinforced the rat's behaviour but would have had the opposite effect of deterring it. And a negative punishment would be something that took the food away when a lever was pressed.

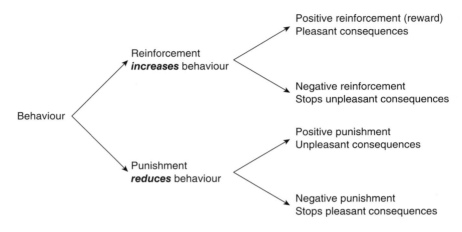

FIGURE 5.1

If a particular stimulus occurs regularly with a reinforcer, that stimulus itself can become a positive reinforcer. This is the principle behind 'click training' which is used by many dog-owners and trainers. The dog is taught to make an association between the clicking sound and the reward of food. The click can then be used on its own as a reinforcer, with the advantage that it can be given *at the same moment* that the behaviour you want to reinforce is happening. Of course, if you don't ever follow a click with food, the connection between click and food will in due course become extinct, and the click will no longer be effective as a reinforcer.

Skinner and the Mind

As we've noted, behaviourists study observable behaviour rather than processes within the mind. But Skinner was at pains to say that he was not denying that there were such things as thoughts and feelings, or that these were important. What he did argue was that we are accustomed to think of such things in the wrong way.

He wrote, for example, that 'what is felt or introspectively observed is not some non-physical world of consciousness, mind or mental life, but the observer's own body'. What went on in that 'world within the skin' was, he argued, the product of the external environment which 'made its first great contribution during the evolution of the species, but [which] exerts a different kind of effect during the lifetime of the individual, and the combination of the two effects is the behaviour we observe at any given time'.

His point is that, when we explain things in terms of what is going on inside our minds, we are not really explaining anything. For example: if you say 'I did X because I was angry', this begs the question as to what 'anger' really is and what causes it.

'When what a person does is attributed to what is going on inside him', Skinner wrote, 'investigation is at an end' (1974: 17, 18).

Schedules of reinforcement

Skinner's experimental work consisted essentially of altering the patterns of reinforcement and seeing the effect this had on behaviour. To give one example, Rat 'A' is rewarded with a pellet every time it pushes the lever. Rat 'B' only gets a pellet every 20 times it pushes the lever. Not surprisingly, rat 'A' learns lever-pushing behaviour more quickly than rat 'B'. But now suppose that both rats stop being given food pellets at all for lever-pushing. For which rat would lever pressing behaviour become extinct more quickly? People tend to guess that rat 'A', which had always been rewarded for lever-pushing, would be slower to give up pushing the lever. In fact, though, experimental evidence shows that it is the opposite that is the case. The rats that are only rewarded occasionally for lever pushing go on trying to push the lever for longer. They learn the behaviour more slowly – and they also unlearn it more slowly.

Shaping

As we've said, Skinner's techniques resemble those of animal trainers – and some of his students did in fact go on to become animal trainers. He and his co-workers set themselves tasks like training pigeons to play skittles in a miniature bowling alley or to knock a ping-pong ball to and fro (Skinner, 1960). You clearly can't get an animal to learn a behaviour as complex as this in the same way as you get it to learn something simple like lever-pushing. If you adopted the method of just waiting for the bird to start playing skittles by chance, and then reinforcing this behaviour, you would wait forever. What Skinner did was this:

- ensured the pigeon was hungry
- established a strong conditioned connection between food and a certain sound (for instance a clicking sound, as described above)
- every time the pigeon did anything even vaguely approximating to the required task, he made the clicking sound and then gave it the food. (This was important because a click can be done at precisely the moment that the behaviour he wanted to reinforce occurred.) For example, he might start by making the clicking sound every time the pigeon pecked at the ball
- once ball-pecking had become established, he would then move on to another stage and, let's say, only click when the ball was pushed in the general direction of the skittles
- once that was established, he would then take it a stage further and, say, only click when the ball was knocked more than a certain distance in that direction
- and so on …

This process is called *shaping* and is a powerful training technique with many applications. Its particular strength is that it avoids setting the person or animal being trained up to fail. At every stage, the trainee is encouraged to continue to produce operant behaviour: in other words, to keep trying. By contrast, if the pigeon was only to be rewarded for completing the full task, *none* of its intermediate behaviour would be reinforced, and so it would have no reason to even begin to change its behaviour in the right direction. Or if the pigeon were trained by punishing it for doing the wrong thing, then this would have the effect – as a result of generalisation – of reducing active behaviour of any kind.

Discrimination

Using techniques like this, it has been possible not only to teach animals to do complicated tricks, but also to teach them extraordinary feats of discrimination. For example, pigeons (not known for their large brains) can be taught to distinguish a photograph of one person from 100 other people, even if they were all taken against the same range of backgrounds and even if that one person was shown in 100 different poses (Herrnstein et al., 1976).

The strength of different reinforcers

Learned behaviours normally extinguish over time, if they are not reinforced – positively or negatively – any longer. As we've seen, the rates of learning and 'unlearning' a given behaviour depend in part on the schedules of reinforcement used. But the kind of reinforcer used also makes a difference. Interestingly, an exceptionally powerful *positive* reinforcer has been found to be the drug morphine. When rats received an injection of morphine for pushing a lever, lever-pushing never completely became extinguished, even if morphine stopped being given and even if the experiment was carried on past the time when there could possibly still be an actual physical dependency on morphine (Walker, 1984: 63).

The only other means of shaping behaviour comparable in power to this were strong positive punishments such as a powerful electric shock. (We believe that there are strong ethical arguments against giving animals powerful electric shocks, but we are reporting the findings of experiments where such things have been used.) Given such a shock for pushing a lever, an animal might never push that lever again, regardless of the length of time that had passed (Azrin, 1959, cited in Pierce and Cheney, 2004: 156). Given the tendency of responses to generalise, this means that positive punishment like this can have a generally inhibiting effect on learning.

Indeed, in some adverse circumstances, the behaviour that animals learn is to *do nothing at all*. In yet another cruel experiment, Martin Seligman (1975) subjected one group of animals (call them group X) to electric shocks in an environment where they were strapped in and could not do anything to get away. A second group, Y, was not subjected to this experience. Both group X and group Y are then given a shock-avoidance task (that is, a task where they are given shocks which can be stopped by, for example, pressing a lever). What was found was that the group X animals performed less well on the shock-avoidance task than the group Y animals. A simple behaviourist explanation would be that the group X animals had (of necessity) been doing nothing when the shocks stopped in the first part of the experiment. The behaviour of 'doing nothing' had therefore been negatively reinforced, so that this was the behaviour that they adopted when placed in the second situation. This phenomenon was called 'learnt helplessness'. Perhaps it helps to explain how some people become very passive and unable to help themselves.

Before moving on, you may like to pause to look at the relevance (or otherwise) of what we have been discussing to human development, bearing in mind that all the findings discussed so far are based on experiments with dogs, rats and pigeons.

ACTIVITY 5.2

1. Skinner found that the rats unlearned behaviour more slowly when that behaviour had only intermittently been reinforced. Can you think of any parallels here with attachment theory?
2. Can you think of situations where human beings are placed in a similar situation to the helpless rats in Seligman's experiments? Can you think of instances of 'learnt helplessness' in human life?

COMMENTS ON ACTIVITY 5.2

1. One parallel that may have struck you is that children who have been anxiously attached – whose attachment behaviour has only intermittently been reinforced – find it harder to cope with moves, let go of old attachments and make new attachments, than children who have been securely attached.
2. Many children in abusive situations are in much the same position, since the abuse is something outside of their control. Certainly, depression in adult life is a common result of childhood abuse, as is a feeling of not being in control. People in institutional care – old people, for example, or people with mental illness – often experience a huge reduction in their control over their own lives, and often exhibit a kind of learnt passivity (there will be more on this in Chapter 11). You may also have been struck by the fact that these animals were in a no-win situation. Children in seriously abusive situations can be in the same position: the most dangerous thing in their lives is also their only source of physical care. You'll remember that attachment theorists suggest that the most dysfunctional form of anxious attachment – disorganised attachment – arises in these kinds of circumstances.

Cognition and Behaviour

Although Skinner, Watson and others tried to avoid any sort of speculation about what was going on in the minds of humans and animals, and to focus purely on the observable and measurable phenomena of behaviour and stimuli, the experimental evidence does make such an approach hard to sustain. There are phenomena which cannot easily be explained without postulating internal maps or models that animals and humans carry in their minds, and thanks to advances in neuroscience we now have much more knowledge about how the brain works than we did in Skinner and Watson's day. An increasing recognition of the role of cognitive factors has led to cross-fertilisation between the separate cognitive and behaviourist branches of psychology that existed in the mid-twentieth century.

One result of this has been the development of *cognitive behaviour therapy* (usually known as CBT). This brief, focused therapy is based on the work of Aaron Beck (1963, 1964, cited by Westbrook et al., 2011: 2–3). It is widely used in the NHS in the UK to help people to change thought patterns and behaviours that are causing them problems. It uses the ideas of learned behaviour, conditioning and reinforcement which we have already described, but, unlike earlier behaviourism, it also takes account of what is going on in people's minds, and a CBT therapist will help clients to recognise their negative thought patterns as part of the process of learning to change their behaviour. These negative thoughts are understood as being based on a system of core beliefs and 'schemata', which are information-processing structures built up from early childhood (Westbrook et al., 2011: 355). We have already met the term 'schema' in our discussion of Piaget in Chapter 4, but it is used more widely in CBT to include emotional as well as cognitive, physical and behavioural dimensions.

To bring about changes in behaviour, CBT uses reinforcement by setting clear, achievable goals in partnership between therapist and client, maybe starting with very small steps (see the discussion of shaping above). For example, somebody with agoraphobia might start by aiming to be able to stand on their front doorstep, or they might not aim to do anything at all, but to keep a record of the pattern of their negative thoughts about venturing outside. The important thing is the reinforcement they gain from completing the task successfully.

ACTIVITY 5.3

Think again about Malik, described at the beginning of this chapter, whose behaviour disrupts his class and prevents him from learning. If you were his teacher, how might you go about understanding and dealing with this behaviour using some of the ideas we've outlined above?

COMMENTS ON ACTIVITY 5.3

You may have thought about the two types of conditioning, classical and operant.

Malik's running around and shouting is not a self-evidently involuntary behaviour, like the salivating of Pavlov's dogs. One could see that a teacher could **shape** it through operant conditioning, using reinforcement to discourage the disruptive behaviour and encourage the desired behaviour of focusing on learning. We talked earlier about the kinds of reinforcement Malik may be obtaining from his behaviour; the positive reinforcement of the attention he gets, and the negative reinforcement of the distraction from a task he finds difficult and stressful.

However, operant conditioning gives us quite a limited and mechanistic view of a teacher's role, which does not take account of the different personalities, backgrounds and experiences of children (as opposed to rats and pigeons). You may have gone on to think about using insights from cognitive behaviour therapy by engaging Malik himself in the process of changing his behaviour, exploring negative thought patterns and ensuring that any goals you set for him are achievable. Finding out from him what he is thinking and feeling will help you as his teacher to decide what kinds of reinforcement will be most effective. If he is primarily seeking attention, you could ensure that he gets this for good behaviour just as much as for bad behaviour, and you might also be looking out for any reason why he might be looking for attention at the moment (perhaps a new baby in the family, or a parental separation) and exploring his feelings about this, so that they get the attention they need. If the main problem is that he finds the work too hard, you could explore his negative thoughts about this ('I'm stupid'; 'It's no good trying; I'll never be able to do it') and ensure that the tasks he is set are achievable, if necessary with extra learning support, so that his learning behaviour is reinforced by the reward of success and he no longer needs to distract himself and others from learning.

Observation and Social Learning Theory

One cognitive factor that can be demonstrated to be a part of learning in animals – and which we all know to be a part of learning in human beings – is *observation*. Animals consistently learn tasks more quickly if they have previously observed other animals completing them, than if they are only taught by the traditional operant conditioning procedures. In fact, learning from observation seems to be very deep-rooted. (In the last chapter we mentioned the fact that one-day-old babies, for example, can be shown to be able to copy simple movements such as sticking out the tongue.) Albert Bandura (1977) explored observational learning in human children. In his basic experiment, a child is shown a live or filmed model doing something, and is later observed to see how much of the model's behaviour she copies. Bandura identified several variables that influenced the amount of copying that occurred:

- Children were more likely to copy models identified as high prestige in some way. (Advertising agencies have presumably discovered the same thing, since they routinely use celebrities to endorse products.)
- They were more likely to copy models similar to themselves in some way.
- They were also more likely (not surprisingly) to copy models that they had seen rewarded for their actions.
- He also found that there was a distinction between acquiring the capability of performing a task and actually copying it. So, for example, children who didn't mimic a certain action after seeing it, could do so if asked (again, perhaps, not a very surprising finding).

Bandura's work formed part of the basis for an area of psychology known as social learning theory, which uses ideas from learning theory to look at how we acquire complex social behaviour. This can be applied to any aspect of social behaviour, for example, how do we learn the behaviour that is characteristic of our culture or our social class? However, we want for the rest of this chapter to concentrate on just one area, which is obviously a crucial one in the study of human development: the acquisition of gender roles.

But before going any further, you may find it useful to look at the following activity. This will give you an opportunity to consider what you have read so far about learning theory by trying to apply it to the question of gender roles.

ACTIVITY 5.4

Looking back at the ideas from learning theory which we've discussed (operant conditioning, classical conditioning, observational learning, generalization, discrimination, etc.), consider how these might apply to the way that children learn different 'masculine' or 'feminine' gender roles.

COMMENTS ON ACTIVITY 5.4

Ideas you may have mentioned are:

- Different behaviours are positively or negatively reinforced, by parents or other adults (that is, aggression is encouraged more in boys, playing with dolls is discouraged, etc.).
- Observational learning means that boys will tend to copy male role models (at home, on TV and elsewhere), and girls female role models. Boys will also tend to copy males who are seen as successful and having high status, while girls will tend to copy famous, high-profile girls or women.

- From an early age different stimuli are offered, even in connection with meeting basic needs for food and warmth (girls are given pink cups, boys blue, for example).
- You may also have considered ways in which connections learnt in one context tend to generalise to others – or children may learn to discriminate very subtly different clues as to what is appropriate for boys and what for girls.

Learning and the Acquisition of Gender Roles

Men and women – and boys and girls – behave in different ways in all kinds of respects. Until recent times, most people would have assumed that this was mainly the result of 'nature' – boys and girls are simply born different – but there has been a growing awareness that many, and some would argue most, of these 'masculine', and 'feminine' characteristics are the result not of nature but of nurture. From a sociological point of view, one would say that gender roles are 'socially constructed': that is, created by the particular circumstances and dynamics of a particular society. From a psychological perspective (the main perspective of this book), one would say that they are *learnt* – and learning theory provides some ideas about the mechanisms through which this might come about.

For the remainder of this chapter we will give a brief tour of some of the research in this area, concluding with some evidence that at least part of the difference between boys and girls *is* to do with 'nature' (see Golombok and Fivush (1994) for a fuller account of this topic).

Differences in Attitudes to Masculinity and Femininity

Gender stereotypes can be very different in different societies. In ancient Greece, for example, there was once a crack army regiment consisting entirely of gay men. The Sacred Band of Thebes, as it was known, apparently played a crucial part in many battles. In our own time, gay men still tend to be stereotyped as 'unmanly', and homosexuality has only recently been permitted in the British and American armed forces, but in the ancient world, men whose sexual preference was for other men were sometimes seen as being *more* manly than men whose preference was for women (see Boswell, 1996: 62–4). And in Iranian culture, the familiar stereotype of most Western cultures is reversed, with men being seen as more emotionally expressive than women (Epstein, 1997, cited in Bussey, 2011: 613).

Operant and classical conditioning and gender roles

Many researchers have suggested that behaviours such as aggression or dependency are differentially rewarded depending on whether they are produced by boys or girls. Baby boys have been found to be given more physical stimulation than girls, whereas girls are touched and talked to more (see Golombok and Fivush, 1994: 77–88).

Boy and girl children are also exposed to different learning environments. Different toys are given to them, or different things are drawn to their attention: 'Look at that fire engine, John!' or 'Look at that pretty dress, Jane!' There is clear evidence that children *are* differentially reinforced for taking part in what are seen as 'gender-appropriate' and 'gender-inappropriate' activities. So, even if it were not the case that things like aggression and dependency per se are reinforced differentially, play *is* selectively reinforced that will develop different patterns of behaviour – a form of 'shaping'.

As we noted above, appropriate activities are even colour-coded in our culture to assist children to choose the 'right' activities, and to allow them to generalise their social learning about gender. To give an example from the personal experience of one of the authors: a 9-year-old boy is going through a Lego catalogue, pointing out the space models, cowboy models, aircraft models and so on. Coming to a page depicting models made with pink bricks, he instantly dismisses it as 'girlie stuff', turning to the next page without a second glance. The 'pinkstinks' campaign recognises and challenges the power of this kind of colour-coding (Pinkstinks, 2008).

Children are actively discouraged from what are seen as 'gender-inappropriate' activities. Interestingly, researchers have found that boys are more likely to be discouraged from 'girl-appropriate' activities than vice versa, and that fathers more than mothers do the job of discouraging them (Leaper and Friedman, 2007). Girls are not discouraged from 'boy' activities to the same extent, but are equally discouraged by both parents (Langlois and Downs, 1980). Other children also exert pressure to conform to accepted gender-roles, and again, boys are more likely than girls to be discouraged by their peers from activities which are seen as gender-inappropriate (Blakemore, 2003).

There are also more subtle messages which children receive from parents and teachers which help to build up their core beliefs about what they can and can't do, which are less obviously based on gender. Research show that parents tend to underestimate their daughters' competence in sport and maths, while overestimating it for their sons (Bussey, 2011: 619).

Observational learning and gender roles

Bandura showed that children are sensitive to the characteristics of the model they use, and are more likely to copy those that seem 'like them'. It therefore seems likely that children will tend to model themselves on the same-sex parent. (The picture is complicated by the fact that, in a traditional family or in a single-mother family, or indeed a modern primary school, where women teachers heavily outnumber men, role models are of course much more to hand for girls than for boys.)

However, Bandura and others (such as Perry and Bussey, 1979) have found that children's copying of role models is subtler than one might think. Children will notice the behaviour of a large number of models of both genders and work out which behaviour is more *typical* of their own sex. Experiments have been carried out in which children were shown a number of models, male and female, choosing between pairs of items. If all the members of one gender were seen to have made the same choice, then, if the children were presented with the same options, they would tend to make the same choice as the models of their own gender. When one member of one gender was noticed by the children to consistently make choices different from the majority of their gender, then the children would tend to discount this person as a role model. The implication of this seems to be that, even if a boy sees his father changing the baby's nappy, for example, or a girl sees her mother mending the car, they are much less likely to copy this behaviour if their wider experience suggests to them that this is not typical behaviour for the respective genders.

Interestingly, some experiments have also found that girls will imitate male role models more readily than boys will imitate female role models, the exception being when boys perceive a female role model to have power. You will remember that Bandura (1977) found that children would be more likely to copy models they saw as prestigious or powerful. In a society where more power is still held by men, this appears to mean that both boys and girls will be more prone to try to copy men in the main, but that both boys and girls will imitate women when they perceive them as having power.

Other factors in gender differentiation

Social learning theory suggests a number of mechanisms whereby children learn gender roles, although it does not have anything to say about how those different roles arose in the first place – a sociological question of the kind that we will discuss in Chapter 10.

We should also note that the fact that roles can be clearly shown to be shaped by learning in very many ways, does not rule out the fact that there may be some actual biological differences (nature as well as nurture). In fact there is evidence that the hormonal differences that exist between boys and girls prenatally do actually have some influence on behaviour. (See Golombok and Fivush, 1994: 43–50, for details of the experimental evidence here.) For example, there is a condition called *congenital adrenal hyperplasia* which results in abnormally high levels of androgen (a male sex hormone) in the bloodstream. Babies with this condition who are genetically female will have internal female organs but external organs which resemble male organs. Some of these children have been raised as boys, and seem to socialise normally as boys. Other children with the same condition, however, have been treated by surgery and by hormone treatment so that the children appear and grow up as girls. Comparisons have been made between these girls and other children. Even though they are treated as girls from an early age, it seems that they are more interested in 'masculine' toys than other girls and spend more time playing with boys, suggesting that the early high doses of androgen, even if subsequently corrected, have predisposed them in some way towards more stereotypically 'boyish' behaviour (Berenbaum and Hines, 1992). There is also evidence that these girls are more likely than other girls to grow up defining themselves as bisexual or lesbian, thus suggesting that the prenatal exposure to the male sex hormone predisposes them to be sexually attracted to women (Golombok and Fivush, 1994: 51).

This is not to say that learning is not a major factor, but it does seem clear that some actual biological differences – nature as well as nurture – may underlie the social stereotypes of masculinity and femininity.

Learning Theory and Human Development

As already noted, gender roles are only one of many areas to which learning theory and social learning theory can be applied. Social learning theory could also be used, for example, to look at the ways in which different patterns of behaviour are learnt by people from different social classes or ethnic backgrounds, differences which, again, in the past have often been seen as innate rather than learnt.

Learning theory has its limitations: there are biological factors and cognitive factors in development which cannot usefully be explained merely in terms of learnt connections. It can also be misused (as Aldous Huxley's satire colourfully illustrates). But it can be useful as a way of understanding the influence of the external environment in shaping our behaviour. This kind of learning could be seen as one of the basic building blocks upon which the construction of social roles is based.

The following activity is an opportunity to consider the value of this point of view in a practical context.

ACTIVITY 5.5

Suppose you are a member of staff on a team that provides support to adults with learning disabilities living in supported group homes in the community, the aim of the team being to promote independence. One of the group home residents, Angie, arrives in your office having got in a muddle with her benefits, with the result that she currently has no money and is in a very distressed state.

You give her some sympathy, calm her down, make her a cup of tea and then go off and sort the whole thing out on the phone with the benefits office.

Angie is very grateful.

But what could be the drawbacks of this response from a behavioural point of view – and what might have been a better response?

COMMENTS ON ACTIVITY 5.5

While Angie saw your response as helpful and has no complaints whatsoever, you may not have really done her a good turn if your aim is to promote independence. What you have done is to reinforce the behaviour of bringing her problems to you to sort out (positive reinforcement being provided by the tea and sympathy, and negative reinforcement being provided by the anxiety of having no money, which has now been taken away). You might have done better, for example, to have talked Angie through what she needed to do, given her a phone and then given her the tea and the encouragement after she had sorted it out for herself. That way you would have been reinforcing her own problem-solving behaviour.

Incidentally, the learning is not all one-way in such situations. Just as you were reinforcing Angie's 'helpless' behaviour, she was no doubt reinforcing your helpful behaviour by being happy and grateful when you had sorted it out for her. This seems to us to be a common pattern in the work of the helping professions: dependency can be rewarding for both the professional and her client, so it keeps getting reinforced.

You might also have considered how both your behaviour and Angie's might be unconsciously influenced by the socially constructed stereotypes that you have each learned and internalised about disability and gender. You may both find it difficult to overcome the assumption that because Angie has a learning disability she won't be able to manage a difficult situation like this. And might you both also have some gender-related assumptions about confidence, independence and problem-solving?

Chapter Summary

- In this chapter we considered the tradition in psychology known as connectionism, behaviourism or learning theory, which explores the ways in which we connect events and actions. We began by looking at the work of Pavlov and the basic concepts of 'classical conditioning'.
- We looked briefly at J.B. Watson (who coined the word 'behaviourism') and considered the idea of learnt connections based purely and simply on proximity.
- We looked at operant conditioning (conditioning that links behaviour with particular stimuli) and the work of B.F. Skinner in this area.
- We described the concept of 'learned helplessness' and looked at stress.
- We then looked at cognitive aspects of learning which cannot easily be explained in purely behavioural terms, and then at observational learning and at social learning theory.
- We discussed the application of learning theory to the question of how children acquire distinct gender roles.

Up to now we have looked at general theories of human growth and development, most of which have focused mainly on childhood. In the next section, however, we will look not at a particular theory, but at a particularly crucial stage of life: adolescence, the time of transition from childhood to adulthood.

Further Reading

 ### On Learning Theory/Behaviourism/Behaviour Analysis

Baum, W. (2005) *Understanding Behaviorism: Behavior, Culture and Evolution.* Oxford: Blackwell.

Pierce, W.D. and Cheney, C.D. (2004) *Behavior Analysis and Learning.* Mahwah, NJ: Lawrence ErlbaumAssociates.

Powell, R., Symbaluk, D. and Macdonald, S. (2002) *Introduction to Learning and Behaviour.* Belmont, CA: Wadsworth.

 ### On Cognitive-Behavioural Therapy

Westbrook, D., Kennerley, H. and Kirk, J. (2011) *An Introduction to Cognitive Behaviour Therapy,* 2nd edn. London: Sage.

 ### On Gender Role Development

Bussey, K. (2011) 'Gender Identity Development', in S.J. Schwartz, K. Luyckx and V.L. Vignoles, (eds) *Handbook of Identity Theory and Research.* London: Springer, pp. 603–28.

Golombok, S. and Fivush, R. (1994) *Gender Development.* Cambridge: Cambridge University Press.

6 WHO AM I GOING TO BE?

ADOLESCENCE, IDENTITY AND CHANGE

- Culture and biology 106
- Transitions 107
- Identity versus role confusion 110
- Relating to others 116
- Sexuality and adolescence 118
- Problems in adolescence 121
- Adults, adolescents and attachment 123
- Coping skills and resilience 125

The transition from childhood to adulthood is of course in part a biological process: a time of physical growth and change, a time when secondary sexual characteristics appear, the stage at which for the first time we become capable of reproduction. But the stage of life between childhood and adulthood which we call 'adolescence' is only partly defined by biology. It is also a psychological transition and it takes place, and is shaped by, its social context. It is seen differently in different societies, just as childhood and adulthood themselves are seen differently. And since society itself is constantly changing, the social context is different in each generation, and the experience of adolescence itself is different as a result.

This is true too of other transitions in life and we will begin this chapter by looking at two questions which are relevant to other stages and not just to adolescence: firstly, the interaction between social and biological factors in development, and secondly, the psychology of transitions in general. At the end of the chapter, we come back to another topic which is important to thinking about adolescence but which also has wider relevance: the nature of *resilience*.

Culture and Biology

Segregation between adults and children has become more marked in industrialised societies, where children go to school while adults either go to work or work at home. In pre-industrial societies (that is to say, in Western Europe and America in the past, and in many developing countries around the world today), both adults and children are involved in similar daily activities and routines, for example, in caring for domestic animals or harvesting crops. There is, of course, still a biological transition between childhood and adulthood, but the change in *role* (see Chapter 10) may be in many ways very much less pronounced.

The significance of adolescence is therefore different in non-industrial cultures, and the period of transition tends to be briefer. Marriages will tend to take place much earlier, for instance, particularly for girls. Adolescence as an extended transitional stage which is distinct both from childhood and adulthood is in some ways a modern, Western invention (the word 'Western' is used loosely here to refer to the industrialised world). A teenager from the Pacific island of Samoa commented that she had never heard of adolescence until she left her own country and came to New Zealand:

> … Sometimes I think that we [in Samoa] are children for most of our lives. … It does not matter how old you are, [for] if you are not considered worthy or responsible enough by your elders then you will not be treated as an adult. You really have to earn your place in the Samoan culture. So adolescence as a developmental stage is foreign to our culture. (Subject #3, Tupuola, 1993, cited by Kroger, 2004: 5–6)

Of course the major biological changes we associate with adolescence *are* common to all cultures – the onset of fertility, rapid growth and physical and biochemical change. But, even within a single cultural context, each individual will experience these changes in a different way. The changes do not take place at the same time, or in the same order, for boys as for girls (the growth spurt usually starts earlier in girls). There are also substantial differences in the timing of these changes from one individual to another.

> Early maturing boys feel more positive about themselves and about their bodies … are likely to be more popular, and to do well in their schoolwork …
>
> [But] a number of writers have shown that girls who mature significantly earlier than their peers are less popular (among other girls), more likely to show signs of inner turbulence … and to be less satisfied with their bodies. (Coleman, 2011: 34)

Here we see the timing of biological changes interacting with an individual's social environment (an early maturing girl may be less popular with her peers), just as in the earlier quotation from a young Samoan we saw the interaction of biological changes and cultural context (growing up in Samoa feels different to growing up in New Zealand). As in so many areas of human development, the experience of adolescence, for any given individual, is not simply biological, not simply a matter of individual psychology, and not simply a socially constructed phenomenon either, but a complex interaction between all of these elements.

In this chapter we will be looking primarily at adolescence as it occurs in Western industrialised societies. But it is important to remember that, even in this context, young people go through this transition with many different cultural expectations. (The importance of social context is something that we will focus on in particular in Chapter 10.)

Transitions

We have used the word transition a number of times now, and it is an idea we will return to later in this book when we look at other stages of life: the mid-life transition, the transition to parenthood, the transition to old age. But since the transition from childhood to adulthood is one of the biggest transitions we have to make, this seems an appropriate point to look at transitions in general and what is involved in them.

Transition is defined by the *Concise Oxford Dictionary* as 'passage or change from one place or state or act or set of circumstances to another'. Any such change in human life involves a psychological readjustment, a coming to terms with an ending and a coming to terms with things being different. Even an event as trivial as a cancelled evening out involves an adjustment of this kind. We may be annoyed, disappointed, temporarily at a loss as to what to do with ourselves until we have accepted that the evening we had in mind is not going to happen and we begin to plan a new one. Major events, though, require substantial psychological work which may take months or years and may never be fully completed. Think of a bereavement, winning a million pounds in a lottery, the birth of a child, a divorce …

Various models have been proposed to describe this process of adjustment, often originating in the study of bereavement (see Chapter 12), bereavement, of course, being one of the most extreme and difficult transitions that most people ever go through. The following summary of the stages involved in dealing with transitions is paraphrased from Sugarman (2001: 144–9), who herself draws on Hopson (1981). As with other stage models discussed in this book, the reader should not be deceived into thinking that people necessarily progress through stages in an orderly, linear fashion. In practice we move back and forth before reaching the end of the process, and we may sometimes never reach the end.

1. **Immobilisation**: this is the initial response of being stunned, frozen, dazed. (Typical comments which we make in the aftermath of both positive and negative events are: 'I can't believe this is happening', 'It feels like a dream', 'It hasn't sunk in'.)
2. **Reaction**: (a) elation or despair: after a period of time, our initial stunned response gives way to a sharp mood swing (either up or down depending on the nature of the event). (b) minimisation: this initial post-shock reaction is typically followed by some kind of minimisation. 'For a positive transition', as Sugarman writes, 'the feelings of elation

become dampened as more ambiguous or less desirable concomitants of the transition become apparent or are confronted … Similarly, the importance or likely impact of a negative event may be played down' (2001: 146).

3. **Self-doubt – (and sometimes depression)**: this phase is characterised by fluctuations in energy level, doubt as to our own ability to manage ('I was really pleased to get this new job', we might say, 'but now I'm wondering whether I'm really up to it') or perhaps self-blame ('If only I'd not let her go out that night, she'd still be here today.') It may involve considerable anger and depression.

4. **Accepting reality and letting go**: until now we have been hanging on to the old order of things as they existed prior to the new event. There has been an element of denial and we have been clinging on in defiance of the new circumstances. At some point, these old attachments have to be broken in order to allow us to move on. These may include ties of affection to other people, or to old habits, or old beliefs. We may feel grief and anger at this, but if we are not completely stuck, there will be a gradual recognition of the need to put the past behind us.

5. **Testing**: as we let go of the past, we become free to explore the new circumstances in which we find ourselves. We can try out new identities and start to form new attachments.

6. **Search for meaning**: 'putting the past behind us' does not mean denying that it ever happened. During this phase, we look back at the past from our new viewpoint, reappraise it and try to make sense of it.

7. **Integration**: the transition process is complete. 'We feel "at home" in the new, post-transition reality' (Sugarman, 2001: 148). New behaviours and new ideas about ourselves have become part of our sense of our own identity.

Successful negotiation of a transition puts a person in good shape to deal with other transitions in the future. But a transition which has not been successfully negotiated may make it difficult for people to cope successfully with adapting to new life changes. To give a simple example, it is difficult to make a commitment to a new partner if one is still attached to and grieving for a previous partner.

The following exercise invites you to consider and compare the way we adjust to different kinds of event:

ACTIVITY 6.1

1. You have been planning an exciting holiday with a partner or friend for some time and are much looking forward to it. Not long before the day of your departure, your friend applies for a new job which will mean that he/she can't come on the holiday and it will have to be cancelled. Suppose you have just received the phone call. What would your initial reaction be – and what stages would you then go through?

2. Out of the blue, your partner announces that she/he has found someone else and wishes to end your relationship. What would your initial reaction be and what stages would you then go through?
3. Looking back at your own teenage years and early adulthood, can you chart the stages you went through between the time you thought of yourself as a child and the time you thought of yourself as an adult?

COMMENTS ON ACTIVITY 6.1

1. We suspect that you will have found yourself going through stages of disappointment, anger at your friend, guilt for feeling angry and so on, but eventually reaching a point where you were able to give up on the old plan and either make some new plan, or rearrange the plan for a later date, so that instead of grieving over what did not happen you are once again looking forward to something that will happen in due course. You might even have found some advantages in having postponed your original plan.
2. Obviously, this would be different in every individual situation. We would guess, though, that there would typically be an initial reaction of disbelief, followed by distress and attempts to change the partner's mind, or to cling onto some elements of the old relationship, for example, by saying you wished to remain friends. This could be seen as attempts on your part to minimise and normalise the situation. Self-doubt and anger with your partner would likely follow for a long period before you reach a stage of being able to let go of the attachment and perhaps begin to think about new ones.
3. People take many different paths through adolescence, but you will probably have noticed yourself experiencing grief at the loss of childhood (when Christmas presents stop being exciting, for example) and ambivalence and fear about becoming an adult, but then gradually coming to terms with the change.

Although two of these questions relate to major life changes and one relates to a comparatively temporary problem, we are suggesting that there will have been a somewhat similar pattern of response in each case.

Transitions and adolescence

The transition from childhood to adulthood is not a sudden event like, say, a bereavement or a lottery win, but it is nevertheless an event to which we have to adjust. We have to adjust to becoming a sexual being and to forming new kinds of relationships, to having new responsibilities and new freedoms, to having to earn a living and choose an occupation that will, to some extent, define us. As with other transitions, adolescence involves a letting go (of childhood and everything that goes with it); it involves forming new attachments (with an increasing emphasis on relationships with friends and sexual partners); and above all (as we will discuss shortly) it involves trying out new identities and building a new adult identity with which to embark on adult life.

But is adolescence really a single transition, a single event, or is it really a number of different ones? Graber and Brooks-Gunn (1996) suggest that we should look at adolescence as a transition containing a number of distinct 'turning points' and they suggest that dealing with these turning points is more difficult when, for instance:

- *Atypical timing* of turning points creates additional stress. For example, as discussed earlier, an unusually early or late onset of puberty, which puts a young person out of step with his or her peers, may be difficult and stressful.
- *Too many* turning points come together, so that there are too many things to deal with at once.
- *Context* is not supportive of change. As we'll discuss shortly, some family environments are not supportive. Nor are some school environments. To varying degrees, society in general may not be supportive. A young person who finds he is gay may find he has less support, for example. A disabled young person may find that society is resistant to allowing her an adult status (something we discuss in Chapter 8).

Identity versus Role Confusion

As discussed in Chapter 2, Erik Erikson offered a stage model that divided the whole lifespan into eight stages of which adolescence was the fifth (see p. 38). Each of his eight psychosocial stages was marked by a distinctive life 'crisis' or task, a reasonably successful resolution of which would provide the individual with qualities which would assist with other tasks ahead (see Table 2.2, on p. 39). And he described the characteristic crisis of adolescence as *identity versus role confusion*. Erikson was writing in very different times. His book *Identity, Youth and Crisis* (Erikson, 1994) was first published in 1968. Nevertheless, his ideas about identity development in adolescence remain influential and have been the basis of much research.

Erikson thought that during the adolescent stage, a combination of rapid growth, sexual maturity and a growing awareness of adult tasks ahead, leads to a questioning of the 'sameness and continuities relied on earlier' (Erikson, 1980 [1959]: 94). Of course, children do have a sense of identity before adolescence but, as we move towards adulthood, we need a sense of ourself that will be able to deal with new demands and expectations that come with being an adult. Successful resolution of this stage will lead to a secure sense of 'ego identity': the individual has developed a defined personality within a social reality which she understands and has a secure sense of herself as a consistent person. Of course, as is the case with all the crises that we face at various stages, there is no guarantee that we will successfully resolve this stage during adolescence itself. This depends in part on the 'inner capital' (p. 94) we have been able to accumulate as we negotiated previous crises, just as in future crises in adult life, we will draw on the inner capital we manage to accumulate as we negotiate the adolescent transition. 'The danger of this stage is *identity diffusion*' writes Erikson (1980 [1959]: 97, original emphasis). Losing the security of old continuities and samenesses when new ones are still not in place can be very frightening. We may adopt a whole range of different strategies to avoid facing the situation we find ourselves in, or to manage the anxieties which it provokes. 'To keep themselves together', for instance, adolescents often '... temporarily overidentify, to the point of apparent complete loss of identity, with the heroes of cliques and crowds' (p. 97).

Identity status

Looking further into the way that adolescents negotiate this difficult business of finding a new identity, James Marcia (1966), and Kroger and Marcia (2011) defined four different kinds of 'identity status' found among adolescents. These are:

1. **Identity diffusion** (see Erikson's use of this phrase above): an identity status characterised by the avoidance of commitment and indecision about major life issues, and by escape into diversionary activities intended to avoid anxiety. The stereotypically 'difficult' teenager who lies in bed, watches TV and refuses to think about or discuss the future might be said to be in a state of identity diffusion. Gullotta et al. comment that in their dealings with others, identity-diffused young people tend to be tense and insecure. As they note, 'how hard would it be to present yourself to others if you have no idea who you are?' (2000: 83).

2. **Identity foreclosure**: a status characterised by the acceptance of others' values (those of parents, for example, or teachers), rather than self-determined goals. The teenager who does not seem to question or rebel against adult expectations at all might be said to be in a state of identity foreclosure. Such a young person might seem to adults to be less of a 'problem' than the identity-diffused teenager, but in fact in Eriksonian terms is likewise failing to tackle the challenges of this stage because she is relying on introjection and identification rather than seeking her own identity. Gullotta et al. comment that 'foreclosed late adolescents have relatively constricted personalities' and are 'immature in their social behavior styles ... frozen in their developmental progression, rigid in their overcompliance, and generally unadaptive' (2000: 84).

3. **Moratorium**: a status of intense identity crisis characterised by active attention to major decisions and exploration of possibilities for the future, but not yet resolved in firm commitments. So, like the identity-diffused young person, a young person at the moratorium stage is avoiding making a commitment, but is doing so constructively, because it is constructive to consider actively all the options before making a serious decision. Moratorium is an *uncomfortable* position, which individuals may be tempted to avoid by opting for foreclosure.

4. **Identity achievement**: individuals with this status have resolved their crises and made firm commitments to ideals and plans, based on their own thinking and not simply on ideas imposed by or uncritically accepted from others. In Erikson's terms, they have successfully negotiated the challenge of this stage of life.

Two of these statuses – moratorium and diffusion – are characterised by lack of commitment to particular goals or values while two – foreclosure and achievement – are characterised by commitment to a particular set of goals and values. But in another sense, moratorium is closer to identity achievement because they are both about actively seeking a new adult identity, while diffusion is closer to foreclosure in that both are about avoiding the anxiety involved in such a search.

These kinds of identity status are not *stages* in identity formation, in that young people do not necessarily move through them in linear order. In fact, as discussed above in relation to transitions (and elsewhere in the book in relation to stage models of various other kinds), stage models in general are usually a considerable simplification of the uneven process of development. But if you refer back to the 'transitions' stages discussed earlier (pp. 107–8), one could say that foreclosure and identity diffusion relate to the early three stages. Moratorium might be said to correspond to what were referred to there as 'letting go', 'testing' and 'search for meaning', and identity achievement to 'integration'.

One of the features of Erikson's model is that at later times of transition, we may revisit unresolved issues from earlier stages. As we'll discuss in the next chapter, the mid-life transition is sometimes marked by revisiting issues that were prematurely foreclosed in adolescence or at the beginning of adult life. For example, permanent relationships or careers or parenthood entered into too early may, when revisited later, be seen as examples of foreclosure: commitments entered into prematurely in order to avoid the anxiety of leaving matters unresolved.

Gullotta et al. (2000: 92–3) suggest that patterns of identity diffusion would tend to be characteristic of young people from rejecting, detached families. Identity foreclosure would tend to be a pattern with child-centred families in which there is strong pressure to conform to the values and beliefs of the parents. Moratorium is, they suggest, characteristic of active families which encourage autonomy, self-expression and individual differences. They associate identity achievement in adolescence with homes with 'high praise, minimal parental control and secure attachments'.

ACTIVITY 6.2

Drawing on your own adolescent experience, (or that of other people you know), think about how the process of identity achievement unfolded. Can you identify examples of foreclosure, moratorium and diffusion?

COMMENTS ON ACTIVITY 6.2

Looking back, did you have some regrets about risks not taken? These might be areas of foreclosure, such as taking advice that led you to go straight from school to take the qualification route to a safe career, ignoring the voice in your head that urged you to travel the world or pursue your passion for making music. Or maybe you settled down with your first boy- or girlfriend, and the relationship didn't turn out well as you both matured and grew apart? On the other hand, you may be appalled by some of the risks you took in the course of finding your way in life. Perhaps too, you remember the discomfort of the moratorium stage, when you felt confused and uncertain what you wanted or were capable of, and wanted independence one minute and security the next. Often it will only be with hindsight that the process of identity achievement can be seen at all clearly; the difference between identity diffusion and moratorium is largely whether one emerges from it or not; at the time they may feel very much the same.

Neurological development in adolescence

The rapid psychological changes that occur in adolescence have a neurological underpinning, as well as environmental, cultural and biochemical ones. Much has been discovered in recent years about the structure and functioning of the adolescent brain, and this area of research continues to develop rapidly.

It used to be thought that brain development was complete by the end of childhood, but it is now known that during adolescence the brain develops almost as rapidly as it does during the period of infancy which we discussed in Chapter 3. And along with this development, as in the early years of life, goes a process of synaptic pruning, as those neural pathways which are not reinforced by use disappear, while those which are regularly used become more efficient. Another process occurring in the brain during this period is an increase in myelination. Myelin is a substance which sheaths and protects the brain cells and neural pathways, making the brain function more efficiently but at the same time restricting its capacity for change (Music, 2011: 188).

The limbic system, the area of the brain that drives both emotion and the exploration of new behaviour, and therefore risk-taking, is also developing rapidly during adolescence, while the frontal lobes, which are associated with self-regulation and what is called 'executive function', do not catch up developmentally until early adulthood (Hare et al., 2008, cited in Music, 2011: 188). Understanding this helps to make sense of the impulsive and sometimes extreme behaviour which is typical of adolescence, and is part of the experimentation involved in the process of identity formation.

Hormonal changes also contribute to these behaviour patterns. Hormones are of course involved in the process of puberty, but are also part of the process of brain development. For example, dopamine, the feel-good hormone, is a powerful neurotransmitter, facilitating connections between neurons in the brain, and its production increases markedly during adolescence (Ernst and Spear, 2009, cited in Santrock, 2012: 88). Another hormone which becomes more active in adolescence is melatonin, which regulates sleep patterns, and research has now shown that there is a biochemical basis for the adolescent's difficulty in getting out of bed in the morning, while wanting to stay active late into the night (Carskadon and Acebo, 2002, cited in Coleman, 2011: 36).

All this rapid development makes the teenage brain particularly vulnerable, while also making risk-taking behaviour more likely. It has been shown that drugs and alcohol are more likely to do lasting damage to the brain in adolescence than in later life (Crews et al., 2007, cited in Music, 2011; 189).

Another part of the brain that develops rapidly in adolescence is the system which connects the left and right hemispheres of the brain. This means that complex information can be processed more readily and in a more sophisticated manner (Giedd, 2008, cited in Santrock 2012: 88). This makes possible the higher level of cognitive functioning that characterises Piaget's formal operations stage, which we described in Chapter 4.

Moral development

One aspect of this capacity for more sophisticated cognitive functioning relates to moral judgements. Lawrence Kohlberg (1927–87) spent his academic career developing a theory of moral development which has been influential in the fields of philosophy, psychology and education. Piaget had already done some work in this area; Kohlberg built on this to identify three levels of moral development, each broken down into two stages, making six stages in all, which can be summarised as follows in Table 6.1:

TABLE 6.1   Kohlberg's Moral Stages' (summarised from Kroger, 2004)

Pre-conventional morality	1.	Avoiding punishment
(childhood)	2.	Instrumental – self-interest within relationships
Conventional morality	3.	Mutual expectations within relationships
(early adolescence)	4.	Upholding society's rules
Post-conventional morality	5.	Social contract – rules not absolute
(late adolescence/adulthood)	6.	Personal system of moral principles

The progression is from a simply behaviouristic avoidance of unpleasant consequences like punishment and disapproval through a deepening understanding of the nature and obligations of one's relationships to others, both in the closer bonds of family and friendship and in the wider networks of society, ultimately moving beyond adherence to rules, laws and social conventions to develop a personal sense of morality, or conscience. Adolescence is a key period for the development of moral judgement, which requires the ability to move beyond black and white thinking and consider complex factors in relation to each other. As Kroger points out, Kohlberg saw this development of moral reasoning as an important part of identity formation (Kroger, 2004: 91). He also believed that education could play an important role in moving children and young people from a lower stage to a higher one (Kohlberg, 1980).

Kohlberg's research method involved posing hypothetical dilemmas such as the 'Heinz dilemma', in which Heinz is unable to afford an expensive drug for his sick wife. He is unable to persuade the manufacturer of the drug to sell it to him at a lower price, and so he steals it. The research subjects are invited to consider and evaluate the morality of Heinz's actions. His work following the same individuals over a period of time supported his hypothesis of a stage theory – people did not return to a lower level once they had reached a higher one, and further research has also confirmed this (Kroger, 2004: 113). However, he also found that many people never reached the highest level, even in adulthood (Colby et al., 1983).

Research also confirms a link between Piaget's stage of formal operations and the more advanced stages of moral reasoning. But as Kroger points out, '… cognitive level appears as a necessary but not sufficient condition for one's mode of moral reasoning' (Kroger, 2004: 113).

It is important to note that Kohlberg's research looked at judgement and reasoning rather than action, which is a very different thing, and that it is based on hypothetical rather than real-life situations. There is evidence that people react to real-life dilemmas with a lower level of moral reasoning than they use in considering hypothetical questions (Kroger, 2004: 109). Kohlberg's theory has been questioned in other ways too, for example in relation to gender and cultural specificity (see Kroger, 2004, Chapter 4 for a full discussion of this). However, his work remains important in highlighting the moral dimension of development and the role of education in supporting this.

Identity, ethnicity and culture

Establishing an identity in adolescence can present particular challenges for young people who are members of ethnic minorities. One reason for this is that they may be faced with competing – and very different – models of adult identity. A British Muslim teenager of Pakistani descent, for instance, has to define her own identity not only in relation to the norms of the majority (white, Western, secular) culture, but also to those of her family's culture, which may subscribe to radically different values in relation to religion, sex, the role of women, marriage, family, authority, and so on. For ethnic minority teenagers, trying to establish a separate identity from their own parents, while at the same time taking pride in their identity as a member of the tradition which their parents represent, requires the '… capacity to surf between two cultures and negotiate their identity in such a way that they maintain their links with their family and achieve full citizenship' (Sabatier, 2008: 186).

Not surprisingly, therefore, ethnicity has been found to be a more important identity issue for those from minority cultures than it is for those from the majority culture (Phinney and

Alipuria, 1990). And the same study found self-esteem among young people from ethnic minorities in particular to be correlated with their interest in and commitment to their own ethnic identity. Phinney (1989, 1993) has also proposed a model of ethnic identity development, based on Marcia's categories which we discussed earlier, in which there is a move from 'unexamined ethnic identity' to 'ethnic identity search' to 'achieved ethnic identity' through the processes of exploration, resolution and affirmation.

We need to be aware that recent scholarship in this area is increasingly recognising the complexity of ethnic identity. Different social identities, such as gender and sexual identity, intersect and interact with ethnic identity, and 'it is important not to assume homogeneity in ethnic identity experiences within or among ethnic minority groups' (Umaña-Taylor, 2011: 803, 805).

Relating to Others

Having talked about what is going on 'inside' young people during adolescence, we'll now consider what adolescence means in terms of relationships with other people. This is of course a two-way question. How do adolescents relate to others – and how does the behaviour of others affect adolescents?

Autonomy and the peer group

There are considerable cultural variations in the amount of autonomy that smaller children are given. There are also large cultural variations in the amount of autonomy that even an adult can expect. However, it must fairly generally be the case that one of the changes that normally occurs in adolescence is that young people are given, and expect, more autonomy. There are several kinds of autonomy though, which don't necessarily all go together. Steinberg and Silverberg (1986), looking at levels of autonomy among 12- to 16-year-olds, thought it would be more useful to break the idea of autonomy into several categories. These were:

- *emotional autonomy*, in which the individual relinquishes childhood dependence on her parents
- *resistance to peer pressure*, in which the individual becomes able to act upon her own ideas, rather than conform to those of peers
- *a subjective sense of self-reliance*, in which the individual feels free of excessive dependency on others, takes initiatives, and has a feeling of control over her life.

What these researchers found in their survey of young people was that as 'emotional autonomy' increases, 'resistance to peer group pressure' decreases. There seemed to be a kind of trade-off. Young people become more reliant on their peer group as they become less reliant on their family of origin.

Ryan and Lynch (1989), however, argue that what Steinberg and Silverberg's first category really measured was not emotional *autonomy*, but emotional *detachment*. Their view was that children who scored high on this measure are actually lacking in emotional support at home and so tend to compensate by relying heavily on their peer group. In their view, securely attached adolescents were actually better placed to achieve genuine autonomy than emotionally detached ones, who would tend to be easily led by their peers rather than genuinely determining their own course in life.

Gender differences

Stage models of development (at adolescence and other stages) have often been guilty of offering male development as the 'norm', and either ignoring female development or tagging it on as an afterthought. Freud's Oedipus complex is a case in point. And, as Carol Gilligan has pointed out, Erikson's well-known developmental chart ('Stages of a Man's Life') also seems to assume that the 'male' developmental route is the primary one.

In her influential book *In a Different Voice*, Gilligan (1982) suggested that girls construct identity in a different way to boys, characteristically linking identity to *intimacy* while boys are more prone to link identity to *role* and to ideas of *autonomy*. She contrasts 'a self defined through separation', which she suggests is characteristically male, with 'a self delineated through connection', which she sees as characteristically female (Gilligan, 1982: 35). She notes that, while Erikson does himself suggest that 'for women, identity has as much to do with intimacy as separation, this observation is not integrated into his developmental chart' (Gilligan, 1982: 98).

Drawing on the work of Nancy Chodorow (1978), Gilligan argues that 'given that the primary caretaker in the first three years of life is typically female, the interpersonal dynamics of gender identity formation are different for boys and girls' (1982: 7), because girls experience themselves as being alike to their main carers while boys experience themselves as being distinct.

> Since masculinity is defined through separation and femininity is defined through attachment, male gender identity is threatened by intimacy while female gender identity is threatened by individuation. Thus males tend to have difficulty with relationships, while females tend to have problems with individuation. (Gilligan, 1982: 8)

Gilligan was concerned with moral development (she was originally a colleague of Kohlberg's) and here she found significant gender differences, with women tending to give more weight to relationships and the responsibility of caring for others, while men gave more weight to abstract principles of justice and law.

We don't want to make sweeping generalisations about differences between male and female behaviour. But it is definitely worth thinking about Gilligan's suggestion that the characteristic female route to establishing an adult identity is different from the characteristic male one, built on very different foundations.

Sexuality and Adolescence

The biological foundation on which the social and psychological phenomenon of adolescence is built is the onset of sexual maturity. For both boys and girls, coming to terms with new sexual feelings and new social pressures about sex is, of course, integral to adolescence and a major driving force behind the changes that occur during this stage. 'Adolescents ... cannot simply add new sexual feeling to an old self' (Cobb, 1995: 129). These new feelings (and the new social expectations that go with them) are one of the main reasons that an adolescent needs to build a new self.

How this happens varies enormously between individuals, cultures and points in time. As Jeanne Brooks-Gunn and Roberta Paikoff observe, 'the study of sexuality is a perfect example of why person, time, context and period must be considered simultaneously' (1997: 190). Among other things, this means that the experience of one generation is only partly relevant to the experience of the next. The authors of the present book, for instance, both grew up in the 1960s and 1970s, a period when sexual norms were very different to those that apply today. Contrary to stereotypes about the permissive '60s, sexually explicit material is much more widely available in 'Western' countries at the beginning of the twenty-first century than it was then (ranging from explicit sex tips in magazines aimed at teenage girls, to images of sexual acts readily available on the internet) and there is generally (though not universally) more acceptance among the parental generation of sexual activity by teenagers. It is not surprising that findings by researchers suggest that young people are becoming sexually active at a younger age than they were in the 1960s or 1970s (Coleman, 2011: 134–6).

But in spite of what appears to be a much higher degree of frankness about sex and sexuality than existed in previous generations, or exists now in more traditional cultures, sexuality remains a difficult area. Young people receive mixed messages from the world around them – on the one hand, there are injunctions to abstain from sexual activity outside of committed relationships, while on the other hand, there is the pressure to prove themselves and acquire status through sexual experience – with boys continuing to receive different messages to girls. And perhaps it is not just a question of mixed messages but of a certain ambivalence about intimacy which is part of the condition of being human. 'The struggle between intimacy and autonomy ...', observe Brooks-Gunn and Paikoff, 'is played out on the sexual stage as well as in relationships with parents, ... peers, and siblings' (1997: 209).

Societies differ but in any society adolescents have to come to terms with physical changes, respond to new desires and manage new expectations, in a wider context that also includes managing sexual risks, negotiating intimacy and autonomy, maintaining the esteem of their peer group and taking account of the expectations and sanctions of the adult world. How they meet these challenges is in turn influenced by a range of factors. A number of studies look, for instance, at the factors linked to the age at which young people become sexually active. Laflin et al. (2008) found that higher academic achievement and (perhaps not surprisingly) importance attached to religious belief were both factors associated with sexual abstinence in boys and girls in a US sample. L'Engle et al. (2006) found that adolescents exposed to more sexual content in the media are more likely to be sexually active. Crockett et al. (1996) found that the most significant factor influencing the timing of the start of sexual activity was parental circumstances. Being the children of separated parents and having a mother who was a teenage parent were factors which, for both boys and girls, were associated with becoming sexually active earlier. Whitaker and Miller (2000) found that teenagers who talked to their parents about sex were likely to initiate sexual activity later than teenagers who did not, with peer influence being stronger on the latter group, as would be predicted from the work of Ryan and Lynch discussed earlier.

But, while a lot of research studies look at questions like the timing of first sexual intercourse, the experience for young people is of course a good deal more complicated than can be captured simply by statistics relating to specific events.

Sexual identity

Becoming a sexual being is part of the whole process of identity formation. Like other aspects of identity formation, it depends not just on an individual developmental process but on the family, social and cultural context in which this takes place, as we have described above. Attitudes to sexual activity depend on the meaning that young people attach to sex, and how sex fits in with their wider picture of themselves and the world.

Young people do not simply begin to engage in sex as a result of being 'slaves to their hormones' though of course biology is part of it. (Hormones are important but their effects are mediated by social context: see Moore and Rosenthal, 2006: 74 ff). There are a whole range of reasons why young people choose to engage in sex, or abstain from it. Brooks-Gunn and Paikoff (1997: 200), for instance, cite African American sources suggesting that some girls consent to sex as a price to pay for the protection conferred by boys against other boys. And sexual activity may be important too as a marker of growing up or for the status it confers within a young person's peer group. Janet Sayers cites the recollections of a woman in her forties recalling her experience of her first kiss:

> All we talked about [when we were 13] was had you been kissed, and had you had your periods. All the girls were desperate to be kissed. I don't think it mattered if it was a gorilla that kissed them. It was more a thing to tell my friends – that I'd had my first kiss – rather than the kiss itself. (Sayers, 1998: 88)

It will not come as a surprise to many readers that researchers find differences in the attitudes of boys and girls, with boys tending to see sex as a means of demonstrating their status and maturity, while girls tend to see it more as an expression of love and intimacy (Moore and Rosenthal, 2006: 133–6), though these differences can be overstated, and are probably not as marked as they were in the past.

Other factors apart from gender play a part here. The same authors also report less marked differences between boys and girls among 'a middle-class Anglo-Australian sample' as compared to the differences between boys and girls among homeless teenagers (2006: 135). Most (though not all) boys and girls in the middle-class group identified 'love, caring and affection' as the primary motivation. Among the homeless group, though, while girls also identified 'love, caring and affection' as their primary reason for engaging in sex, 'many of the homeless boys responded to the harshness of their lives with an unequivocal rejection of romantic values' (2006: 135).

To what extent gender differences are due to biological difference, and to what extent they are due to different 'sexual scripts' inculcated by social conditioning, is difficult to unravel (see the discussion on gender differences in Chapter 5), but research does confirm that the 'double standard' does still exist in terms of messages given to boys and girls about the acceptability of sexual behaviour. Discussing a review of 30 different American studies on this topic carried out since 1980, Mary Crawford and Danielle Popp conclude that, while some groups 'still endorse the absolute double standard that prohibits sexual intercourse outside marriage for women, more generally the orthodox double standard has made way for double standards that are subtler but perhaps equally effective as a means of social control' (2003: 22–3). For example, girls continue to be labelled as 'sluts' by their peers if considered to be too sexually active, but there is no equivalent word for promiscuous boys.

Different 'sexual scripts' may even alter something as basic as what people mean by 'having sex'. Diamond and Savin-Williams (2009) discuss the differing definitions revealed in a number of in-depth studies of adolescent sexual behaviour. Girls tended to take a narrower view than boys, and were less likely to count anything other than full intercourse as 'having sex', which is consistent with the kind of double standards already discussed (2009: 482). Young people in the US who had pledged not to have sex outside marriage for religious reasons also took this narrow view, in some cases retracting the disclosures of sexual activity which they had made a year earlier (Rosenbaum, 2006, cited in Diamond and Savin-Williams, 2009: 483)

The extent to which people define their desires in relation to their social learning and their expectations of themselves also becomes apparent when we unpack the concept of sexual identity. *Sexual identity, sexual orientation* and *sexual practices* are different things, which may or may not be congruent with each other. Our *sexual identity* is how we define ourselves (for example homosexual, bisexual, heterosexual), *sexual orientation* describes our sexual preferences and desires, and *sexual practices* describe our actual behaviour. (Coleman, 2011: 147). Figures from a longitudinal study of US youth show that significantly more young people admitted to having experienced same-sex attraction than would define themselves as gay or lesbian (Savin-Williams and Ream, 2007, cited in Savin-Williams, 2011: 681–2). This anomaly can be explained by the fact that although Western societies have moved a long way in the last half-century towards a greater acceptance of different sexualities, assumptions about sexuality are still overwhelmingly *heteronormative.*

Even now gay and lesbian young people will pick up the message from many different sources that being gay is not an acceptable identity, that it is not compatible with being a 'real' man or a 'real' woman – and so on. In the UK, for example, young people would have to cope with the widespread use of the word 'gay' as a term of abuse among their peers. And this is even more the case with acceptance of transsexual and transgender identities.

Recent research and writing about adolescent sexuality has moved towards a more inclusive view, in which sexual diversity is normalised rather than defined as a problem. An example of this is Dillon's model of sexual identity formation, which can be applied equally to people of all sexualities (Dillon et al., 2011: 658). His model moves from what he terms compulsory heterosexuality (the heteronormative assumption) through exploration and experimentation to commitment. He links it with Marcia's model of identity formation, where the developmental task is to steer between the extremes of diffusion and foreclosure to reach a personally congruent identity which can be owned and lived. It is also important to note, as Savin-Williams does, that sexual identity is not just an issue for adolescence which is then settled for life (Savin-Williams, 2011: 681). It can, and often does, change in the course of adulthood.

Problems in Adolescence

In the UK media and public debate, adolescents, teenagers or youths are frequently depicted as *problems*. There is – and has been for many years – a great deal of adult concern about youth crime, anti-social behaviour, teenage pregnancy, drug and alcohol use and so on. But the stormy and rebellious stereotype of adolescence can easily be overstated. For the majority, adolescence is not an exceptionally stormy period. In some cases, in fact, it could be argued that adolescence is *not stormy enough*, since a lack of any challenging behaviour during adolescence might sometimes indicate that a young person had opted for 'foreclosure', rather than risking the state of 'moratorium' required to build a genuine adult identity.

Not everything the adult world sees as problematic is a problem for the young person concerned. Adolescent psychologists today tend to approach the problems of adolescence by looking at the factors that contribute to risk and resilience and take a view that focuses on strengths rather than problems. This positive youth development model has become particularly influential in the US (Lerner et al., 2009). However, it is true that a number of problems come to the fore in adolescence, or peak at that time, and we will consider some of these.

The incidence of depression, for instance, is relatively high during adolescence (Seroczynski et al., 2003). This may in part be linked to hormonal changes, but it is also a product of the multiple challenges involved in this period of life: as we noted earlier, depression is a common feature of transitions of all kinds. Drug and alcohol use also becomes widespread, although patterns vary considerably from country to country, and also over time. A longitudinal study of American high school pupils shows a peak of substance use from the mid-70s to the early 80s, then a decline, followed by another rise in the early 90s, since when it has levelled off. Patterns also varied considerably for different drugs (Chassin et al., 2009: 725). A survey of the health behaviour of adolescents across Europe and the US carried out for the World Health Organisation in 2009–10 (Currie et al., 2012) found that in England 22 per cent of girls and 31 per cent or boys drink at least once a week at the age of 15, and 43 per cent of girls and 38 per cent of boys of this age report having been drunk on at least two occasions (155–7). Twenty-four per cent of 15-year-old girls and 22 per cent of boys had used cannabis, and 9 per cent of both boys and girls had done so in the last 30 days (166–7). Some countries in Europe had higher rates than this, and others lower. Boys mostly reported higher rates of drinking and drunkenness, but the gender gap narrowed between 1998 and 2006 (161).

Eating disorders usually appear in adolescence or soon afterwards. 'Anorexia nervosa … occurs primarily in pubertal girls, and bulimia nervosa generally appears in slightly older teenage girls or women in their early twenties' (Polivy et al., 2003: 523). Suicidal behaviour – very rare in childhood – also sees an abrupt rise in adolescence (Windle et al., 2000: 261), though the incidence of such behaviours varies considerably according to the particular social context. (In the USA, for example, suicide rates are more than twice as high for Native Americans aged 15–24 as for the rest of the population [Seroczynski et al., 2003: 558].) At present, in both the USA and the UK, attempted suicide and deliberate self-harm are much more common in girls than boys, but completed suicide is more common in boys (Coleman, 2011: 122; Seroczynski et al., 2003: 557).

Adolescence is also a peak time for criminal behaviour, with the peak age for offending in England and Wales being 18 for boys and 15 for girls (Coleman, 2011: 116). There is evidence that criminal careers tend to start in adolescence and that if you get through adolescence without graduating into crime, then you are much less likely to become criminal later. For example, an American study (Wolfgang et al., 1987) found that of young people who had not offended in adolescence, 81 per cent still had no criminal record at 30. In other words, only 19 per cent of those who had not offended in adolescence had then gone on to commit offences subsequently. By contrast, out of juvenile offenders, 45 per cent were still chronic offenders in adulthood.

There are different ways of looking at the emergence of deviant behaviour in adolescence and researchers have identified and explored both socio-economic factors and familial ones. Barber (1992) suggests that a developing individual needs both psychological autonomy and behavioural boundaries. Young people whose parents have difficulties with allowing them psychological autonomy will tend to be more likely to withdraw and have internalised problems. Young people whose parents have difficulties with setting behavioural boundaries will tend to have external problems, such as delinquency. This seems to connect with the studies cited by Gullotta et al. (2000) which we mentioned earlier, suggesting that 'identity-diffused' young people tend to come from rejecting, detached families, while 'identity-foreclosed' young people come from conformist, child-centred families.

Deviance and identity

But if deviant careers begin in adolescence, this is not so different from any other kind of career. You would probably find a significant proportion of doctors showed some sort of interest in medicine when they were still adolescents, for example. So the choice of a criminal career (or any other 'deviant' career) may not necessarily differ that much in pattern from socially approved career choices. And many writers on the subject would say that the choice of a deviant career is in fact an attempt to establish some sort of adult identity. Jessor and Jessor (1979), for example, saw deviant behaviours as 'functional'. They were attempts to obtain some autonomy and control. Reicher and Emler (1986) likewise argued that delinquency can be a positive choice, a way of establishing a reputation and proving oneself. After all, many of the adolescent behaviours which worry adults – smoking, drinking, having sex – are in fact attempts to feel more adult by doing the 'things that adults do'. In the absence of other alternatives, criminal activity too may be a way of achieving the things that adults are supposed to do in the world: developing skills, providing for oneself and others, showing courage ...

Some adolescent girls perhaps choose to become pregnant at a very early stage for similar reasons. Being a parent is, after all, a recognised adult role, an adult *identity*, and for some it must seem like the only adult identity that is attainable. Coleman (2011: 151–2) notes that teenage pregnancy is highest in urban areas, and among the most socio-economically disadvantaged groups. There is a higher incidence among girls brought up in care than in the general population. The following is the explanation given by a 16-year-old for her decision to become a parent:

> ... when I got to around 14, I was in a children's home and all I felt was that no one loved me, no one ever loved me, no one ever would love me, and that's when I decided I wanted me own family, and so that's what I done. (A 16-year-old participant in a study by Dennison and Coleman, 1998, cited in Coleman, 2011: 151)

Adults, Adolescents and Attachment

Adolescence is not something that occurs to individuals in a vacuum. We have already alluded to the wider social context within which it occurs (and without which we would have no distinct concept of adolescence at all). We will look now at the more immediate context, the context of family and relationships with adults.

Factors that make for a successful adolescent transition to a confident adult identity seem to include:

- Parental involvement and connectedness with young people. 'Diffused' young people have been found to score lower on the scale for emotional attachment to parents than other young people and lower on independence (Perosa et al., 1996; Willemsen and Waterman, 1991). Seeking autonomy is not about ending close relationships with parents and family, but actually takes place most effectively within the context of close relationships with both parents.

- Parental acceptance of conflict and of their children's own emotions. 'Absence of conflict has characterised the family environment of foreclosed family relationships' writes Kroger (2000: 108, citing Perosa et al., 1996; Willemsen and Waterman, 1991) while Bronstein et al. (1993) conclude that where parents accept and support non-hostile expression of emotions by their children, this is linked with their greater ability to cope with the transition from childhood into adolescence.

- Parents' ability to set firm boundaries, without being controlling or unresponsive. As Kroger (2000: 52) puts it, referring to work by Baumrind (1991): 'An authoritative (in which warmth and nurturance are coupled with firm control) rather than an authoritarian or permissive parental style of child rearing has been associated with greater self-reliance, social responsibility and achievement motivation in later childhood and adolescence.'

Maccoby and Martin (1983) classified parenting types on two dimensions ('demandingness' and 'responsiveness') resulting in the four categories shown in Table 6.2.

Research seems to show (Coleman, 2011: 90–91) that on measures such as self-esteem and avoiding risk behaviour such as drug use, adolescents brought up in 'authoritative' families score the highest. Adolescents brought up in 'indulgent' households are on average less mature, more irresponsible and more conforming to their peers. Adolescents brought up in 'indifferent' households are more impulsive and more likely to get involved in high-risk behaviour.

TABLE 6.2 Parenting types (after Maccoby and Martin, 1983)

		Demandingness	
		High	Low
Responsiveness	*High*	Authoritative	Indulgent
	Low	Authoritarian	Indifferent

Another way of putting all this would seem to be that the adolescent transition takes place best within the context of a *secure attachment* and that young people with an insecure attachment to their parents or carers will find it harder to establish a secure adult identity. Bowlby's *secure base*, you may remember, was something that the securely attached child was supposed to be able to internalise and carry forward as a source of confidence and security in adult life.

What we would also predict from attachment theory is that those adults who themselves experienced insecure, and particularly disorganised, attachments to *their* carers as children, will find it harder to provide this kind of security to others, perhaps particularly during the challenging and testing time of the adolescent transition. Parents who were themselves insecurely attached, for example, may find it difficult to reconcile being firm with being caring and supportive, and may attempt one at the expense of the other, or lurch unpredictably between the two. They may need help with striking this balance.

Coping Skills and Resilience

In recent years, there has been an increased interest in the nature of the resilience that enables some individuals to recover better than others from traumatic or stressful events. However, we need to beware of thinking of resilience simply as a character trait that some people have and others do not. It is important to look at resilience as it interacts with risk, which in this context refers to the stress factors that may affect young people's lives. These factors can be at an individual, family or community level, and they often tend to occur together; for example, poverty is likely to be accompanied by poor physical and mental health for the individual and/or other family members, insecure housing, limited educational opportunities and so on. The more stress factors a young person is exposed to, the greater the likelihood of a poor outcome (Appleyard et al., 2005, cited by Coleman, 2011: 212). Some stress factors are to do with the normal transitions and changes of adolescence, while others may come from specific events, such as illness, bereavement or moving to another school, town or country. And some, like poverty, are chronic, while others, like a serious accident, are acute. All in all, risk and the way it interacts with resilience in adolescence presents a complex picture which requires a 'multilevel approach' (Compas and Reeslund, 2009: 562).

What qualities and/or coping strategies enable some adolescents to deal more successfully with stresses? Working to promote resilience seems an interesting alternative to responding to problems after the event.

Researchers in this area have identified two broad groups of ways in which people respond to stressful events:

- emotion-focused – aimed at managing the uncomfortable feelings that the stressor evokes (there are several possible sub-categories of this: for example, approaches based on rumination as against approaches based on distraction)
- problem-focused – aimed at tackling the stressor itself (Lazarus and Folkman, 1984, Lazarus, 1993, cited in Frydenberg, 2008: 39).

It would seem that emotion-focused coping strategies become more common with age, while problem-focused strategies are not closely related to age (see Compas, 1995). In fact, which is the best approach to take will depend in part on the situation. In situations which it is possible to control, a problem-focused strategy is appropriate, but in situations which it is not possible to control, an emotion-focused strategy is more appropriate and in fact a problem-focused approach is likely to be counter-productive, since it will not work and will therefore add to feelings of failure and inadequacy. Beardslee and Podorefsky (1988), for example, in a study of teenagers with depressed parents, found that those teenagers who recognised that they could not cure the depression itself coped better.

Successful coping in this and other studies seemed to be linked therefore not only to emotional factors, but also to cognitive factors (the ability to think through a situation, see it from different points of view, and arrive at a realistic appraisal of the extent to which it can be controlled).

Coping skills can be taught and Compas (1995) reports several pieces of research evidence which show, for example, that the teaching of basic coping skills in school does have positive outcomes.

Frydenberg (2008: 23–4) suggests that there is a third group of coping strategies which could be described as 'dysfunctional coping'. This would include things like turning to drugs and alcohol. In Frydenberg's (Australian) study, these seem to become more prevalent at the age of about 15. Frydenberg also notes an increased tendency towards self-blame in the older adolescent group, and the importance of friendship networks in enabling young people to cope effectively with stress, suggesting that young people with specific social skills deficits will generally be more vulnerable to stressful events. Teaching social skills then becomes another strategy for promoting resilience.

The coping strategies used by boys and girls tend to be different, in line with the gender differences we have already noted in relation to intimacy and autonomy. Girls are more likely to turn to family and friends for support and assistance, while boys are more likely to adopt a problem-focused approach rather than talking to others about how they feel (Coleman, 2011: 219).

Like risk factors, factors contributing to resilience can be considered at individual, family and community levels (Garmezy and Rutter, 1983, cited in Coleman, 2011: 215). Evidence from a number of longitudinal studies highlights the importance of the presence of a consistent and reliable adult (not necessarily the parent); '... the role played by one adult who cared about the individual, and who was available at significant turning points, appears to be absolutely central to the development of resilience in the face of adversity' (Coleman, 2011: 216).

We will conclude this chapter with an activity which invites you to apply some of the ideas we have been discussing to a kind of situation where adults and adolescents often find it difficult to understand each other.

ACTIVITY 6.3

Ben is an able boy. Up to the age of 15 he performed well at school, particularly in maths and science, and expressed a keen interest in a career in medicine, which was a source of considerable pride to his parents. They themselves both left school at 16 and now run a small convenience store, and they have cherished the hope that their son, who is their only child, would become a doctor ever since his talent for science became evident in primary school.

But from the age of 15, Ben's motivation began to slip. He turned in poor homework, or, increasingly, simply failed to complete homework at all. He began to miss classes, and sometimes whole days of school, and, when in school, he was often disruptive, talking and joking in class and distracting other pupils.

When teachers attempt to challenge him about this change in his level of motivation, he shrugs, and is monosyllabic, reluctant to engage in any kind of dialogue. He is just the same at home, refusing to discuss the situation with his parents. When pressed he simply walks out, staying out very late with friends with whom he smokes cannabis, drinks, plays video games and watches TV. His performance in exams has plummeted. Medical school, and indeed university at all, will cease to be an option unless he does something about this. But when this is pointed out to him, and he's asked what his plans are, he refuses to answer.

'It's as if,' his mother says, 'he thinks he can just spend the rest of his life smoking weed and watching TV with his mates.' His father, with some bitterness, adds, 'I notice he doesn't mind helping himself to food out of the fridge whenever he wants it, though. I wonder how he thinks it gets there?' Both parents work long hours, opening the shop at 6am, and closing at 10pm, and they feel that Ben is throwing away opportunities that they would dearly love to have had.

What can be said about Ben's current identity status? How might his parents and other adults be most helpful to him?

COMMENTS ON ACTIVITY 6.3

Ben would seem to be exhibiting the obvious signs of identity diffusion, in that he is simply showing no willingness to work on or think about the problem of what he is going to do in the future. Since of course he will at some time have to earn his own living, one could argue that he is simply in denial, 'hiding his head in the sand'. And of course this not uncommon among teenagers, enjoying the autonomy that comes with the approach of adulthood, but dreading the responsibilities that adulthood also brings.

However, things may be a little more complicated than that. It would appear that the expectation that he become a doctor has been placed upon Ben from an early age by his parents. It may be that medicine doesn't appeal to him. Or perhaps, whether it appeals to him or not, the fact remains that if he simply pursued that career, he would always feel as though it was something that he'd accepted, rather than something he had chosen. In other words, what seems to his parents and teachers like Ben recklessly abandoning a clear and promising career path may in fact for Ben be the only way he knows of avoiding identity foreclosure.

(Continued)

(Continued)

This is not to say that his diffused state is a viable long-term option, but it may be a way of putting on the brakes, until such time as he is ready to move into a state of moratorium and start exploring options for himself. He might feel more supported if he could be reassured by his parents that more than one option would be fine with them. It will also be helpful for him if his parents, while expressing their concern and providing clear boundaries, can find ways to convey to him that he is loved and valued for who he is now and not just for what he might become. If there are other significant adults in his life besides his parents and teachers, maybe people who can be role models for a variety of different paths into adulthood, this will be helpful too.

Chapter Summary

- In this chapter we began by looking at the relationship between biology and culture (a version of the nature–nurture question) with particular reference to puberty, which is both a biological change and a culturally determined one.
- We then looked at another general topic with particular relevance to adolescence – the psychology of the characteristic stages which human beings go through when responding to new circumstances of whatever kind.
- There is a general consensus that achieving an adult *identity* is the major challenge for young people going through adolescence and we looked at the various stages and factors in the development of a sense of identity. We considered the question of ethnic and cultural identity.
- We looked at recent research findings about the development of the adolescent brain, and at cognitive and moral development in adolescence.
- We then looked at the changing nature of adolescents' relationships with others, including their parents and with their peer group. We looked at the concept of autonomy and how it relates to identity. We looked at gender differences in relation to identity and at suggestions that the relationship between autonomy, identity and intimacy is different for girls and boys.
- We then considered how boys and girls adjust to themselves as sexual beings.
- We then considered the increase in crime and self-destructive behaviour that occurs in adolescence and how this relates to the discussion about identity.
- We looked at different parenting styles and how the behaviour of adults and the quality of adult attachments impact on the adolescent transition.
- Finally, we looked at another topic which is highly relevant to adolescents but is important at every stage of life: the quality of *resilience*.

Many of these themes will be carried on into the next chapter where we look at early and middle adulthood and the changes and transitions that occur within the long period from the end of adolescence to the beginning of old age.

Further Reading

Coleman, J. (2011) *The Nature of Adolescence*, 4th edn. Hove: Routledge.
An account of the whole range of issues relating to adolescence, put in a social context.
Frydenberg, E. (2008) *Adolescent Coping: Advances in Theory, Research and Practice*. Hove: Routledge.
Kroger, J. (2004) *Identity in Adolescence: The Balance between Self and Other*, 3rd edn. London: Routledge.
Moore, S. and Rosenthal, D. (2006) *Sexuality in Adolescence: Current Trends*, 2nd edn. Hove: Routledge.

7 ACTING LIKE A GROWN-UP

CHALLENGES OF ADULTHOOD

- What do we mean by 'adult'?   131
- Development, continuity and change   132
- Stages and transitions   136
- Identity and intimacy   138
- Generativity   140
- Young adulthood   141
- Middle adulthood   144

When does adulthood begin? As we saw in the last chapter, in some cultures the onset of adolescence is seen almost in itself as the beginning of adulthood. But in Western industrial countries an adolescent is legally still a child and adulthood is a later and distinct status, though there is little legal consistency about when it starts. In Britain, for example, under the age of 16, a person cannot give legal consent to sex and is required to attend school. At 16 it is legal to marry with a parent's consent and to finish schooling (although in England, unlike Wales, Scotland and Northern Ireland, you must remain in some form of education or training until you are 18). You can hold a driving licence from the age of 17, but you cannot buy alcoholic drinks in a public bar or vote until the age of 18 (though in Scotland 16- and 17-year-olds were allowed to vote in the 2014 referendum on independence). In many American states it is illegal to buy alcohol until the age of 21, although in some states the age of consent is 18. And, according to Kroger (2000), in New Zealand a person can vote at 18 but cannot enter into a legal contract until the age of 20. But still, roughly speaking, in industrial countries a boy or girl is legally recognised at somewhere between the age of 18 and 21 to have become fully adult.

We will treat one part of adult life – old age – as separate by giving it a chapter on its own (Chapter 11). This is because it has a number of characteristics that mark it out as rather distinct, though we don't wish to imply that old people are not also adults. In the present chapter we are going to look at early and middle adulthood – the periods, roughly speaking, from 20 to 40, and from 40 to the onset of 'old age' – which cover the largest part of most people's lives.

Though adulthood may be a single legal status, one might question whether it makes sense in psychosocial terms to see adults at very different ages as necessarily having a great deal in common with one another. Does a young woman of 20 have more in common with an 80-year-old than she does with a girl of 15, for instance? On the other hand, if we try to divide adulthood up, like childhood, into several distinct developmental stages, this too can present problems because there are so many different routes through adult life.

Our perspective on the ages and stages of life is powerfully determined by our point of view, the point that we ourselves have reached. In revising this chapter for the second edition we noticed how much the first edition had emphasised the mid-life crisis (Chris Beckett was 40-something at the time) and we also noticed that it had defined 60 as 'old age', which no longer seemed appropriate (Hilary Taylor's 60th birthday had passed as this chapter was finalised for the second edition). We could both remember a time when the age of 40 seemed to us like the beginning of old age – but of course it feels very different to us from our present viewpoint. Both authors will be in their 60s by the time this third edition appears in print.

What do we Mean by 'Adult'?

When we say 'let's sort this out like adults' or tell someone to 'grow up and stop acting like a child', what do we actually mean? What is the essential quality that marks out adulthood and prompts us to label some adults as childish, or adolescent, when they fail to conform to it? Before going any further, you may like to consider your own views on these questions.

ACTIVITY 7.1

With apologies to any younger readers, we are assuming that you are at some stage in your adult life. Looking back on your own experience, or at the experience of others:

At what point in your life did you start to think of yourself as an adult? Why? What had changed from how you were before?

If we divide adult life up into young adulthood, middle adulthood (middle-age) and late adulthood (old age), which group do you belong to? Is it easy to decide? How do you view adults in the other two groups? What is different about them and what do you have in common with them, that you do not have in common with adolescents or children?

COMMENTS ON ACTIVITY 7.1

Many adults would say that they don't actually feel like an adult to themselves. (We probably all have times when we wish the real grown-ups would come along and solve our problems for us.)

Nevertheless, there is a time in life when we stop thinking of ourselves as a boy or a girl and start thinking of ourselves as a man or a woman. This may or may not coincide with the time that the rest of the world starts to see us in that way; it will probably relate to Marcia's process of identity achievement, which we discussed in the last chapter.

As to the quality that distinguishes adult life from childhood or adolescence, we can't guess what you decided about this, but in discussions with groups of adult students, the word that tends to come up is 'responsibility'.

In the end, all verbal categories are arbitrary. In English we have one word, 'adult', which covers people of a wide range of ages. What does seem to be a common theme, though (as noted above), is an expectation that, having reached adulthood, a person must take responsibility for themselves and for others around them. As we pointed out earlier, this is reflected in laws which allow adults to take on responsibilities which are restricted or forbidden for younger people. It is also reflected in the use of the words 'childish', 'immature' or 'adolescent' to refer to adults seen as acting irresponsibly. This is not to say that children and young people cannot act very responsibly. In Britain alone, the 2011 census showed that almost 178,000 under-18s were acting as carers for family members with disabilities or health problems (Carers UK, 2014). It is also the case that, for some adults, it may be a struggle to get society to let them take responsibility for their own lives (for adults with disabilities, or for older people, as we'll discuss further in Chapters 8 and 11). And there is a growing trend for young people to remain economically dependent on their parents for some years after they have become legally adult. For example, in most circumstances the benefits and student finance systems in the UK regard young people under the age of 25 as at least partly the financial responsibility of their parents.

But we would probably agree that young carers are in danger of 'losing out on childhood' if they are expected to take on too much responsibility, and we would probably also agree that in most circumstances it is inappropriate to treat older people or disabled adults like children who cannot make choices for themselves.

Development, Continuity and Change

As we have noted, the period of 'adulthood' covers by far the largest part of our lives, but these years have historically attracted much less attention from those who study and theorise about human development than have the years of childhood. This is beginning to change, but in 1978 Levinson, in the introduction to his study of a sample of 40 American men, described adult life as 'one of the best-kept secrets in our society, and probably in history generally' (Levinson, 1978: ix). Durkin explains this apparent lack of interest in adulthood by observing that many developmental psychologists have tended to take the view that the process of development is completed with the achievement of adulthood (Durkin, 1995: 597).

It is certainly the case that some perspectives on adult life emphasise the stability and continuity of the personality as developed through childhood and adolescence, while other 'stage models' focus on continuing change and development. The course of adult life is a complex interplay between the biological, the psychological and the social, between who we are, the kind of world we find ourselves living in, the choices we make, and what happens to us. The passage of time is not in itself a sufficient framework for understanding adulthood and its challenges. We need to be able to look at it in a number of dimensions at the same time – and we need to take into account that, as adults ourselves, we are participant observers and our point of view will alter according to where we stand.

Lifespan development

The branch of psychology which looks at development across the whole of life, and not just childhood, is known as 'lifespan psychology'. This is not a unified theory, but a broad perspective encompassing a number of academic disciplines, including sociology, history, anthropology and biology. Baltes (1987) identified the seven main principles of the lifespan perspective:

- development is a lifelong process
- development is multidimensional and multidirectional
- the process shows plasticity – that is, it can be affected and changed by life experience and circumstances
- it involves both gains and losses
- it is an interactive process between the individual and their environment
- it is culturally and historically embedded
- it is a multidisciplinary field of study.

It is interesting that Baltes developed his thinking about lifespan psychology from a starting point of studying the problems of ageing – as Kierkegaard observed, life can only be understood backwards, but it must be lived forwards (Kierkegaard, 2001 [1843]: 18).

There are some links between this perspective and the more sociological life course approach, which we will also consider in Chapter 10. This has developed in recent years in response to a world where social structures and cultural norms are constantly changing, as a way of understanding how this shifting landscape affects human development at an individual level throughout the life course.

Continuity

Though important processes of change and development can be traced in adult life, it is also possible to see aspects of continuity across the lifespan. The work of McCrae and Costa (who, like Baltes, approach the lifespan perspective from a starting point in gerontology, the study of old age) on personality in adulthood is based on a number of American longitudinal studies, where the same group of people are studied over a long period of time. These studies suggested, to researchers' surprise, that personality remains relatively unchanged after the age of 30 (McCrae and Costa, 2003: vii). They proposed a five-factor theory of personality based on basic traits which they maintain are consistent over the course of life: neuroticism, extraversion, openness, agreeableness and conscientiousness. These 'Big Five' traits have since been widely used by other personality researchers as a basis for their work.

The different attachment styles which we discussed in Chapter 3 are an aspect of our personalities which seem to be carried over into adult life, and have a profound influence on our choice of partner, our intimate relationships, and also on other important areas of life such as our interactions with our workplace and our community. The work of Mary Main and others has demonstrated the persistence of these patterns of attachment, and she has developed the Adult Attachment Interview, which is used as a diagnostic tool in psychological work with adults, including couple therapy (Main and Goldwyn, 1994). In the interview, adults are asked to describe their childhood experiences and relationships, and the manner in which they do this is used to assess their attachment style. Main's four categories of adult attachment – secure, dismissing, preoccupied and unresolved – correspond to the secure, avoidant, ambivalent and disorganised attachment behaviours which can be observed in babies and young children. Security is measured by the degree to which the adult interviewed is able to engage with the interviewer to tell a coherent story about their childhood, with an integrated balance of positive and negative feeling. *Dismissing* adults will have difficulty in recollecting childhood experiences and feelings, while *preoccupied* adults' narratives will be full of unprocessed negative emotion. *Unresolved* states of mind in adulthood are the legacy of the dysfunctional parenting that leads to disorganised attachment in childhood, and for unresolved adults feelings and fears from the past are constantly intruding into the present, making it difficult for them to manage relationships, particularly with partners and children; '… early loss, abuse, neglect and trauma, if unresolved, retain the power to seriously disturb thought and feeling across the lifecourse' (Howe 2011: 183).

Attachment behaviour in adults is seen, of course, in their choice of partner; the couple relationship is the natural successor to the attachment to caregivers in infancy and childhood and the hope is that it will become a secure base for adult life. But it is different from early attachment relationships because it is interdependent, with each partner both providing and seeking a secure base. When things go well, partners will move flexibly between the dependent and depended-on positions. Securely attached adults, who are comfortable looking back at their childhood selves from an adult perspective as described above, are more likely to be able to do this.

The process of choosing a partner – the chemistry of 'falling in love' – ultimately defies analysis, whatever theories are advanced. However, it is clear that early attachments are influential – as we noted in Chapter 2, we will often choose a partner who has something in common with one of our parents. Other unconscious processes at work involve mirroring, splitting and projection, which we also discussed in Chapter 2. Clulow and Mattinson suggest that in forming relationships we are working to a script which goes:

> I love someone who reflects part of myself, sometimes a hidden or unacknowledged part of myself; I feel good with a you who either shares my feelings, expresses them for me or helps me defend myself against them. (Clulow and Mattinson, 1989: 52)

While attachment styles may tend to be lifelong, adults can continue to change and develop through their closest relationships, those with partners and with children. We have already seen how crucial the parent–child relationship is to the child's development, but the extent to which adults are changed by the experience of parenthood is often overlooked.

Narrative

One perspective on the life course is to see it as a narrative, a story with a beginning, a middle and an end. We have been influenced by that approach in this book in deciding to begin it with the story of the birth of a baby. The viewpoint here is that of the individual whose life is under discussion – what sense do they make of their story? Is it a comedy, a tragedy or a romance? Among others, Dan McAdams has developed a narrative theory which sees a person's life story as 'a personal myth that an individual begins working on in late adolescence and young adulthood in order to provide his or her life with unity or purpose and in order to articulate a meaningful niche in the psychosocial world' (McAdams, 1997: 5). According to McAdams, different elements of the narrative emerge at different developmental stages, with the narrative tone, images and themes being laid down in childhood, the belief systems and characters developed in adolescence and young adulthood, and the narrative denouement in middle adulthood, with later adulthood given over to review and evaluation.

As we have seen in the discussion of adult attachment above, the ability to construct and communicate a narrative of one's early life is an indication of secure attachment, which in turn leads to a greater resilience in coping with life's difficulties. In a more recent book Dan McAdams argues that those individuals who are most productive and dynamic (he uses Erikson's term 'generativity', which we will discuss in more detail later) are those who can tell a positive story of their lives:

Narrative research shows that especially productive and caring American adults often identify an early advantage in their lives that (they believe) established for them a secure and coherent inner self. (McAdams, 2005: 139)

In a review of recent developments in personality psychology, McAdams (2010: 536) concludes that '… personality develops as a dynamic constellation of dispositional traits (the person as actor), characteristic goals and motives (the person as agent) and integrative life stories (the person as author)'. In thinking about adult life we are considering a complex phenomenon which resists generalisation, and about which we need to be able to hold in mind different perspectives at the same time. Many of the theories we discuss in this chapter and in the rest of this book are based on specific research studies, of a particular group of people in a particular geographical and cultural location at a particular point in history, and it is important to bear that in mind when deciding how useful these theories are in shedding light on our experience here and now. We will be looking in more detail at the importance of the wider social context to an understanding of human growth and development in Chapter 10. In the rest of this chapter we will take a broadly chronological approach, because this is the most accessible way of thinking about it – but it is not the whole story.

Stages and Transitions

The best known stage theory of adulthood is Erik Erikson's. We have already discussed his stages of childhood and adolescent development in Chapters 2 and 6, and we gave an overview of his model of development through the human lifespan in Chapter 2 (p. 38–40).

There have been many other stage theories advanced, and Sugarman's book on lifespan development gives a comprehensive overview of these. There is a broad difference between those lifespan models which describe a process of growth and development followed by a process of decline in later life and those which describe a pattern where the period of growth and development is followed by a period of specialisation and integration (Sugarman, 2001: 68). These contrasting narratives of pessimism and optimism will clearly be of great significance when we come to look at old age. Some models focus more on cognitive and maturational factors, and some, like Erikson and Levinson, give more emphasis to socio-cultural factors.

Daniel Levinson (1978) produced a stage model of adult development in a book called *The Seasons of a Man's Life* (a book which popularised the concept of the 'mid-life crisis', which we will discuss later). He proposed that adult life for men typically unfolded through a series of stable (structure-building) stages and transitional (structure-changing) phases. Others have also focused on transitions, for instance Lowenthal et al. (1975) whose work was based on interviews with men and women at the point of leaving school, marriage, children leaving home and retirement. We have already looked at the transition cycle proposed by Hopson (1981) in Chapter 6 (pp. 107–8) and we will return to the subject of transitions when we discuss family systems in Chapter 8.

Transition is concerned with change, which involves loss. This is most obvious in sad life events such as bereavement or divorce, but elements of loss are also present in happy events such as marriage and graduation, as familiar roles and contexts give place to new ones. Life events, both predictable and unexpected, play a significant role in determining the course of adult life. They can also have an impact on stress levels and affect physical and mental health, and this is particularly likely when several significant life events occur within a short space of time. Holmes and Rahe (1967) compiled a ranking of the life events most likely to cause stress. The top ten most stressful events include, as you would expect, close family bereavement, divorce or separation, imprisonment, personal injury or illness, redundancy and retirement, but it is interesting that they also include the positive changes of marriage and marital reconciliation. Other positive events such as pregnancy and the birth of a child also rank highly, as does change in financial status or employment, irrespective of whether it is for the better or for the worse. When this ranking was re-examined in 1995 it had not changed significantly, except that the overall levels of stress experienced had risen, and marriage had moved down the list, presumably because it does not now usually involve the same degree of lifestyle change as in the past (Sugarman, 2001: 143).

Although transitions are important, and it is helpful to pay attention to them as we consider development in adult life, we must be wary of seeing stage theories as a neat progression from one stage to the next. Erikson himself made no such claims for his model and objected to writers who tried to make an *achievement scale* out of his stages, or made the assumption that at each stage 'a goodness is achieved which is impervious to new inner conflicts or to changing conditions' (Erikson, 1995 [1951]: 247 [footnote]).

We would suggest that what is most useful about stage theories is the insight that new developmental tasks become progressively more difficult if other developmental tasks have not yet been completed. This basic idea is common to all theoretical models in the psychodynamic tradition. In attachment theory, for example, establishing a secure base is seen as the necessary precursor to confident exploration of the world.

Returning to Erikson's stage theory, the table on page 39 shows how his stages of adult development fit into the whole model. Erikson divides adulthood into three stages, the first two of which, early and middle adulthood, are our focus in this chapter. But we suggest that it is useful to start by looking at Erikson's developmental themes in adolescence and adulthood more broadly across adult life, before we come back later in the chapter to consider the more specific features and problems of young and middle adulthood. Linking stages of development simply with the passage of time can be too simplistic. Life is more complicated than this.

It is also helpful to think of change as proceeding according to a 'social clock' as well as a biological clock, as suggested by Neugarten et al. (1965). This describes the effect of social and cultural norms and expectations about the 'right' time to make life decisions and transitions such as getting a job, settling with a partner or having children. And of course these expectations will differ across different cultures and social groups and in different historical periods. An example of this is the increase in recent years in the average age at which women have children. This reached 30 for the first time in England and Wales in 2014, having been increasing steadily since 1975 (ONS, 2014a). This trend is mirrored in most Western countries. Reflecting on the factors which might be influencing this change will suggest that changes in employment patterns, gender roles and economic pressures are all playing a part.

Identity and Intimacy

Erik Erikson saw the challenge of early adulthood as being the establishment of intimate relationships with other adults, following on from (and building on) the earlier adolescent struggle to establish one's own identity:

> The strength acquired at any stage is tested by the necessity to transcend it in such a way that the individual can take chances in the next stage with what was most vulnerably precious in the previous one. Thus the young adult, emerging from the search for and the insistence on identity, is eager and willing to fuse his identity with that of others ... even though [this] may call for significant sacrifices and compromises. (Erikson, 1995 [1951]: 237)

His suggestion was that only when we are secure and confident in our own identity can we take the risks involved in genuine social and sexual intimacy of a lasting kind. He went on to say that 'the avoidance of such experiences because of a fear of ego loss may lead to a deep sense of isolation and consequent self-absorption'. Some empirical support for his view that identity achievement is an important prerequisite for successful adult relationships is provided by an extremely long-term study by Kahn et al. (1985), who looked at the progress of a group of male and female college students over an 18-year period from late adolescence to their late 30s. The researchers found that those who seemed to have established a strong sense of their own identity during college also had the more enduring marital relationships 18 years on. Men who seemed to lack a well-developed sense of identity in late adolescence were more likely to remain single into mid-life. But women who had likewise had difficulty in establishing a secure identity in late adolescence had usually gone on to marry, but then typically had had problems in maintaining stable marital relationships.

As this study illustrates, it clearly is not the case that everyone enters adulthood having successfully resolved the issues of adolescence and, as Kroger (2000: 151) comments, 'a number of existing longitudinal studies of adolescent identity development have produced samples with fewer than half of subjects attaining the status of identity achievement by young adulthood'.

The task of identity formation may well continue into adult life, like other tasks associated with earlier stages of development. Most people would probably agree with Erikson that establishing intimate adult relationships is an important theme in early adulthood. Erikson added that some partnerships amounted to 'an isolation *à deux*, protecting both parties from the necessity to face the next critical development – that of generativity' (1995 [1951]: 239). This is one way in which identity development can be foreclosed, as we discussed in relation to adolescence in Chapter 6. And couple relationships often run into difficulties when one partner wants to continue with the development of their identity and the other does not. This may lead to conflict over whether and when to start a family, but it can also lead to problems when one partner develops a different and broader outlook on the world, perhaps through travel, a new job or a university course.

Levinson identified five main tasks in early adulthood. These were:

1. *Forming and living out a 'Dream'* – by 'Dream' is meant a kind of vision that a young man has of what his life – and himself as an individual – is going to be about. Many of the men in their sample reported that there was some conflict between following their 'dream' and meeting external demands on themselves.
2. *Forming 'mentor relationships'* – Levinson found that it was typical for men in early adulthood to establish a relationship with someone older, but not old enough to be a parent (half a generation older, perhaps) to provide support and guidance. An older sibling can for some people be a mentor figure, or perhaps a more senior workmate.
3. *Forming an occupation* – Levinson saw this as something more than just finding a job, which may be a short-term decision. It is more about what kind of work identity one is going to seek to establish in the longer term.
4. *Forming love relationships* – here is Erikson's intimacy, but given less prominence.
5. *Forming mutual friendships* – what Levinson actually found was that a lot of the men in his sample did not in fact have close mutual friendships with other men (or non-sexual friendships with women), but that this was felt to be a gap. So he suggested that this was another task of early adulthood.

Levinson's original study was about men and did not pretend to be universally applicable to men and women, but studies of transitions in adult life for women have been carried out (Levinson and Levinson, 1996; Roberts and Newton, 1987) which have suggested that broadly similar patterns exist for women as for men. One difference seems to be that, while Levinson's men tended to formulate their dream in terms of individual career goals, women – even very career-orientated women – tended more to construct 'dreams' around family relationships. This fits with Carol Gilligan's thesis of the 'different voice' of women, which we discussed in Chapter 6.

Generativity

Generativity versus stagnation, in the Eriksonian scheme of themes, is associated most strongly with parenthood and reproduction, arising naturally from the previous stage of intimacy:

> Generativity, then, is primarily the concern in establishing and guiding the next generation, although there are individuals who, through misfortune or through special and genuine gifts in other directions, do not apply this drive to their own offspring. (Erikson, 1995 [1951]: 240)

The focus on the production of the next generation associates this stage most strongly with middle adulthood, but of course many people are still in early adulthood when they become parents for the first time. It makes sense that intimacy precedes generativity in psychological development (just as sex precedes childbearing in a purely biological sense), but clearly they are not two distinct stages.

However, Erikson viewed generativity as something associated with participating in society and working towards goals beyond one's own immediate needs, as well as just with the bringing up of children. He made the connection, for example, between generativity and work. (This link is paralleled, as he noted, in Marxist thinking where both 'production' and 'reproduction' are seen as the means by which a particular social system perpetuates itself.) But again, occupational role is as important to many in early adulthood as it is in middle adulthood.

With the move into middle adulthood, there is a change of focus. Summing up the concerns raised by adults aged 40–65 whom she interviewed, Jane Kroger writes:

> Although issues directly related to biological changes were not frequently mentioned, change in procreational and sexual capacities were clearly on the minds of some participants. However of greater interest for most seemed to be a new psychological awareness of their own mortality and how meaningfully to fill whatever time there was that remained for them. In addition, the wish to contribute to the welfare of the general community surfaced in ways not described by previous age groups. … And … community recognition of individual contributions was highly valued by many in the process of midlife self-definition. (Kroger, 2000: 168)

Erikson's concept of generativity is quite difficult to pin down, and his proposal to link it to middle adulthood seems inappropriate when he also links the idea to parenthood. Nevertheless, Kroger's comments perhaps illustrate a certain quality that is typical of middle adulthood (though not unique to it), in which there is a concern to contribute to – and be recognised by – the wider community.

We will now consider some of the distinctive features of young adulthood and middle adulthood, and the kinds of issues and problems which may typically arise.

Young Adulthood

There are a number of features of early adulthood which, if not universal, apply fairly widely to this age-range in modern industrialised societies:

- It is the peak time for human physical performance in most areas. Muscle tone and physical strength, for example, peak at around the ages of 25–30.
- Most people leave their parental home during this period and set up home separately.
- Most people marry or set up a couple relationship during this period.
- Careers tend to be established in this period.
- Many people have children during this period.

Most of these things are of course culture-specific, as we'll discuss further in Chapter 10. In traditional, pre-industrial cultures, the idea of a career may be unknown in the Western sense. Marriage and leaving the parental home may take place in a very different way. There have also been changes in Western culture in recent years, with a trend towards a longer period of education and dependence on parents, and more fluidity of relationships and later childbearing. This pattern led Jeffrey Arnett (2004) to suggest that the years between adolescence and the end of the 20s should be seen as separate developmental stage, characterised by freedom, exploration and instability, which he terms *emerging adulthood*.

You will remember from Chapter 4 that Piaget's four stages of cognitive development concluded with the 'formal operations' stage, which he described as being attained in adolescence. While there is no qualitative change in thinking comparable to those changes which occur in childhood, there will be further cognitive changes through learning from experience as adulthood progresses. In adult life there are often specific tasks to perform, at work or at home, so that cognitive development may become more specialised and focused on particular areas. Sugarman (2001: 85–7) discusses some of the psychologists who have suggested frameworks for understanding subsequent cognitive development in adulthood. More recently discoveries about the brain's capacity to change and develop throughout life in response to experience (as described, for example, by Norman Doidge, 2007), have given neuroscientific confirmation to the understanding of cognitive development as extending beyond childhood and adolescence. We also saw in the last chapter that Kohlberg saw moral development as extending into adulthood.

Difficulties in young adulthood

One limitation with models such as the ones we have been discussing is that they are essentially descriptive. For those who are working with young adults and who are looking for practical tools to help them in their thinking, this may be frustrating. In rather the same way, a car mechanic seeking guidance on how a particular type of engine works and what is likely to go wrong with it, might not find it very helpful to be given purely descriptive information about how a sample of cars behaved over their working life. Of course there is not and never will be a human equivalent of a car service manual, but there are many people who are having difficulties with the demands made upon them as young adults, and who are struggling with the issues of identity, intimacy and generativity which we have been discussing. Their difficulties may become apparent through, for instance, offending behaviour, drug or alcohol misuse, relationship and parenting problems or mental health problems. These issues may bring them into contact with professional services of one kind or another. So it may be helpful to consider the following scenario and see whether any of the ideas we have discussed so far are of any assistance.

ACTIVITY 7.2 ♫♫

KARL

Suppose you are a community psychiatric nurse working in a drug and alcohol service, and that one of your patients is a man named Karl, aged 24. Karl left school at 16. He has never had a job that lasted longer than a few weeks. He has a long string of criminal offences (burglary, shoplifting). He is a heroin addict and is believed to have been a heroin user since the age of 17. He has two children by two different partners. Both partners have said that he has been violent towards them. A child protection agency has established that Karl recently left his youngest child (Sarah – aged 6 months) on her own when he went out to obtain drugs. He is attending youth services at the insistence of the child protection agency, who have made it clear that they will take steps to prevent Sarah remaining in Karl's care if he does not address his drug habit. Sarah's mother, Liz, who is 17, is also a drug user. She is often depressed, and has little self-esteem. In spite of Karl's violence towards her, she cannot imagine leaving him as she looks to him for security.

If you look at Karl specifically as a young adult, within the cultural expectations of young adulthood that now exist, does this illuminate his problem in any way? (In other words, what is there about being a young adult in particular that may contribute to his problem?)

And what about Liz? In what ways are her problems similar to Karl's and in what ways are they different? Supposing you yourself were 24 years old, what difference might this make to how you work with Karl? And how about if you were 54?

COMMENTS ON ACTIVITY 7.2

Clearly drug use, criminal activity and so on are not unique to early adulthood. But it may have struck you that the expectations which are placed on young adults may be a pressure for some which could lead to drug use, offending and so on. Whatever the limitations of models such as that of Levinson, most people would agree that tasks like establishing a 'Dream', forming love relationships and forming an occupation are indeed typically associated with early adulthood – and that not being able to manage them would be seen by many as a kind of failure.

Karl will be aware of these expectations, but in attempting to meet them (to establish intimate relationships, to become a parent, to enter the world of work.) he may in effect be trying to run before he can walk. The sense of failure that results may well be a contributory factor in his drug use and violence, even though the end result of such behaviour is to set him back even further. And his partner Liz is suffering from a similar sense of failure, but we can see how the gender difference leads them to adopt different coping strategies which bring them into conflict with each other. Liz is trying to deal with it by clinging to intimacy at all costs rather than struggling for the kind of autonomy that Karl is trying to achieve through his violent and criminal activities.

The reason why these adult demands are so hard for him to meet may well be because he has entered adult life without the necessary resources that would come from the successful resolution of challenges earlier in life. He almost certainly did not achieve a secure identity in his adolescent years. He may very well have never acquired the capacity to trust that comes from having one's needs mirrored in infancy. Perhaps any work with him will need to start by helping him to feel less ashamed of having to learn to walk before he can run.

Additionally, we need to be aware of the social dimension which is sometimes missing from purely psychological models. Karl's problems may well be rooted in his personal history, but they may also be exacerbated by his social environment. For example, he may come from a community where there are few educational or employment opportunities. If Karl was black, racism could have put additional obstacles in the way of his entering the world of employment.

Finally, on the question of your own age and how this might affect your work with Karl, it may have struck you that if you were the same age as Karl, he might find this very threatening, since you have managed to achieve a position of responsibility and authority which has eluded him. This is something you might need to bear in mind. He might well find it less threatening if you were 54 (old enough to be his parent), though other difficulties might arise if he has difficulty relating to his own parents, or if part of his problem is that his own parents have not let him grow up (see Chapter 9 for further discussion of this).

You may also like to consider how your gender and ethnic background, as well as your age, might impact on your work with Karl.

Middle Adulthood

The age of 40 is often seen as a marker of mid-life, a pivotal point. Levinson (1978) found in their sample of men that 80 per cent had been through a period of some personal turbulence about the 40 mark, and this popularised the notion of the mid-life crisis (though other researchers, e.g. Farrell and Rosenberg (1981) have found less extreme patterns of conflict). However, the idea had been around for a lot longer. Carl Jung (1875–1961) had a serious mid-life crisis which led to a mental breakdown. This personal experience led him to develop the concept of individuation, which he saw as the developmental task of the second half of life, opening up the possibility of a new kind of creativity after the focus on relationship and reproduction in the earlier years of adulthood. Individuation can be described as 'a kind of Pilgrim's Progress without a creed, aiming not at heaven, but at integration and wholeness' (Storr, 1973: 89). In 1965, Elliott Jaques wrote a paper entitled 'Death and the mid-life crisis', which explored the effect of reaching mid-life on creativity by examining the careers of artists and writers, as well as drawing on material from his psychoanalytic experience (Jaques, 1965). He concluded that the challenge of this particular transition is to be able to accept the knowledge of one's own death, and to find a creative way of living with this knowledge.

This puts the mid-life transition in stark terms. So when we say jocularly that 'life begins at 40', we may either be denying the reality that we are already half way through it, or else recognising the possibility of a different kind of new beginning – or quite possibly a bit of both! It seems a natural point at which to review commitments made in earlier life and consequently also a time when men and women sometimes decide to end some old commitments, and strike out in new directions. (Levinson found, for example, that this was a common time for divorces and house moves.)

This is a phase of life which necessitates – as do the changes in adolescence – a reappraisal of one's identity. And the mid-life crisis may not only parallel adolescence in some ways, but may also include elements of adolescent behaviour. If you have seen the film *American Beauty* you will remember, for example, how the hero got himself sacked by insulting his boss, bought himself a showy and expensive car, and developed a crush on one of his teenage daughter's school friends, while his wife threw herself into a torrid affair with a work colleague.

Among the issues commonly encountered at this stage of life are the following:

- *Some physical decline* – this is not sudden, of course, but from this time onwards we are likely to become more aware of things such as greying hair, skin wrinkles and so on, as well as a gradual reduction in physical performance. Athletes, for example, will be past their physical peak. Clearly, exercise and a good diet can slow this down, but the very need to be aware of such things may for many people be a change. We are also likely to become more aware of peers who have suffered serious health problems.
- *A decline in fertility for women* – during their 40s, women's fertility reduces. What happens at a biological level is that the ovaries start to miss out on hormonal signals from

the pituitary gland to release eggs. The pituitary then produces more hormones to compensate. (This is an example, incidentally, of a biological 'feedback loop' – a concept we will return to in Chapter 9.) So hormonal balances change until, at around 50 or 55, the ovaries stop functioning and a woman reaches the menopause: the end of the reproductive phase of her life. Research tends to show (see for example Whitbourne, 1996) that the menopause is a transition whose impact has been somewhat exaggerated in popular mythology, but nevertheless it is an important and fundamental change to be adjusted to.

- *Adolescent children and the 'empty nest'* – parents in middle adulthood and onwards have the experience of their children growing up and leaving home. As we've noted, this can fall at very different times for different people. Parenting an adolescent provides many new challenges and may bring up unresolved issues from the past. The impact of children actually leaving home is also likely to be an event which has very different meanings for different people. The impact of the 'empty nest' on a woman who has devoted herself principally to childcare and homemaking may be greater, for example, than the impact on men or women whose energies have gone into their career.
- *Fewer career options* – career changes become more difficult, because, qualifications being equal, employers tend to favour suitably qualified younger men or women to older ones. (One example of this attitude is provided by the information given on its website by the Australian High Commission in London to prospective skilled migrants: 'You must be under 50 when you apply.')
- *Own parents entering old age* – the older generation getting old and dying becomes a fact of life from this point onwards. It may become necessary to provide care for parents or other elderly relatives. Or the death of parents may result in major reappraisals of one's own position in the world.
- *Letting go of dreams* – a man of 40 once remarked to one of us that from now on he was going to have to accept that he was just an ordinary person. Certain hopes and dreams that may have provided direction in earlier life may now have to be relinquished. If you haven't become a rock star yet, it is unlikely to happen now. In some cases, the dream to be relinquished may be the dream of becoming a parent.

One could perhaps summarise the mid-life transition as a time of life when it becomes necessary to relinquish an identity as 'young'. Clearly, as with all such transitions, there is likely to be an element of grieving and denial involved in this. However, if one can let go of young adulthood, new possibilities open up. Many of the challenges associated with middle adulthood which we listed above have positive as well as negative sides. Children leaving home can free up time and energy for other projects. Letting go of old dreams too can be a release from a pressure, as well as a source of sadness. In some cultures menopause itself is apparently positively welcomed (Neugarten et al., 1963). Even the death of parents, however sad in itself, is quite often experienced as a freeing from old ties, and some people report, following the death of a parent, that they feel like an adult for the first time.

For many in middle adulthood, accumulated experience is a valuable resource. When recognised by others, this is a source of authority. (Most people in senior positions in politics, business and elsewhere, for example, are in middle adulthood.) Mallory (1984) found that 'identity achievement' increased with age (using Marcia's terminology which we discussed in the last chapter), while 'identity diffusion' decreased. Mallory found that identity achievement was higher for men and women aged 40–47 than for men and women aged 30–37 (for whom 'foreclosure' ratings were higher). This would suggest that, on average, the over 40s were more secure in their own identity than young adults.

Difficulties in middle adulthood

As we said earlier in relation to young adulthood, the ideas we have been discussing are quite descriptive and may seem to be of limited use when it comes to practical questions. Again, the best way of testing them may perhaps be to look at some examples of difficulties that might be faced in middle adulthood and consider how to approach them.

Of course the difficulties faced by adults in their middle years can come into all the same categories as the younger adults we discussed earlier, but the most common problems will change: specifically, adults in this age range are more likely to be having difficulties with adolescent children, and far more likely to be caring for elderly relatives. Loss of career through redundancy, ill health or early retirement is also more likely in middle adulthood.

The following activity looks at two case examples of adults in their middle years.

ACTIVITY 7.3

What themes do you notice in the following two cases? If you were a mental health worker, what approaches might you take in trying to help?

- Jill (50) – coming from a large African-Caribbean family, Jill incurred the anger of both her parents as a young woman when she chose not to start a family, in order to pursue a career in the Civil Service, her ambition being to become the first black woman to head a government department. She works extremely hard, and very long hours, and has always had a fairly limited personal life. As a result of her ability and efforts, she has risen to a senior post in the Department of Health, overcoming both sexist and racist obstacles. However, a few months ago she had a heart attack and had to take extended sick leave, with the possibility that she would not be able to return to her old job and would have to consider early retirement. She became very depressed during her enforced idleness and made an attempt on her own life. She is now in hospital being treated for depression.

● Sue (45) – the youngest of four, and the only girl, in a suburban white British family, Sue grew up with parents who pushed their sons to achieve, and seemed to value their daughter's achievements very little. Sue didn't leave home until the age of 24 when she married an older man and became a housewife and mother. She is proud of her two confident, well-adjusted children, both of whom have now left home. She has recently started a job as a learning support assistant in a local school, which she very much enjoys. But her mother has now died and her three brothers now expect Sue to give up her part-time job to care for her father, pointing out that all three of them are the main breadwinners for their families, while Sue's income is small and she is supported financially by her husband. She agrees with them about her duty, but the prospect fills her with such dread that she has become ill.

COMMENTS ON ACTIVITY 7.3

Loss of a career and caring for older parents are both themes which become more common in middle adulthood. For both women, work was important to their identity and the loss of work – or the threat of it – was a blow. For both women, these typically middle-adulthood challenges may also interact with painful issues from earlier stages of life, as well as with gender and perhaps cultural issues. Caring responsibilities are more likely to be carried by women than men throughout their adult lives, and as a result they are more likely to face difficult choices between career and family.

In Jill's case, it would appear that she had to cut herself off from her family of origin to some extent in order to pursue her career. It is also possible that she may have had some regrets about not having children, but felt she had to make a choice between career and children (it would be more unusual for a man to feel that he had to make such a choice). Having made significant sacrifices in order to invest in her career, the possible loss of it must be a major blow. She has built an identity for herself around her career, rather than around personal relationships. On what is she now going to build a sense of meaning and purpose in her life?

Sue's family background seems to have resulted in her settling for 'identity foreclosure'. She never established herself as an independent adult as a young woman and perhaps only managed to escape the parental home by accepting a new parental figure in her much older husband. However, she has gained some confidence from doing a good job as a parent and the 'empty nest' has for her been an opportunity to spread her wings and to begin to seek an identity of her own. This is now being placed under threat by the pressure from her brothers to once again subordinate her own needs to those of other people. This has brought up old struggles, never fully resolved, from her earlier years.

(Continued)

(Continued)

As a mental health professional (social worker, psychiatric nurse, occupational therapist, psychologist or support worker) you might use a counselling or cognitive behavioural approach to help these women to express their feelings about the difficulties they are facing and to understand them in terms of the ideas we have outlined above, and to try to find a more positive way of responding to their situations. In Jill's case this might involve exploring the possibility of reconnecting with her family and cultural roots, from which she seems to have become alienated. In Sue's case, she may need support to question the family assumptions she has grown up with about gender roles and become more assertive about her own needs. For both of these women the loss, or threatened loss, of occupational role is significant, and insights from the Model of Human Occupation (Kielhofner, 2008) used by occupational therapists may be very relevant. This focuses on the three aspects of human occupation, productivity, play and activities of daily living, as they are carried out over time and in a social and cultural context.

Many adults in middle years, as well as younger adults, will have had difficulties in dealing with the challenges of earlier stages, and this may make it more difficult to deal with the new challenges that they now face. And many, however well they faced previous challenges in their lives, will have extra challenges piled on them which they had not expected and which will force them to radically revise their expectations. In addition, the two things may come together: new challenges and old issues. Old unresolved issues ('baggage', as some people call it, or 'unfinished business') may be brought to a head in middle adulthood by a new crisis that was unexpected but is nevertheless typical of middle adulthood: difficulties with adolescent children, the break-up of a marriage or long-term relationship, loss of a valued career, the needs of ageing parents. This kind of interaction between old issues and new events will be explored further in Chapter 9, when we look at family life cycles.

So in understanding the challenges of adult life we need to be aware of past issues as well as present ones. There is a third factor, too, which we need to consider, which is the opportunities and options available for meeting these challenges. These will vary hugely for different people in different social circumstances, and we will explore this in Chapter 10. So we would suggest that as individuals our progress through life will be shaped by three distinct sets of factors:

- the nature of the challenges that we face
- the legacy of the past
- the opportunities available.

The first of these three is often the only one that is visible. This means that, when working with people in difficulties, we have to bear in mind the other two. They may in reality, like the submerged part of an iceberg, be the largest part of the problem. We also have to bear in mind that present challenges, and how they are dealt with, will in turn becom part of the legacy that a person carries into the future. This is why it is important not t try to solve other people's problems for them, but to try to help them resolve problem for themselves.

Chapter Summary

- In this chapter, we looked at what is meant by 'adult'. While there is a huge difference in the issues faced by adults at different ages and in different circumstances, a common theme is that adults are expected to take responsibility.
- We then looked at different ways of thinking about the course of adult life. We discussed lifespan development and themes of continuity and change and the narrative approach.
- We considered stage theories and the importance of transitions, and the effect of life events on development in adulthood.
- We then looked at themes of identity, intimacy and generativity across the course of adult life, using Erikson's theory as a basis for our discussion, but also considering others' work on these themes.
- We then looked at specific features of young adulthood, and discussed the kinds of problems that may be characteristic of this life stage.
- In the next section we looked at the mid-life transition and middle adulthood. We looked at the themes that are common to this period, and some of the typical problems that can occur.
- We concluded this section with a more general discussion about the interaction between challenges in life, unfinished business from the past, and the different opportunities that are available to different individuals in different circumstances.

In the next chapter we will look at the particular challenges faced by people with disabilities as they embark on and progress through adulthood, and in the chapter after that we will shift our focus from the individual to the family. For families collectively, as well as individuals, face challenges, carry legacies from the past, and adapt to many different circumstances.

Further Reading

Durkin, K. (1995) *Developmental Social Psychology*. Oxford: Blackwell.
He gives a very comprehensive overview of research studies dealing with adulthood.
Howe, D. (2011) *Attachment across the Lifecourse*. Basingstoke: Palgrave Macmillan.
Kroger, J. (2000) *Identity Development: Adolescence through Adulthood*. London: Sage.
Sugarman, L. (2001) *Life-Span Development, Frameworks, Accounts and Strategies*, 2nd edn.
    Hove: Psychology Press.

8 ACCESS TO ADULTHOOD

GROWING UP WITH A DISABILITY

- Defining disability   151
- Impairments and developmental pathways   153
- Families, children and disability   159
- Adolescence and disability   162
- Disability and adulthood   165

In a delivery room in a maternity hospital, a mother is about to give birth after an eight-hour labour. There are four people present: the mother herself, the baby's father, a midwife and a doctor. Everyone is trying to encourage the exhausted mother ('Keep pushing!', 'You're almost there!', 'Don't forget your breathing!')

Then the father shouts out excitedly, 'I can see its head!'

Suddenly, a fifth human being is in the room ...

This account of a birth is identical to that at the beginning of Chapter 1. But let us suppose now that, as the baby emerges into the world for the first time, the four adults present become aware of a birth defect not previously picked up by antenatal tests: the baby's fingers are missing perhaps, or she has no eyes. Imagine how different the reaction will be in these circumstances to what it would otherwise have been.

Many impairments are picked up antenatally, and many others do not become apparent until some time after birth, so this is only one of a number of possible ways in which parents find out that their child has an impairment of some kind. And of course impairments are not always present at birth, but can develop later as a result of illness or accident at any point through the course of life. But imagining the response of the people present at the child's birth should help to illustrate a point that we will keep coming back to in this chapter: disability is not just about impairments, but also about the reactions of others. Disability may seem to be about the absence of a limb or of a functioning sense organ, or about a difficulty with learning, development or mental health, but it is never simply about the one individual who is directly affected, but always also about the way these things impact upon and are responded to by those around the individual person concerned: by their families, by their peers, by their neighbours, and by society as a whole.

One thing that can hold people back from growing and developing their lives is being 'infantilised', being treated as if they were infants. Old people are often infantilised ('Are we going to eat up all our pudding today, Mr Jones?'). So are women ('Don't you worry your pretty head about this'). So, at least in some contexts, are men ('He's just a big kid'). Black people have been infantilised in all kinds of ways in recent history (fully grown black men could find themselves addressed as 'boy' by white people in apartheid-era South Africa). And disabled people are certainly often infantilised. In all kinds of ways, disabled people can find themselves prevented or impeded – by society at large, by particular organisations, by anxious and overprotective loved ones – from moving through the stages of development which we have been discussing so far in this book.

People with disabilities may find themselves permanently in a dependent status. They may face formidable obstacles to having a satisfying work career, or of making a contribution to the community. They may also be discouraged from having sexual relationships, or having children. So, not only do people with disabilities often have difficulty gaining access to many facilities that other people use, from buses to toilets to public buildings, they may even have to struggle to gain access to the rewards and responsibilities of adulthood itself. For this reason, it seemed important, in looking at human growth and development, to devote some space to looking in particular at the developmental issues faced by people with disabilities, although within the scope of this book we can only give a very general overview.

Defining Disability

As we have outlined above, disability can take many different forms and can affect people at different stages of their lives. It is a complex concept, both because it covers such a wide range of conditions and because it involves an interaction between the individual and society. The terminology used in this area can be confusing too. You will find that some writers use the word *disability* to refer to the actual physical difficulties encountered by the person with an impairment (the inability to walk, for example, in the case of a person whose impairment is having no legs) and *handicap* to describe the social restrictions resulting from that. In common parlance, 'disability' or 'handicap' are often used interchangeably to cover all these different meanings, though handicap is now thought to have negative connotations. Many terms that have been used in the past to describe different impairments have acquired – or have always had – deeply negative connotations: 'spastic', 'idiot', 'moron', 'imbecile', 'cripple'. We will discuss the power of language to stereotype and exclude in Chapter 10 (p. 193), but for the moment we will recognise that terminology will inevitably shift over time as thinking and understanding change, and that it is important to listen to the preferences of people with disabilities themselves when we choose our words.

Social and medical models

There are really two aspects to the problems faced by people with a disability:

- The purely physical or organic aspect (which might be a missing limb or a non-functioning sense organ, for example). This we are going to call impairment.
- The aspects resulting from the attitudes of the rest of society. This we will call disability.

So, to give an example, the fact that a person has no legs is, in the terms we are going to use, an impairment. The fact that this person finds it hard to get around, on the other hand, is a disability, and would be more or less of a disability depending, for example, on the layout of streets and buildings and help with mobility that was available in the particular community in which that person lived.

The definitions we are using are those of the Union of the Physically Impaired Against Segregation (UPIAS, 1976), an organisation of disabled activists described by Colin Barnes (2012: 13) as 'undoubtedly the most influential organisation in the history of social model thinking'. They reflect what is called a *social* model of disability, as opposed to a *medical* model. The social model is based on the idea that it is normal for a society to contain individuals with mental and physical impairments. Disability is a consequence of *society's* failure to recognise this and to make provision for the inclusion of such people in mainstream activities.

In contrast to the social model, which sees disability as being something created by society, the medical model sees the disability as being purely to do with the individual concerned.

The social model can be overstated. As Tom Shakespeare points out, not all of the problems faced by people with impairments are within the power of society to abolish, and 'there is a danger of ignoring the problematic reality of biological limitation'. (2014: 28). Yet it is certainly the case that the degree to which an impairment causes disability does depend on the social context. Short-sightedness or long-sightedness, for example, are undoubtedly impairments, but they are not serious disabilities in a society where spectacles are available to everyone. Dyslexia is an impairment but the extent to which it is a disability depends on the importance of writing in a given society, and the availability of help with writing. On the American island of Martha's Vineyard, there was for a period such a high incidence of congenital deafness among the population that it ceased to be regarded as abnormal and even most hearing people learned to use sign language. This is an instance where profound deafness, while still clearly an impairment, was not a serious disability (Quinn, 1998).

Towards a more integrated model

The last four or five decades have been a period in which disability studies have developed as an academic discipline, alongside a user movement that has become increasingly articulate and influential in developing thinking about disability. 'The combination of political activism and scholarship has helped generate a shift in perceptions of disability both nationally and internationally' (Barnes 2012: 23). Disability is increasingly seen as a human rights issue, as set out in the United Nations Convention on the Rights of Persons with Disabilities, adopted in 2006. This recognises in its preamble that:

> '… disability is an evolving concept and … results from the interaction between persons with impairments and attitudinal and environmental barriers that hinder their full and effective participation in society on an equal basis with others' (UN, 2006).

The WHO *World Report on Disability* (2011: 3–4) begins its answer to the question, 'what is disability?' by stating that it is '… complex, dynamic, multi-dimensional and contested', and goes on to say that it '… should be viewed neither as purely medical nor as purely social … A balanced approach is needed, giving appropriate weight to the different aspects of disability'.

Although service users' voices have been influential in developing the social model, language can be a barrier for people with learning difficulties who want to participate in research, just as steps and narrow doorways can be a barrier for wheelchair-users. A mixed group of learning disabled and non-learning disabled researchers collaborated to produce an article giving the learning disabled researchers' views on what they needed and what should be done to make things better for learning disabled people (Docherty et al., 2010). Writing about the social model of disability, they say that:

> Anne Louise Chappell (1998) says that learning disabled people are left out of the social model of disability. The social model of disability is in writing, so that professionals can look at it. It's not accessible to learning disabled people. We might want to study the social model ourselves, but we can't because it isn't accessible. It should be in pictures and large print. (2010: 434)

Once again, we find – as we have already found in relation to gender roles in Chapter 5 and adolescence in Chapter 6 – that when something appears at first sight to be an essentially physical or biological matter, this turns out to be only the starting point. The biological fact exists, but its impact on the individual depends on the social context and on the meanings that society assigns to the biological fact.

Impairments and Developmental Pathways

Impairments vary greatly both in kind and degree and one must be careful not to generalise about them as if they were all the same. The principal areas are as follows, though within these categories there are still large differences, and many people have more than one type of impairment:

- learning impairments (impairments that affect cognitive ability)
- motor impairments (which affect mobility and/or other abilities involving muscle control such as speech or use of the hands)
- sensory impairments (which in practical terms means blindness and deafness – the lack of the ability to smell would also be a sensory impairment, but would not result in serious disability, because for human beings smell is not of primary importance either for communication or for finding our way about).

Although advocates of the social model are quite right to draw our attention to the fact that disability is in large part a socially constructed phenomenon, an impairment in itself can constitute an obstacle to an individual developing along the same path as people who do not have impairments, even if the individual concerned is given all possible support. A person with severe learning difficulties, for instance, may not necessarily be able to move through all the stages of intellectual development envisaged by Piaget, even in optimum conditions.

Hodapp (1998) suggests that if we compare the development of children with impairments to that of children who do not have impairments, we can look at several different aspects:

- *rate* of development
- sequence of development (does development progress through the same stages, or does it progress in a different order?)
- structure of development (do developments in one area relate to developments in other areas in the same way?).

Not surprisingly, research shows that the rate of development does vary, as it does in the general population, but interestingly it appears that the sequence of stages is broadly the same. All children seem to move along analogous paths, albeit at different rates, contrary to a widely held stereotype that children with learning difficulties in particular are somehow static.

When it comes to structure, there are differences. Piaget's model envisaged that development occurred across a broad front, with analogous stages being moved through, across a wide range of areas – language development, spatial understanding and so on. You may remember from Chapter 4 that there are some disputes about whether development in different areas really does all proceed together in this way, or whether it is more modular. Certainly, when it comes to people with impairments, there do seem to be important variations in the structure of development depending on the type of impairment.

Learning impairments

Among children with learning impairments, there are differences in the structure of development depending on the nature of the impairment. Children with Down syndrome, for example, are strong on social skills but slow on language and mathematical skills.

Children with Williams syndrome (a much less common genetically determined condition which also affects physical and intellectual development) are strong on language skills and social skills, but weaker on skills such as drawing and other spatial skills (see Hodapp, 1998: 54). But while children with specific impairments will experience particular problems in particular areas, the extent of developmental delay in these areas is also undoubtedly linked to context, the expectations of parents, teachers and carers, the type of encouragement or discouragement that is offered, and the extent to which compensatory input is offered in particular areas of difficulty.

Motor impairments

Studies of the development of children with motor impairments (such as Cione et al., 1993) have found that these children tend be behind other children developmentally in a general sense, but fall behind especially in areas such as development of the concept of 'object permanence' (as discussed in Chapter 4). This is perhaps not surprising given that motor impairments will make it more difficult to explore and manipulate physical objects.

'Motor impairments' have a variety of causes. They can result from cerebral palsy, for example, which is caused by brain damage at an early stage of development – and can result in learning as well as motor impairments. Or they can result from hereditary conditions such as spina bifida, which is a spinal problem and can lead to muscle weakness in the lower half of the body, including sometimes problems with bowel control. Some other motor impairments are the result of physical injury.

Just as with learning impairments, the *structure* of development has been found to differ from one type of motor impairment to another. Children with spina bifida–hydrocephalus often have verbal abilities well in advance of their performance abilities, while children with cerebral palsy seem to develop their abilities more evenly, though on average they are behind children who do not have impairments (see Hodapp, 1998: 150–54).

Sensory impairments

Blind children tend to be slower at developing skills in the areas of object permanence than do sighted children (Warren, 1994). Without sight, a blind baby has far fewer cues than a sighted baby to tell her that an object still exists when it is out of reach, and often no cues at all. So it is not surprising that blind children take longer to grasp this concept.

Lack of sight leads to delays in a number of other areas of development. Motor skills and spatial skills are slower to develop (see Brambring, 2007). 'Babies move for the purpose of reaching something or someone that interests them', as Dale and Salt observe. 'Without vision, babies may not know that there is something to reach' (2007: 685). Language skills also develop in slightly different ways. Blind children are apparently slower in grasping the difference between 'this' and 'that' (Anderson et al., 1993). They are also apparently less prone than other children to 'overgeneralise', for example by using the word 'dog' to refer to all animals, but *more* prone to 'undergeneralise', for example by using the word 'dog' as if it referred to one particular dog only (see Hodapp, 1998: 132). Without sight, a child is less well placed to notice similarities between objects in the world at large.

In the case of deaf children, as one might expect, it is language development that takes a different course from that of hearing children. But here there are some interesting complications which again serve to illustrate the pervasive role of context and culture in human development. These arise because, in the case of deaf people, there are distinct and separate languages. In the USA, the main sign language used by deaf people is American Sign Language (or ASL), while in Britain it is BSL. Apart from being signed rather than spoken, these languages have their own quite distinct grammar and sentence structure. 'ASL does not resemble English or BSL, but relies on agreement and gender systems in a way that is reminiscent of Navajo or Bantu' (Pinker, 2007: 24). But deaf children, in Britain and the USA, when they learn to read and write, learn English, and they will have to use English in some form to communicate with most hearing people. This means that when studying the language acquisition of deaf children, it is necessary to bear in mind that they may be working simultaneously on acquiring two quite distinct language systems. Researchers have found that deaf children who are exposed to sign language from an early age acquire it in much the same way – and in the same time scale – as hearing children acquire speech. The deaf babies of deaf parents even apparently 'babble' in signs at the age of 10–14 months (Petitto and Marentette, 1991).

Deaf children who acquire sign language at an early age from deaf parents are at a developmental advantage as compared to deaf children who are taught sign language at a later stage, having grown up with hearing parents. Meristo et al. (2007) found that the former group performed at a level similar to hearing children on tests of 'theory of mind' reasoning (see Chapter 4), while children in the latter group lagged behind on these tests. This reflects the findings of Greenberg and Kushe (1989) that children who are deaf and whose parents are deaf as well progressed educationally more rapidly than deaf children whose parents have their hearing. This is likely to be due to a number of factors. Deaf children of deaf parents are able to acquire sign language in the same informal way that hearing children acquire spoken language, whereas deaf children of hearing parents tend to be behind in all aspects of language development. But, more generally, deaf parents would understand without having to think about it, the particular needs of deaf children (for example, the need to find visual ways of getting a deaf child's attention). Rather like the deaf inhabitants of Martha's Vineyard in the past, deaf children of deaf parents grow up in a family environment where deafness is 'normal'.

Emotional development

This discussion on impairments and developmental pathways has so far related to issues to do with the acquisition of specific skills. But if impairments may result in children taking different developmental routes in respect of cognitive development, is it possible that impairments can also result in different pathways in respect of emotional development or the development of personality characteristics? You may remember that we noted in Chapter 4 that there was necessarily a close relationship between cognitive development and emotional development.

The following activity is intended to help you think about the particular challenges faced by people with disabilities.

ACTIVITY 8.1

Below are the favourable outcomes which Erikson proposed for each of his eight stages of development:

1. trust in the environment
2. a sense of autonomy and self-esteem
3. the ability to initiate activities
4. a sense of competence and achievement
5. the ability to see oneself as a consistent and integrated person
6. the ability to experience love and commitment to others
7. the ability to be concerned and caring about others in the wider sense
8. a sense of satisfaction with one's life and its accomplishments.

What obstacles might stand in the way of achieving these outcomes for:

- a person with a sensory impairment?
- a person with a learning impairment?
- a person with a motor impairment?

COMMENTS ON ACTIVITY 8.1

The following are a few suggestions:

In the absence of appropriate help, a child with a sensory impairment such as blindness, attempting to find her way in a world designed for sighted people, might well have difficulty establishing a sense of trust in the environment.

Similarly, in the absence of appropriate support, a person with cerebral palsy, who was unable to do things such as walk, dress herself or use the toilet, might have difficulty with a sense of autonomy.

(Continued)

(Continued)

A child with learning difficulties, in the absence of appropriate help, might well have difficulty in developing a sense of competence, when comparing herself with other children.

Appropriate help, in all these cases, would need to include both resources that provide practical assistance (for example a wheelchair, mobility training, Makaton sign language) and the attitudes of those who provide it. Helpers need to understand the importance of enabling the person they are helping to do as much as possible for themselves, rather than just focusing on getting a task done, if they are to support them to realise their full potential. There are obviously resource implications here too; equipment and adaptations can be costly, and providing sensitive and empowering help will often take longer.

All of us, whether or not we are disabled, carry 'unfinished business' from the earlier stages of our life, and all of us find it hard at times to meet the challenges made on us in the here and now. People who have disabilities may have to carry additional emotional baggage from the past as well as deal with exceptional challenges in the here and now. Commenting on the high incidence of mental illness among people with learning impairments, Howells (1997) observes that:

> They [people with learning impairments] have few opportunities to exercise choice, their expectations are low and they suffer from overprotection. Little scope exists to develop social networks beyond the family and paid carers. The result is too great an emotional investment in too few people. This, in turn, increases the significance of loss through bereavement and changes in staff. (Howells, 1997: 77)

On the other hand, it may be a mistake to attempt to apply models such as Erikson's too literally to people with disabilities. Stage models impose a particular pathway. For example, Erikson, like Freud, speaks of toilet-training as a very basic way in which children learn about taking control of their own lives. Clearly, this is not an option for someone whose impairment means that she will never be able to control her bowels. But this should not be taken to mean that she cannot develop a sense of being in control, merely that she needs to find other pathways in order to give her that experience, and help with finding those pathways may be one of the things others can provide. (Erikson himself acknowledged, incidentally, that the significance of bowel control in emotional development depends on 'whether the cultural environment wants to make something of it' [Erikson, 1995 (1951): 71]. He wrote that the Sioux, for example, placed little or no emphasis on toilet-training in the sense that it is understood in European culture.)

Families, Children and Disability

In February 1972, a yellow and red calico duck beanbag sat expectantly in the crib in our new house … At 6 a.m. the morning before Valentine's Day I delivered our long-hoped-for child, a baby girl. The physician placed her briefly on my stomach, moved her to an examining table, and said, 'In just a few minutes, I'll come to the recovery room to talk with you.' When he stepped in, we heard 'Your baby shows signs of Down's syndrome (DS). Do you know what that is?'

… As I drank refreshing orange juice in the recovery room, Peter sat with his head in his hands, contemplating the necessary calls that would stun our parents about their first grandchild. We plunged into an unfamiliar world of confusion, numbness, disbelief. 'What's the baby's name?' a nurse asked.' We haven't decided.' We knew this was not Rebecca, the name selected for our baby if it were a girl. Within a few hours we decided on a name farther down our list, 'Sarah,' and added Kathleen as the middle name. Unconsciously, the naming process signified our recognition of the loss of our expected child and represented our first step in acknowledging the child who had arrived instead.

Over the 32 years of Sarah's life, enormous changes have occurred in our society, which now offers children and adults with disabilities, and their families, support … that did not exist in 1972. Yet, there remains, unchanged, parents' common experiences of loss, mourning, and chronic grief, which extend throughout the life span and are exacerbated at times of transition. … (Riesz, 2004: 371–2)

The birth of a child with an impairment is an event to which a whole family has to adjust. But how the family copes with this challenge – and the extent to which the child will be welcomed, supported and helped within the family, will depend both on the wider social context, and upon the characteristics of that particular family. At the societal level, widely held cultural beliefs might be a factor (in some cultures, the birth of a child with a disability is viewed as a punishment from God), while at the family level each family will have its own unique beliefs and ideas about disability, and about many other related questions, probably built up over several generations. Some families might set great store by sporting achievement, others by intellectual achievement, and these families might be particularly affected by the birth of a child with physical or intellectual impairments. These factors can be described as 'vertical stressors' as opposed to 'horizontal stressors' that operate at a particular time, like the birth of a child with an impairment. And it is when vertical and horizontal stressors intersect that things become especially difficult for a family (McGoldrick et al., 2011: 9). We will return to this idea in more detail in our next chapter, when we look at family systems theory.

One of the most influential models of what occurs at the point that a mother gives birth to a child with an impairment was that offered by Solnit and Stark (1961). They proposed that the birth of a child with an impairment was in some senses a bereavement. Parents had to go through a period of mourning for their dreams of a 'perfect' child and this would involve going through the stages associated with grieving: shock, denial, sadness and anger, adaptation and reorganisation.

It is worth thinking for a moment about what it means, not for the parents or the wider family, but for the *child herself* if her birth, instead of being a joyful event, is the occasion for mourning, as was the case with Sarah, the child with Down syndrome whose birth was described above. It is not an ideal start in life.

Some readers may not feel comfortable with the idea of describing the birth of any child as being like a bereavement, but no one can seriously dispute that such a birth involves a major adjustment. The arrival of a child is a stressor in most families and the arrival of a child with an impairment is undoubtedly more of a stressor on the family system than the arrival of a child without an impairment. The capacity of the family to cope depends on a number of factors. Minnes (1988), looking in particular at families with children who had learning impairments, categorised these factors under the following headings:

The child's own characteristics

The families of children with Down syndrome seem to cope better – on measures of stress and depression – than those with children with some other kinds of intellectual impairment. This is probably due in part to the fact that Down children tend on average to be affectionate and sociable, and to be less prone to difficult and challenging behaviour patterns than some other learning-impaired children. But it is perhaps also because the syndrome is well known and there are well-developed support networks.

The resources of the family

Minnes broke this down further into 'internal' and 'external' resources:

- By 'internal' resources are meant the personal characteristics of the family members and of the family as a whole. In particular, coping strategies that are focused on solving practical problems seem to be more adaptive than 'emotion-focused' coping strategies. According to Hodapp (1998: 81), 'In virtually every study, mothers who were focused on actively solving problems seemed better off than those focused primarily on their own emotional reactions.'
- By 'external' resources are meant such things as the family's financial resources and/or the availability of financial help, and the services and support networks that are available.

The family's perception of the child

The family's beliefs are also important. As Hodapp observes (1998: 81), some families may view a child as a special burden or responsibility placed upon them by God. Others may view the additional demands of a child with learning impairments as being 'unfair', and a brake on achieving what they saw as their legitimate aspirations in life. Family perceptions of *specific* impairments are also a factor. Returning to the case of the Down child, the widespread *perception* that Down children are affectionate and lovable may be helpful, as well as in the fact that it is often really the case.

All developmental challenges are challenges for the whole family, and clearly this is very much the case with disability. A family with a disabled child may in some cases have a radically different life cycle from other families. For example, in a family where a child has serious learning impairments, the whole family may need to adjust to the fact that one of its members will never reach a stage of independent adult life.

In fact, the presence of a child with a disability can be a cause of family breakdown. Gath (1977) found a higher incidence of divorce or marital dissatisfaction among parents of children with Down syndrome, while Hodapp and Krasner (1995) found the incidence of divorce among parents of school-age children with visual impairments to be 25 per cent, as against 15.3 per cent among a sample with non-disabled children.

But the presence of a child with a disability can also result in positive growth. Marriages can be strengthened by the arrival of children with a disability, as well as broken, and extended families can be drawn together into a strong, mutually supportive system. Grossman (1972, cited in Hodapp 1998: 70) carried out a study of older siblings of children with disabilities and found an almost exactly even split between predominantly positive and predominantly negative feelings. Feelings of resentment and frustration were reported by 45 per cent, while another 45 per cent described the experience of having a sibling with disabilities as being on balance a rewarding and enriching one. From a family systems perspective (see next chapter), a family's ability to adapt successfully to new challenges depends on its members' capacity to renegotiate the family structure. Perhaps the second group in Grossman's study came from families which had been able to change in this way. Perhaps the families of the first group had become 'stuck', unable to resolve and move on from their initial negative reactions.

Before moving on, you may find it useful to go through the following activity to help you think about families of children with disabilities. You will also find the next chapter dealing with family systems helpful, as it expands on some of the ideas above.

ACTIVITY 8.2

You are a social worker in a children's disability team. You have received a referral from a family who have twins aged 18 months and two older children aged three and five. One of the twins suffered brain damage at birth and has some physical impairment as a result; she is not yet able to walk or grasp and manipulate objects, unlike her twin, and she is also difficult to feed and very unsettled in her behaviour. Her parents are struggling to cope, and their doctor has asked if they can have respite care for their daughter. What factors would you consider in deciding how to respond to this request?

COMMENTS ON ACTIVITY 8.2

This family has a lot to cope with; having four young children so close in age would be stressful in itself without the additional factor of disability. They certainly need support and respite of some kind, but you have probably thought of a lot of questions you would want to ask about their situation before a decision was made about how best to provide this. How much help have the parents had, if any, in coming to terms with their child's disability, and how much is known about its diagnosis and prognosis? What effect has it had on relationships within the family? What resources can the family draw on, both from within their own family culture and from wider family, friends and community? Are there any aspects of the family culture which are adding further to the practical and emotional difficulties of coping with their child's impairment?

Failing to resolve initial negative reactions is a danger for families of children with disabilities and therefore a danger to the child herself, because healthy emotional development is not assisted by negative or ambivalent feelings on the part of one's parents. The process of adjustment will be greatly helped by clear information about the cause of the disability, about what to expect in terms of development and what parents and others can do to help the child reach her full potential. In this situation you would want to check whether all these issues have been fully explored, although of course there are not always clear answers to these questions. Support groups, where parents can access information and share experiences and strategies, can be very helpful.

Another danger is that parents may become so preoccupied with managing the particular special needs of a child with a disability, perhaps out of a desire to make the child become as 'normal' as possible, that they lose sight of the fact that the child has the same universal emotional needs as any other child. Such needs might include needs for fun, cuddles, exploration and so on and also needs for consistent care. This may affect the attachment relationship between parent and child; studies of attachment patterns in children with disabilities show that they are slightly more likely to be insecurely attached than others (Howe 2011: 207). With this in mind, you would want to think carefully about the effect on attachment of respite care which separated this young child from her main carer. There is a difficult balance to be struck here between the parents' needs, the needs of the child and the needs of her siblings, which would need to be sensitively explored with the family in order to come up with a creative and workable package of support.

Adolescence and Disability

The developmental task of adolescence is widely agreed to be the construction of a new identity with which to enter the adult world (see Chapter 6). Components of this identity differ from one individual to another, and also vary between boys and girls, but are likely to include elements of the following:

- Autonomy – increasing independence from one's family of origin, which may include physically leaving home, as well as making one's own decisions and taking responsibility for one's own needs. This is linked to the increasing importance of a peer group as a source of support.
- Sexual identity – a sense of oneself as a sexual being, which arises from learning to successfully negotiate sexual relationships.
- Occupational identity – a sense of oneself as competent and able to provide for oneself and others, which comes from acquiring skills and work habits.

It would be wrong to generalise about all young people with disabilities as if they were a single homogeneous group, for there are enormous differences between the challenges that will be faced by, say, a young person of above average intelligence who is deaf, a person with Down syndrome, or a person who is quadriplegic. Nevertheless, there are some themes which do seem to run through the experience of many adolescents with disabilities.

Autonomy

Young people with disabilities may have their peer-group involvement limited or curtailed in various ways. They may attend special schooling, separate from other young people. In some ways, this may promote peer-group involvement, by allowing young people to mix with others who share the same kinds of experience, but it does also have the effect of isolating young people with disabilities from young people generally. In cases where young people with disabilities attend residential schools, or are bussed to schools at some distance using special transport services, this problem may be particularly pronounced. They miss out on getting to know young people in their own neighbourhood.

Mobility problems may also make street-corner type socialising more difficult or impossible, as can intellectual impairments (some may lack the necessary linguistic or cognitive abilities) and visual impairments. There may be problems with gaining acceptance from non-disabled peers – or even reluctance to admit that they are peers – and difficulties with access, for physical or other reasons, to social and leisure facilities used by non-disabled young people in the same age group.

Becoming independent from one's family of origin may also be complicated – or made impossible – if one is dependent on one's family for basic physical care, such as dressing, bathing or going to the toilet. Whether these needs can be met in other ways will depend on financial resources and/or the availability of publicly-funded services. Parents may also be in a position to hold on to control which they simply would have had no choice but to relinquish with an able-bodied child. For non-disabled children, establishing autonomy typically involves an element of wresting power from adults, as well as being granted it. Young people with disabilities may find this more difficult.

Sexual identity

Exploration of sex and sexual relationships is complicated for young people with disabilities for all of the reasons given above. Even access to information about sex may be more restricted, because adolescents typically acquire sexual information from their peers as well as from adults and, as we've seen, some young people with disabilities have more restricted contact with their peers.

Lollar (1994) makes the point that young people with spina bifida (and this would also apply to some with other conditions) have been subjected throughout their life to highly intrusive examinations and interventions, so that they will not have developed the same boundaries about their bodies as other young people, and may need particular help with this. Some young people with spina bifida may also have limited sensation in the genital area or, in the case of boys, be unable to have an erection.

Protectiveness on the part of parents and other adult carers may also result in a lack of sexual opportunities, which is not to say that protectiveness is necessarily unjustified in the case of young people whose limited cognitive abilities may otherwise place them in situations which they are unable to control or understand. Young people with disabilities are often more vulnerable to abuse and exploitation than are their non-disabled peers (see, for instance, Sullivan and Knutson, 2000).

Occupational identity

Depending on the nature of the impairment, and on the social environment, a young person with a disability may also have much more difficulty than non-disabled young people in finding a job and acquiring skills that will allow her to earn her own living and participate fully in the work of society. Drawing on a UK survey of nearly 24,000 men and women aged 19–59, a government survey found that 71 per cent of disabled respondents had no paid employment, as against 24 per cent of non-disabled respondents (Berthoud, 2006: 32). Though paid work is often an important part of occupational identity, this also includes leisure and social activities and the routines of daily living, and people with disabilities are also likely to face obstacles in these areas. Writing in the foreword to the *World Report on Disability*, Professor Stephen Hawking contrasts his own experience as a person with serious physical disabilities with that of the majority:

> I rely on a team of personal assistants who make it possible for me to live and work in comfort and dignity. My house and my workplace have been made accessible for me. Computer experts have supported me with an assisted communication system and a speech synthesiser which allow me to compose lectures and papers, and to communicate with different audiences.

> But I realise that I am very lucky, in many ways. My success in theoretical physics has ensured that I am supported to live a worthwhile life. It is very clear that the majority of people with disabilities in the world have an extremely difficult time with everyday survival, let alone productive employment and personal fulfilment. (WHO, 2011: ix)

Establishing an identity

So the routes by which people typically establish a separate identity during adolescence may be more restricted, or even closed in some cases, to young people with disabilities. The challenge for these young people and their supporters seems to lie both in challenging unwarranted obstacles and in finding alternative pathways to establishing a secure adult identity.

Disability and Adulthood

In 'Western' industrialised society, adult life is seen as typically including the following:

- moving out of the parental home and becoming responsible for one's own care
- engaging in sexual relationships and establishing a long-term sexual partnership
- becoming financially independent
- raising children
- leaving school and full-time education and moving into a career or occupation
- contributing to the community.

Of course, many people with impairments of all kinds achieve and excel in all these areas. And, of course, disabled and non-disabled people alike may freely choose not to marry or to have children. However, it is also the case that many people with impairments will have difficulty achieving some or all of these goals not because of choice, but because of difficulties created by their impairment and by the attitude of society to that impairment. In some cases, the disability that results can amount to a denial of access to adulthood itself. People with learning difficulties, in particular, are often infantilised by the language that is used about them: 'He is 50, but really his mental age is 5.' The group of learning disabled researchers quoted earlier have this to say about the negative attitudes they have encountered:

> The professionals, care managers, day centre staff, and parents and Joe Public judge us – all of them judge us – and they're frightened of change. A lot of learning disabled adults are in a rubber band system. They say 'You can go as far as that.' But if they see us progressing too far forward they say, 'Oh come back!' and pull us back. ... People say, *'you can't!'* all the time.
>
> You can't get a job.
>
> You can't get married.
>
> You can't have a baby.
>
> You can't have your own house.
>
> You can't go out unless you're with someone else.

You can't get on a university course.

You can't have a normal life.

But now we can, and people need to learn that we can … It's like Wolfensberger (1998) said, people think we're 'forever children' because we don't have the intelligence of a 'normal' adult. To us it's a put down, they put us down. (Docherty et al., 2010: 435)

Moving out of the parental home

The departure of a young adult from the family home is not just an issue for the individual concerned, but for the whole family system, as we will discuss in the next chapter, and indeed for society in general. This is well illustrated by the case of adults with disabilities. Some people with disabilities remain with their parents into adulthood. While this is sometimes a free choice, it may simply be because the young person or the rest of the family are not offered any viable alternative, or perhaps because they cannot *accept* any viable alternative.

Historically, even when young adults with disabilities moved out of the family home, many moved into institutional environments where they continued to be treated as dependent children. This applied particularly to adults identified as having learning difficulties. As Sperlinger reminds us about the situation in the UK:

> When the national health service was set up in 1948, the colonies or institutions which were built originally in the nineteenth century to segregate people with learning difficulties from the rest of society became 'hospitals' in which people were 'nursed' (all of their lives) and their problems were defined in medical terms. People with learning difficulties were seen as sick and in need of treatment. (Sperlinger, 1997: 6–7)

In the 1970s, one of the authors worked in such a hospital. In this institution, adults with learning difficulties, many in their 40s and 50s, were uniformly referred to by themselves and staff as 'boys' and divided into 'high-grades' and 'low-grades'. They were offered no opportunities for sexual relationships, other than furtive ones. They had no choice about when and what they had for meals. They slept in dormitories and had no safe place for personal possessions. They had to ask for toilet paper when they needed it. Cigarettes were issued to them from the ward office. Privileges were withheld as punishments. Yet some of these men were of high enough intellectual ability to be able to read and write fluently. It was a tribute to the human spirit that many of them were still able to maintain a great deal of personal dignity and some very caring long-term relationships. There are no longer hospitals in Britain like this, but the underlying attitude which they represented still does exist.

Historically, as now, many adults with learning or physical impairments would also have remained with their parents throughout their adult life. In the past, life expectancy for people with Down syndrome or cerebral palsy was considerably shorter than it is now, so that parents could generally expect to outlive their children. This is no longer the case, so that we now have people with Down syndrome or cerebral palsy who have lived with their parents into middle or late adulthood, having to move on into other accommodation at a time not of their choosing, but dictated by their parents' deteriorating health, or their parents' death.

Intimacy, generativity and independence

Being an adult is not a question of being completely 'independent', for no one, disabled or otherwise, is really independent – as Peggy Quinn points out, 'each person depends on others for food, electricity, transportation, postal services and many other components of daily life' (Quinn, 1998: 160). She goes on: 'a more appropriate goal is that of *responsible inter-dependence*. … In this case, each person does what she does best and negotiates with others for the goods and services she needs to fill the gaps (Quinn, 1998: 160; our italics). Many disabled people experience a lack of opportunity to experience responsible interdependence, as opposed to childlike dependency.

Disability and old age

We will conclude by noting that, in later adulthood, disability of course becomes much more prevalent. Those of us who are fortunate enough not to have to confront the challenges of disability in earlier life, may well have to do so in old age. But that is a subject we will return to in Chapter 11.

Chapter Summary

- In this chapter, we looked at the interaction of physical and environmental/social factors that together constitute 'disability' (we used 'impairment' to refer to the purely physical/biological aspect). The restrictions that result from disability can in some circumstances amount to a restriction in access to the status of adulthood itself.
- We then looked at different types of impairment – learning impairments, motor impairments and sensory impairments – and considered the particular developmental challenges that each poses. As discussed in previous chapters, there are dangers in imposing a certain developmental pathway as 'normal' and this is apparent in the case of people with disabilities.
- We looked at the family context of children with disabilities, discussing both the initial reaction of a family to the arrival of a child with disabilities and the impact

(Continued)

(Continued)

of disability on a family system (which, it would appear, can be both disruptive and strengthening).

● We then moved on to look at the particular issues faced by adolescents with disabilities, bearing in mind that adolescence is normally viewed as a time of establishing a separate identity.

● We concluded by looking at issues for disabled adults.

This chapter has emphasised both the family and the wider social context of disability. The next chapter will focus on family systems theory and the one after that will look further at the wider social context in which not only disability but all aspects of human growth and development unfold.

Further Reading

Hodapp, R.M. (1998) *Development and Disabilities: Intellectual, Sensory and Motor Impairments.* Cambridge: Cambridge University Press.

Summarises a large number of research findings and covers the Solnit and Stark and subsequent models on the birth of a child with a disability.

Lewis, V. (2003) *Development and Disability*, 2nd edn. Oxford: Blackwell.

Provides separate chapters on the development of children who are blind, deaf, have motor disabilities, have Down syndrome and have autism.

Quinn, P. (1998) *Understanding Disability – a Lifespan Approach*. London: Sage.

Covers each stage of the lifespan in a separate chapter.

9 NO MAN IS AN ISLAND

FAMILY SYSTEMS AND THEIR LIFE CYCLE

- Systems theory — 170
- Systems and families — 172
- The family life cycle — 176
- Stages in family life — 180
- Larger systems — 186

In the previous chapter we showed that a disability is not simply a characteristic of an individual, but is the product of an interaction between an individual and the wider social context in which he or she lives. This is an example of the more general point that human beings do not grow and develop in isolation. As the seventeenth-century poet John Donne famously put it:

> No man is an *Island*, entire of it selfe; every man is a piece of the *Continent*, a part of the *maine* ...
> (Donne, 1962 [1624]: 369)

People form parts of larger systems, pieces of a continent. It is within that context that we become the individuals who we are. But there is more to it than that, for these larger systems themselves are subject to growth and change: relationships change, families change, communities and societies change. So in this chapter we are going to look at the growth and development of systems – specifically at *family* systems – and at how one can view human growth and development in terms of whole families rather than just looking at the growth and development of the individuals within a family. The next chapter will look at the even wider context of society at large.

We have included this chapter because family systems theory seems to provide a useful, unique and important perspective on child and adult development. But in fact family systems theory often goes unmentioned in the developmental literature. Accounts of systems theory and its application to families are found mainly in the family therapy literature, which is naturally orientated more towards the practical task of working with troubled families than towards advancing academic knowledge of human development.

There are many different approaches within the family therapy literature and there is no single 'founding father' or 'founding mother', as with some of the other theoretical models we have discussed, though Gregory Bateson (see Bateson, 1973) is described by one author as 'arguably the most influential early theorist' (Barnes, 2004: 18).

Systems Theory

Originating in the work of the biologist Ludwig von Bertalanffy (1971), systems theory has its roots in mathematics, biology and cybernetics and deals with the way that parts come together in larger wholes. A system is a complex of interacting elements. An example of a very simple system is a room with a heating system controlled by a thermostat. The elements within this system – the room, the heating system and the thermostat – are linked together in a circular relationship: the temperature of the room affects the thermostat, the thermostat switches the heating on or off, the heating affects the temperature in the room and so on, as is illustrated in Figure 9.1.

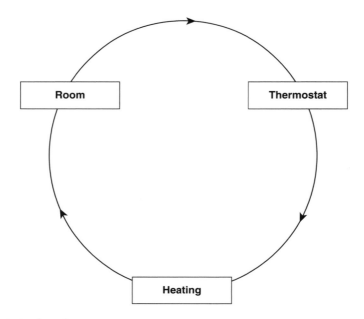

FIGURE 9.1   A simple system

Our bodies are systems like this. They are vastly more complicated, of course, consisting not just of three elements but of a large number of organs and tissues but, as in the example of the room and the thermostatically controlled heating, the different elements interact together. Heart rate and rate of breathing, for example, are affected by the level of oxygen in the blood, and the level of oxygen in the blood is in turn affected by heart rate and rate of breathing.

If you look at it on a smaller scale, each organ is a system made up of a large number of cells. And if you look inside a cell, that itself is a system of interacting parts. Going to the other extreme, human beings are themselves a part of larger interlocking and overlapping systems: families, communities, organisations, countries, the biosphere. Each system is made up of 'subsystems' and is itself in turn a subsystem in even larger systems. There are many different 'system levels'.

Closed and open systems

Systems can be closed or open. A closed system is one which does not interact at all with the surrounding world. In open systems, there is an interaction with the world outside across the boundary of the system. A system has to have *some* sort of boundary to exist as something separate from its surroundings, but that boundary may be permeable.

Living systems characteristically are open systems. They have a semi-permeable boundary which does not cut them off completely from the outside world, but allows them to maintain some sort of equilibrium with it. The amoeba, for example, is a single-celled organism which has a semi-permeable membrane around it. Without the membrane, the contents of the amoeba would simply dissolve into the surrounding water, but if the membrane was completely impermeable, the amoeba would not be able to take in the water, nutrients and oxygen that it needs, or get rid of waste products.

Circularity and feedback loops

Circularity is a feature of systems in general. In a system, the sequence of cause and effect does not just go in one direction. In our thermostat example, one *could* say that the thermostat controls the temperature in the room (because it is the thermostat that turns the heating on and off), but it would be equally true to say that it is the temperature in the room that controls the thermostat (because the thermostat is a mechanism that responds to changes in temperature). The relationship between thermostat and room in this example is what is called a *negative feedback loop*. That is to say, an increase in temperature results in the heating being switched off, which then of course leads to the temperature dropping down again. A *positive feedback loop*, on the other hand, would exist if the thermostat was wrongly wired up so that an increase in temperature had the effect of turning the heating *up*. You can see that a positive loop would result in the room getting hotter and hotter indefinitely, while a negative feedback loop has the effect of maintaining temperature at a more or less constant level.

The term 'positive feedback loop' does not imply that this kind of feedback loop is necessarily beneficial. Positive feedback loops can be very dangerous. To give one example, part of the current concern about global warming is that rising temperatures may set in motion positive feedback loops which will cause even *faster* rises in temperature. (For instance, if higher temperatures result in the release of methane gas from frozen tundra, the methane will have a 'greenhouse' effect which will then result in further warming, more thawing of frozen land and the release of still more greenhouse gases to warm things up still more.) When positive feedback loops have harmful consequences of this kind, we tend to speak of 'vicious circles' or of things 'spiralling out of control'. But positive feedback loops can be beneficial if they result in a steadily improving situation, in which case they are referred to as 'virtuous circles'.

Just as positive feedback loops are not necessarily positive in their consequences, negative feedback loops are by no means necessarily negative in theirs. They are called negative because the feedback dampens down whatever stimulus set them off. In fact, far from being harmful, negative feedback loops are absolutely vital components of all living things, since life needs to maintain a state of equilibrium, or *homeostasis* (from the Greek words for 'same' and 'standing') in order to function. Maintaining equilibrium is of course precisely the purpose of a thermostat (the word comes from the Greek for 'heat' and 'standing'), which is a classic example of a negative feedback loop. Our bodies have their own remarkably efficient thermostatic mechanisms which, unless we are ill, keep our blood within half a degree or so of 37°C, the optimum temperature for our particular body chemistry, in summer or winter alike.

Systems and Families

But what does all this have to do with families? Well, as we have said, every individual is not only a biological system, made up of numerous sub-systems, but herself part of larger systems, including societies, communities, organisations, cultures … and families. A group of people sharing the same environment interact and influence one another in many different ways. And, as Franklin and Warren write:

> if there is … a sufficient level of contact between them, a global structure emerges that influences each of the actors in ways that cannot simply be explained by the impact of one individual on another; the whole is greater than the sum of the parts and cannot be explained completely by breaking it down into parts. … Thus a system is born. (1999: 401)

This applies to all kinds of groups of people. Most of us are familiar with the way that a sporting team or a team at work gradually 'gels together' into some kind of an entity, but of course the members of families typically have a much higher level of contact over a much longer period of time. You may well have experienced the powerful and complex feelings, positive, negative, or both at once, that are set in train when the members of an extended family reunite at an occasion such as a wedding or a Christmas dinner, and the way that old patterns of behaviour, old rivalries and grudges and alliances, can very quickly reassert themselves, even after many years. In such situations, we observe the emergence of an entity that is greater than the sum of its parts.

To look at this entity which we call a family, and to consider it as a system, has the following implications, which have been found useful in practice in therapeutic work with families:

- If families are systems, they have properties which are more than the sum of their parts. So we cannot fully understand the behaviour of an individual in isolation, without looking at the system of which she is part.
- If they are similar to biological systems, families will operate to try to maintain a reasonably steady state. So, if a certain member of the family is habitually behaving in a certain way, this behaviour is likely to be serving the purpose of maintaining a steady state, even if the family members themselves do not recognise this.
- Communication and feedback between the parts of the system (that is, the members of the family) are an important part of the functioning of the system. So that, if we want to understand the family, we have to look at the way members communicate with one another, and not just at each individual in isolation.
- If you want to understand the behaviour of an individual in the family, you usually understand it better in terms of circular causality, rather than of linear causality. That is to say, the behaviour of an individual is not simply the cause of other events in the family, or simply the effect, but is linked to the rest of the family in a feedback loop. As with the thermostat and the temperature of a room, each one both controls and is controlled by the other.
- All systems are made up of smaller systems and are themselves part of larger systems.

Proponents of a systems perspective argue that when we think about human problems and try to solve them, we often fail to bring about change because we focus too much on individuals and not enough on the system of which they are part. A young offender, for instance, is working well with a probation officer and seems to be making excellent progress. But then, for no obvious reason, he seemingly throws it all away and goes out and offends again. There could be many reasons for this, of course, but one possibility is that the probation officer has neglected to look at the family context in which the offender is operating. Perhaps his offending serves some purpose for the family. It may provide a distraction, as we will discuss below, from other more alarming issues which might otherwise threaten the family's integrity. Or perhaps there is a culture within the family that a man must commit crimes to prove his manhood.

To return to the analogy of the thermostat, suppose you find yourself in a rather cold house and, finding a small fireplace in the front room, decide to light a fire. Unfortunately, you fail to notice that the thermostat that controls the central heating is also in the front room. The warmth of the fire causes the thermostat to turn off the central heating for the rest of the house. So, though it gets warmer immediately in front of the fire, the house as a whole gets colder than ever. In order to heat up the house as a whole, you'd need to know about the thermostat and know how to adjust it. Just stoking up the fire without adjusting the thermostat will only generate a local heat, which is not enough to offset the loss of the central heating over all the rest of the house.

To give another analogy, if a group of people are playing poker and one player starts playing rummy, he won't get very far. The rest of the group will stop him from carrying on, or they will evict him from the game. If he wants to play rummy, he needs to persuade the rest of the group to play a different game.

Social workers, relationship counsellors and others who deal with family problems will often find that a particular member of a family – often a child – is identified as 'the problem'. But if they look at it more closely from a systems perspective, they may well find that the problem lies in the whole group, and that the person identified as the problem may actually be performing a *helpful* role for the group, either by providing some kind of safety valve or by attracting outside help. The other family members may complain about this person's behaviour, but it may still turn out that in some way the family *need* this behaviour to continue.

If you are not accustomed to thinking about systems, this can seem quite a puzzling idea. The following activity may help to clarify it:

ACTIVITY 9.1

Mr and Mrs Smith have three children, Mary (18), Ricky (13) and Betty (10). Mr Smith works in the oil industry and this requires him to work abroad much of the time. There have been serious marital problems over the years. Mr Smith has had several affairs and has talked on several occasions of leaving home for good.

Ricky has started getting into trouble. He stays out a lot. He has been involved in shoplifting. He is missing a lot of school, and is under threat of being excluded because of his disruptive, defiant behaviour in the classroom and outside of it.

Mrs Smith has been diagnosed with depression.

Mr Smith has recently taken unpaid leave from work to be at home to support Mrs Smith, resulting in loss of income for the family, and also jeopardising his chance of a promotion to a new post of global operations manager.

Mary had a place at a university 200 miles away, but has now deferred because she is so worried about what is happening at home. She is working in a local shop.

Everyone in the family is very angry with Ricky. Mr Smith is particularly angry, not only about the disruption of his work, but also angry on behalf of Mrs Smith (who John has made ill) and Mary (whose future has been put on hold).

But looked at in systemic terms, what purpose might Ricky's behaviour serve for the family system as a whole? And what might the family need help with to move forward? Looking at this as a problem for the family as a whole, what kind of interventions might be helpful?

COMMENTS ON ACTIVITY 9.1

You probably noticed that one effect of Ricky's behaviour has been to bring his father home more. Children's problem behaviours frequently seem to serve some function for the relationship of their parents. Difficult behaviour can bring together parents who are drifting apart by giving them a task which they have to work on together. Or, by drawing their anger on to himself, a child can prevent them from taking it out on one another. If you have a partner and are a parent, you may well have noticed for yourself how one of your children becomes more demanding when you and your partner are not getting on.

Ricky's behaviour has also had the effect of preventing his sister from leaving home. With a frequently absent father and a depressed mother, he may well have become quite dependent on her for support and is now managing to keep her available to him, and to delay the beginnings of the 'empty nest' transition for the family, which his parents may also be finding difficult, as it will put more focus on their own conflicted relationship. Mary herself may also be finding it difficult to separate from her family; she may be anxious about how her mother will cope, and what will happen to her parents' marriage. She may secretly welcome the excuse to delay her departure.

Having his parents and sister so angry with him cannot be pleasant for Ricky, but it may well be less scary for him than having them angry and rejecting of each other. It may well be less scary for the parents and the rest of the family too.

From a family systems point of view, any intervention would need to shift the perspective away from a view of this as being just Ricky's problem, and towards looking at the operation of the family as a whole. Structural family therapists, for instance, might work on establishing clearer boundaries between, on the one hand, the parental system of the mother and father (they need, one way or another to do the parenting) and, on the other hand, the children, so that Mary and (in his own much less obvious way) Ricky will not have to feel so responsible for looking after everyone.

If you are involved in social work or health visiting or some other profession which involves working with families having problems, you will doubtless have noticed how preoccupied people often seem to get with the question of 'whose fault is it?' or 'who started it?' or 'who is to blame?' Indeed, you may have noticed this within your own family or your own personal relationships. You may also have noticed that arguing about this rarely, if ever, seems to result in a solution.

From a systems perspective, these are simply the wrong questions. They are *linear* questions, applied incorrectly to *circular* systems, which means that arguing about them is a bit like arguing about which came first: the chicken or the egg (or about whether the thermostat controls the room temperature or vice versa.) It is the whole system that needs to be looked at if change is going to come about.

The Family Life Cycle

If we look at family systems rather than at individuals, not only do we need to jettison linear explanations for behaviour in favour of circular ones, we must also set aside linear models of development in favour of *cyclical* ones. By linear models, we mean models such as that of Erikson which sets out life in ascending stages beginning with birth and ending with death. Individuals *are* born and grow older and die in that order but a family is not born and (except in catastrophic circumstances) does not die, and birth follows death within a family almost as surely as death follows birth.

Indeed, it is perfectly possible for a family to be dealing simultaneously with the death of one of its members and the birth of another, and it is a certainty that any family will be dealing with several of Erikson's stages all at the same time, for, as Monica McGoldrick, Betty Carter and Nydia Garcia Preto point out, a family is usually at least a three-generation system, and nowadays often a four or even five generation one (2011: 1). It is not unusual for a family to be dealing with the transitions involved in adolescence, those involved in mid-life and those involved in the onset of old age, all at once, because parents are typically at the mid-life stage when their children reach adolescence, and grandparents are typically at or past retirement age.

When we look at families as systems, growth and development are a cycle and not a line. In fact, even to describe them as a *cycle* is a simplification, because events do not follow one another round and round in order like the cycle of the four seasons. In a family, winter, spring, summer and autumn may all be happening at the same time.

Stressors and system levels

For families, as for individuals, how they cope with these challenges will depend in part on their history. McGoldrick et al. (2011: 7–8) speak of 'horizontal stressors' and 'vertical stressors' (an idea we touched on in the previous chapter). 'Horizontal stressors' are challenges which are thrown up by the passing of time. This includes both *predictable* events, like the birth of a child or the onset of adolescence, and *unpredictable* events, like illness, or redundancy, or divorce, or the discovery that a child has a disability. It also includes events which will be absolutely central to some families' experience but completely alien to others. For example, in the modern world, millions of families are uprooted from their homeland, or broken up, or both, as a result of migration, whether this is for economic reasons or to escape tyranny or war. In other contexts, moving house within a single town may be the only physical move that a family ever has to deal with. 'Vertical stressors', on the other hand, are a sort of inheritance that is transmitted down through the generations of a family. For instance, some families have a history of mental health problems, some are unable to talk about sex, some are preoccupied with educational achievement, some have strong religious or political allegiances stretching back for many generations which individual family members cannot easily challenge, some have a pattern of absent fathers, or of powerful matriarchs, or of difficulties in coping with adolescence, or of drinking and violence. The possibilities are as numerous as families themselves.

You may remember from Chapter 2 that Erikson's model envisaged that different stages in life throw up new challenges ('crises'). These challenges are what we are now calling 'horizontal stressors' (although McGoldrick et al.'s term covers, as we have seen, not only predictable life transitions but also unpredictable events). Erikson also suggested that when we attempt to negotiate a new life challenge, we may have to revisit challenges from previous stages that have not yet been fully resolved. These pieces of unfinished business from earlier stages are what we are now referring to as 'vertical stressors'.

However, Erikson's model deals with individuals, albeit in a social context. The model we are now discussing looks at the horizontal stressors as challenges that are not just encountered by an individual but by a whole family. And it sees the issues from the past which make up the vertical stressors as coming, not just from an individual's own past, but from the history of the family as a whole, perhaps going back for many generations. Adolescence, for example, is not just a challenge for the individual concerned, but for her parents, and perhaps for siblings and grandparents as well. How well the family copes with it will depend not just on the history of the individual young person, but on the parents' own experience of adolescence, and perhaps their parents' before them.

But just as individuals belong to families, so do families belong to wider systems. Each family is part of a community, a social class, a culture, a society. ... Each of these is a different 'system level', and each system level has its own horizontal and vertical stressors. Nations, for instance, have to deal with new events in the here and now (horizontal stressors) but they also have to deal with the legacy of history. If you look at recent events in parts of the world such as Israel/Palestine, you can see how whole societies have to deal not only with the day-to-day 'horizontal' issues that every nation faces, but also with the 'vertical' legacy of fears and aspirations that come from their particular history. Just as individual lives take place within, and are shaped by, their family contexts and family histories, so the lives of families are shaped in turn by their social and cultural contexts.

At any system level, difficulties are likely to occur when a horizontal stressor interacts with a vertical one. That is to say, the most challenging times are likely to be when something that is happening now touches on some painful and unresolved issue from the past. When this happens in a family, 'there tends to be a quantum leap in anxiety in the system' (McGoldrick et al., 2011: 9), which may make it difficult to successfully complete the changes necessary to deal with the new horizontal event and move on from it. For example:

- If you come from a family with a history of difficulties with parenting, or loss of children, the birth of a child will produce heightened anxiety, far above the level of anxiety which this new event would produce in other families.
- If you come from a family where sexual abuse occurred, there are likely to be anxieties through the generations about physical contact and sex – even assuming that sexual abuse itself doesn't recur through the generations, which it frequently does.
- If you come from a family where great store was placed on intellectual achievement, then there will be high anxiety around exams and so on. The discovery that a child has learning difficulties might cause particular problems for such a family.

Often the same theme will emerge in different ways in different generations. A family with problems around the issue of *control* may in one generation be obsessively controlling, and in the next generation have problems with setting boundaries at all. Both these patterns, though apparently opposite, are problems with control. For example, one may sometimes encounter drug addicts who have had great difficulty in controlling their habit or any other aspect of their lives, whose parents are very highly controlled and controlling. While the drug-using child and the controlling parent may seem poles apart, they are both exhibiting difficulties around the question of control.

Probably the best way to look at this question of horizontal and vertical stressors is to consider some examples of how they might work in practice. The following activities may help with this.

ACTIVITY 9.2

Looking at your own family of origin, can you think of any examples of vertical stressors that seem to have been passed down the generations? You may be able to identify these stressors by looking at the kinds of events that your family seems to find particularly difficult, as these would be the occasions when horizontal and vertical stressors interact.

Or consider the following case example and ask yourself what horizontal and vertical stressors are interacting here:

Janice is 42. As a child, she was abused by her stepfather, sexually and physically. Her mother could not cope with her and at the age of 13, she entered the care system. She had several moves within the care system and suffered further abuse there at the hands of a male residential social worker.

She is now a single mother of three sons, each by a different father.

The two older sons are both teenagers and are now completely out of her control. They are not attending school. They are both offending regularly and using drugs. They come and go from the house as they please. They are aggressive and abusive to their mother if challenged.

Janice has asked for professional help with the two boys: she says she has lost it completely with them and she thinks they should be in care.

COMMENTS ON ACTIVITY 9.2

We don't know what vertical stressors you noticed in your own family but in Janice's case, we would suggest that there may be vertical stressors do to with:

- Adolescence – Janice's mother could not cope with her as an adolescent, and she has no confidence in her own ability to cope with her teenage sons. Further exploration might well reveal that a history of children being evicted from the family at adolescence goes back for several generations. It is not hard to imagine that the two boys in turn will find it hard to cope assertively with their own adolescent children when they themselves become parents.
- Male sexuality and aggression – Janice was abused by her stepfather and by a male worker in care. She has not had a stable relationship with a man. She is finding it hard to cope with her sons now they have reached the age of sexual maturity. Again, the history of abusive men might well turn out to have gone back further into the past. And again it is easy to imagine that the two boys will grow up to become men who are abusive to women and girls.

In the last chapter we looked at how disability affects the whole family system, and how the birth of a child with a disability is one of those moments when horizontal and vertical stressors are likely to intersect and react with each other (see p. 159). You may also have professional or personal experience of your own of how families cope with disability.

ACTIVITY 9.3

Drawing on this, can you think of:

- horizontal stressors that might result from the presence of a child with a disability
- vertical stressors that might exist in particular families which might make successful family adaptation more difficult
- stressors that might exist at the system level of the wider society.

COMMENTS ON ACTIVITY 9.3

A child with a disability may place extra stress on a family for the entirely practical reason that she requires more care than other children and therefore makes more demands and takes up more time. The need for care may also go on for longer than for other children. As well as demands on time, there may be additional demands on the family's money, its space and its capacity to ask for outside help.

Vertical stressors would include particular concerns, preoccupations or anxieties which might be triggered by the presence of a child with a disability. We earlier suggested that these might include a preoccupation with intellectual or sporting achievement, but many other issues might be brought to the fore. For example, issues about responsibilities for providing personal care might be highlighted. (Consider a family where, up to now, it has been accepted in practice that personal care is a woman's job, although there has been some resentment about this on the part of the women in the family. What would be the impact of a child who requires enormous amounts of personal care?) Or, in some families where there are anxieties on the part of family members about getting enough care or attention, the arrival of a child with considerable needs for personal care might well increase anxieties and tensions. You will no doubt be able to think of many other instances such as these.

Some disabling conditions, like cystic fibrosis and Duchenne muscular dystrophy, can be inherited, as can some forms of visual and hearing impairment. This may lead to guilt on the part of the parents, combined with complicated feelings about their own genetic inheritance, and also to anxiety about future parenthood, making this both a vertical and a horizontal stressor.

Moving to other system levels, you might have considered the different social context that exists in societies such as some Scandinavian countries, where there is a high level of public provision for children with disabilities, as against societies where there is none, and where making provision is the financial and personal responsibility of the family concerned. You may also have considered the different beliefs, values and prejudices about disability that exist in different social contexts.

Stages in Family Life

Taking a family as opposed to an individual view of human development, we see that each developmental stage – birth, adolescence, marriage, divorce, remarriage, retirement, death – affects the whole family, and not just individual members of it. And each stage sets tasks for the whole family. When your children become adolescents, this poses challenges for you as a parent, as well as for your children. When you grow old and frail and cannot cope with daily life on your own, this poses challenges for your spouse and your children as well as for you. In both cases, there are not just practical problems to be solved, but adjustments to be made to the way the whole family operates. In family systems terminology, a successful transition into a new phase normally requires not only a 'first-order' change, but a 'second-order' change. Alan Carr distinguishes between first- and second-order change as follows:

> First-order change involves a change in the relationships among elements in a system without an alteration in the rules governing those relationships. An alteration in these relationship rules is entailed by second-order change. (2012: 78)

We earlier used the example of a card player who wishes to change from poker to rummy.

McGoldrick et al. offer a table (2011) of family life-cycle stages. We are purposely not showing such a chart here, partly because we want to emphasise that the way that families grow and change is cyclical not linear (the process has no beginning and no end) and several transitions can be taking place at the same time. We also wish to acknowledge, as they themselves take pains to point out, that families do not necessarily all go through the same stages. Many families, for example, have to deal with separation, divorce and remarriage, but others do not. Some families may have to deal with challenges that other families do not have to contemplate at all: migration to other countries, for example, or the complete disruption of family life by warfare.

But we will now look at some of the transitions that families characteristically have to negotiate together. (McGoldrick et al.'s book gives a much more detailed account of these transitions.)

Young single adults leaving home

When a young adult leaves the parental home, this involves a transition for the whole family. Not only does the young adult have to revise his or her role, but the parents and grandparents will need to redefine theirs in relation to the young adult and to the other parts of their lives. Many families find this hard. Some parents encourage the young person to remain dependent, and some young people do indeed remain dependent. Others do the opposite and try to break off contact with their family of origin, thus perhaps denying themselves the possibility of genuinely renegotiating the relationship (so that they remain stuck with a sort of adolescent attitude towards their parents).

Sometimes, young adults find it difficult to leave the parental home at all. It is important to acknowledge that there are some factors at work here that are not just to do with the family, like the difficulties, particularly for young people, in obtaining secure and affordable housing which have increased greatly in the UK in recent years, leading them to continue living with their parents for longer than in the past. These are aspects of a wider system level than the family, the level of society as a whole, which we will discuss in the next chapter. But we also need to consider what might be going on for the other family members, as well as for the young person and the parents. It may be that there is a general anxiety throughout the system about what will happen to the parental marriage after the 'nest is empty'. If so, the young person staying at home may well be the system's attempt to shore this up. We might find, for instance, that there is pressure of various kinds which makes it difficult for the youngest to leave home.

Couples, marriage, separation and divorce

When people come together as a couple, this is usually seen as the joining of two individuals but if we look at families as systems, then the couple relationship involves changing two entire systems which overlap, to develop a third system.

McGoldrick (2011: 207) goes as far as to maintain that 'the lack of resolution of these relationships (with the extended family) is the major problem in negotiating this phase of the family life cycle', even though this may not be recognised by those involved, who may be more likely to focus on problems around money, sex, chores and so on, which are the normal currency of couples' relationship problems. The following are some illustrations of the kinds of problems that can occur with the business of renegotiating family status:

- The couple's parents may interfere too much and the couple may find it difficult to stop this. That is, they may find it difficult to create a sufficiently strong boundary around their own sub-system to allow it to become a genuine system in its own right (you may remember the analogy of the amoeba that would simply dissolve if it was not contained by a membrane). It might be, for instance, that a young man's mother finds it hard to relinquish the close relationship with her son that she had when he was living at home, and he is afraid to hurt her feelings by resisting, and this may create difficulties in his relationship with his partner. Solving the problem may involve not only the couple both changing their behaviour, but his mother accepting that she now has a different role.

- On the other hand, the new couple may go to the opposite extreme, and cut themselves off as an isolated twosome. This could come about as a reaction to the older generation being too intrusive and refusing to deal with the couple as autonomous adults. The couple's attempted solution may cut them off from support which they actually still need and may create difficulties between them. A more durable and helpful solution might involve not only the two of them but also the wider family making, or accepting, changes.

- Sometimes one or both of the members of the couple may still be too enmeshed in their family of origin to be able to invest in a real new system or to accept the implications of the new arrangement. For example, if a man continued to regard his mother as his first point of contact when he wanted to discuss problems and triumphs in his life, he might be effectively excluding his partner from feeling that they are really a couple. Suppose, for the sake of argument, that the couple's sexual relationship broke down as a result, you can see that it would probably be fruitless to try to deal with this in isolation as a purely sexual problem. The underlying problem would be to do with the son and his mother failing to make the adjustments necessary to allow the new couple system to get off the ground. The sexual difficulty is merely a symptom.

Just as becoming a couple requires adjustments of whole systems and not just of the individuals involved, so do separation and divorce, and the forming of new relationships and remarriage, when they occur. There are certain tasks which the members of the couple and the system as a whole need to complete in order to move on. Somehow, each partner needs to achieve an 'emotional divorce' and 'retrieve the hopes, dreams, plans and expectations' (McGoldrick and Carter, 2011: 319) that were invested in the relationship. Yet, at the same time, they cannot cut off completely because, particularly if there are children, the old couple relationship cannot completely cease to exist as a system, but must radically be renegotiated to take into account the new realities. And reconstituted family systems are likely to be even more complex, involving three or four, or even more, overlapping family systems rather than just two, and sometimes involving wide age differences which can cut across generations. For example, an older father with a new baby from a second or third relationship may have grandchildren the same age from a first relationship.

If this renegotiating work isn't done, families can remain in some ways 'stuck emotionally for years, if not for generations' (McGoldrick and Carter, 2011: 318).

Family members becoming parents

Again, this requires a change in the whole multigenerational system and Carter, McGoldrick and Petkov suggest that the need here is for the extended family to 'make emotional and relationship shifts to make a place for the new member' (Carter et al., 2011: 213). Parenthood brings a huge change to a couple relationship as two become three, and all new parents must adjust overnight to the physical, emotional and financial demands of caring for a new baby. When parents experience serious difficulties in making the transition to this new role, this is likely once again to reflect a problem with the whole system, and not just with the couple. Grandparents who have had difficulty in giving up their own role as parents can inadvertently prevent their adult children from feeling like parents themselves, and in some may even actively undermine them, while those who have struggled with aspects of their own parenting role may find it difficult to give the new parents the kind of support they need. And these patterns may well stretch back into earlier generations.

Adolescence

When children in a family reach adolescence, a new phase begins, in that fundamentally different boundaries need to be established. Adolescence is not just something that happens to an individual. Once again, it is relationships within the entire family that need to be renegotiated. In particular, parents at this stage need to change their attitude to control. It is no longer desirable or realistic to attempt to control every aspect of their child's life. Failure to make this shift might lead to the young person giving up on working her own way through to autonomous adulthood (perhaps resulting in 'identity foreclosure' or 'identity diffusion' as discussed in Chapter 6). Or it might result in the adolescent refusing to accept control, and parents getting frustrated at what (to them) feels like impotence.

This phase commonly coincides with the 'mid-life' of the spouses, when they will be concerned with 'major tasks such as re-evaluating their marriage and careers' (Garcia Preto, 2011: 241). At this stage, focusing on parent–child problems can be used to mask marital secrets: an affair going on, perhaps, or a secret wish on the part of one party to divorce. Or if parents are already in open conflict, pre-or post-separation and divorce, this is likely to exacerbate the young person's difficulties while also making it harder for the parents to work together to help resolve them. . Not only can different stages of the family life cycle occur at the same time, but they impact on one another in complex ways.

Family members growing old

When members of a family reach old age, further adjustments are required in the family system for it to be able to cope with the new circumstances. Difficulties in making the adjustment may result from older family members refusing to give up the power they once had (trying to hang on to it through manipulation, for example), or alternatively opting for a passive, dependent role. Or they may result from younger family members, on the one hand, refusing to accept the lessening powers of the older ones and continuing to make the same demands on them as ever, or, on the other, treating them as completely incompetent and refusing to accept that they are capable of doing anything.

When parents become frail and dependent on others for care, the adjustment involved for the whole family system is very considerable, and is likely to churn up old difficulties from the past (vertical stressors). The adult children of the elderly person are confronted, perhaps, with their mixed feelings about their own childhood (when they were the ones who were dependent and the elderly parent was the one with the power). Siblings whose contact may have been limited to social gatherings, may now be forced to work closely together in arranging care for the elderly relative, and old sibling rivalries can often be reawakened.

This stage can often coincide with the previous stage discussed: as grandparents become old, grandchildren may be passing through adolescence.

The systems model of development: summing up

For a model of this kind, it is not necessary to insist that a particular sequence of steps is the only one possible (in different cultures, very different sequences may occur, and within a single culture, there will be many different patterns). What *is* central to a systems model, though, is the idea that, whatever the transitions to be gone through, their successful negotiation is a task for the whole system, not just the individual – and that problems that occur are problems for the whole system too.

Each family system negotiates or fails to negotiate these transitions partly as a result of the absence or presence of vertical stressors, some of which may be unique to that family, some of which may be pervasive in society generally. The implications for practical work with families are that it is important to be aware of the family as a whole, its culture, its vertical stressors and the pattern of relationships that exist within it. Successful transitions require the participation of the wider family system as much as possible.

It may be useful to measure these ideas about stages and transitions in family life against your own experience:

ACTIVITY 9.4

Reflecting on your own experience of family transitions, either as an adult or as a child or adolescent, can you think of examples of how these were successfully negotiated, and of transitions which were more difficult? What were the factors in your family culture that contributed to this? Can you identify any vertical and/or horizontal stressors that were at work?

The transition that almost everyone reading this book will have experienced, or if not, will be contemplating, is the departure from the parental home. How did you yourself negotiate this? (If you are still living with your parents, ask yourself how you might deal with this transition in the future.)

How were you helped or hindered by your parents and other members of your family? Looking back on it, how easy did you make it for them to change their role in relation to you? Was there anything else going on at the same time (that is, a horizontal stressor) that made the process more difficult?

What 'vertical stressors' existed/exist in your family that might have added to the difficulties of this particular transition?

What aspects did you/will you/would you find difficult as a parent dealing with your own children making this transition?

COMMENTS ON ACTIVITY 9.4

Thinking about the transition of leaving the parental home, everyone's experience will of course be different, but the sort of vertical stressors that exist in some families might be:

- a history of parental marriages breaking down following the departure of children
- a history of depression on the part of one or both parents, following the departure of children
- a history of young adults entering into unhappy relationships soon after departure from home.

(Continued)

(Continued)

Horizontal stressors, as well as the transition itself, would be other difficult events occurring around the same time, such as:

- illness in the family
- separation or divorce
- a bereavement
- the family moving house
- a parent experiencing stress at work or losing a job.

Factors which would make this transition easier would be a family culture which encourages independence and self-reliance and parents who are able to let go of their hands-on parental role and move to a different kind of relationship with their adult children while still offering support and a secure base.

In terms of other family transitions, if you are older you may be in a position to see patterns of similarity and difference in vertical and horizontal stressors and in family culture across the generations as you compare, say, the way you were parented with your own experience of parenthood, or your own adolescence with that of your children.

Larger Systems

As we have noted, the application of systems theory to families is something that is usually discussed in books on family therapy, rather than in textbooks on human development, and it has been tested in the therapy room rather than in the psychological laboratory. (This is true also of psychodynamic theory, though the latter has spawned a much larger theoretical literature and has found its way into most of the textbooks on psychological development.) The fact remains, as we hope this chapter has shown, that it offers a developmental model which illuminates areas which might otherwise be neglected by the psychological models discussed so far in this book. No serious theory of human development ignores the context in which people grow and change, but the systemic model is unique in its emphasis on the pattern of relationships that form family systems.

This model does itself have limitations, however. One criticism that can be made of systems models of the family is that, by seemingly taking away responsibility from individuals and locating it in the group as a whole, it is in danger of ignoring the question of power. This is particularly apparent when the model is applied to abusive family situations where, as White et al. (1993: 58) point out, 'taking a supposedly "neutral" stance in therapy sessions tacitly supports the power imbalance which exists in the family resulting in the continued oppression of the victims'.

This has led to some rethinking in systemic family therapy, and to an acknowledgement that:

> [t]he way in which people become drawn into habitual patterns that may not be to their individual liking, for reasons of economic survival [and/or] for protection of their young and their elderly dependants, requires a different lens for examining theory … Choice will also be dependent on relative power related to age. (Barnes, 2004: 18)

This recognition of the political context in which families operate leads us on to a second limitation of focusing on family systems. The question must be asked: why families? For, just as proponents of the family systems model can object to a focus on the individual as being too narrow, so a focus on the family system can be criticised for failing to take into account larger systems. Communities are also systems, as are whole societies and nations. And these bigger systems, like families, themselves grow and change and themselves have enormous importance to individual human development. We noted in Chapter 5, when discussing the learning of gender roles, how difficult it was for one or two adults in isolation to change their child's perception of gender-appropriate behaviour, because of the pervasive influence of the wider society. This is an example of the larger system, at a higher 'system level', being more powerful than the family.

In the next chapter we will look further at this wider social context within which all human growth takes place, and take a look at our subject matter from more of a sociological point of view.

Chapter Summary

- In this chapter, we introduced some basic concepts from systems theory and suggested that these ideas can be applied usefully to human groups, and particularly to families.
- We suggested that by looking at families in a systemic way, a new perspective is gained, which can be lost by more 'linear' and individually focused models.
- We then looked at a systemic approach to the family life cycle, contrasting it to earlier stage theories. In the systems model, development is part of a cycle. (From the point of view of a family, birth follows death just as much as death follows birth.)
- Finally, we suggested some limitations of a family systems perspective. We suggested that it was in danger of ignoring power differentials within a family. In addition, we argued that the family itself, just like a human individual, can be seen as a component of still larger systems.

Some aspects of these larger systems will be the subject of the next chapter, which looks at human growth and development from a sociological perspective.

Further Reading

Barker, P. (2007) *Basic Family Therapy*, 5th edn. Oxford: Blackwell.

Barnes, G. (2004) *Family Therapy in Changing Times*, 2nd edn. Basingstoke: Palgrave.

Carr, A. (2012) *Family Therapy: Concepts, Processes and Practice.* Chichester: Wiley.

McGoldrick, M., Carter, B. and Garcia Preto, N. (eds) (2011) *The Expanded Family Life Cycle: Individual, Family and Social Perspectives*, 4th edn. Boston: Pearson.

All of these books give clear accounts of the systemic model described in this chapter. and McGoldrick, Carter and Garcia Preto's edited collection is the book out of these four that focuses most on life-cycle transitions.

10 IT TAKES A VILLAGE

A SOCIOLOGICAL PERSPECTIVE

- A sociological perspective   191
- Bronfenbrenner's ecological systems theory   192
- Social construction   193
- Social roles   194
- Stereotyping and labelling theory   196
- Divisions in society   198
- Culture and history   203

Let us return yet again to the scenario of the birth of a human being with which we started this book, and which we came back to in the previous chapter. But this time, let us pay more attention to the setting of the scene rather than the leading actors (the child, the mother, the father, the midwife, the doctor). In doing so, we will try to shed more light on some of the questions we asked right at the beginning of this book:

> What will she become? Will she be the prime minister or an office cleaner? Will she be happy? Will she be healthy? Will she be loved? Will she win honours or commit crimes? Will she one day be in a place like this bringing her own baby into the world?

Suppose that the birth is taking place in a hospital in a war zone, with the noise of shelling in the background, a shortage of medical supplies if anything goes wrong, and no safe place to take the baby home to. Or, in a hospital in South Africa serving a community struggling to cope with the ravages of AIDS, to a mother who is HIV positive. Or, in a society where the birth of a girl baby will be greeted with consternation, just because she is not a boy. Circumstances such as these will have a profound effect on the new-born infant and the family into which she is born. And the way we set the original scene makes a lot of assumptions, reflecting what we accept as the norm in our culture and society. The mother will be there, of course, in any cultural context, but for all sorts of reasons, the father may not be. A crowd of other family members may fill the room, or the mother may be alone. The birth may not be taking place in a hospital at all, and this may be by choice or because that alternative is not available. The doctor and the midwife may not be available either, with the skills, resources and technology to deal with any complications that may arise during the labour or the birth. The chances of the happy outcome in our scenario are very different for different countries, and different social groups within each country.

Birth itself is a universal human experience, but the *way* it is experienced will vary hugely according to the social, cultural and economic context in which it takes place. What is true of birth is of course also true for the rest of our lives. How long we are likely to live, for instance, varies enormously depending on where we were born. The World Health Organisation Commission on Social Determinants of Health reported in 2008 on patterns of health inequality, and summarised its findings thus:

> Our children have dramatically different life chances depending on where they were born. In Japan or Sweden they can expect to live for more than 80 years; in Brazil, 72 years; India, 63 years; and in one of several African countries, fewer than 50 years. And within countries, the differences in life chances are dramatic and are seen worldwide. The poorest of the poor have high levels of illness and premature mortality. But poor health is not confined to those worst off. In countries at all levels of income, health and illness follow a social gradient: the lower the socioeconomic position, the worse the health. (CSDH, 2008: 1 [introduction])

In fact, the statistics from this report that made the news headlines in Britain were not those comparing different countries, but those from two different districts of Glasgow, close geographically but worlds apart in terms of wealth. Life expectancy in a poor inner-city district was 54, while in an affluent suburb it was 82 (CSDH, 2008: 32). While one can debate whether some of the factors in adult behaviour which contribute to this huge difference (for example poor diet, alcohol abuse and drug abuse) should be seen as lifestyle choices or socially determined factors, children have no choice about the circumstances into which they are born. Education, for instance, has a key role to play in children's life chances – not just their own education, but that of their mothers – and this is something that most children and parents have no choice about. The WHO report quotes evidence from several studies which show a strong relationship between the educational attainment of mothers and the survival, health and educational attainment of their children. It also reports that in 2008 there were an estimated 75 million children across the world of primary school age not in school.

It is these wider social factors that we want to consider in this chapter.

A Sociological Perspective

'It takes a village to raise a child' is an African proverb (popularised by Hillary Clinton in the title of a book [Clinton, 1996]) which expresses the significance of the wider society in the course of individual development. Opinions vary about the degree to which it is a factor – those who take an individualist perspective would agree with Margaret Thatcher's famous dictum that 'there is no such thing as society' (Thatcher, interviewed by Keays, 1987), while another point of view is that the individual is defined by their relationship to others, and to the groups and communities which are formed by these networks of individual relationships.

What is this alternative view of the individual? Broadly, it is a sociological view. We can only touch briefly on a few relevant sociological concepts in this chapter, but sociological perspectives intersect with and relate to many aspects of what we have already discussed in previous chapters. For example, we have already looked at one model for thinking about the individual in relation to others in Chapter 9: family systems theory. In Chapter 8 we pointed out that 'disability' is not simply a matter of individual impairment but about the way that people with impairments are seen and responded to by the rest of society. And taking it further back, when we looked at object relations theory (including attachment theory) we were considering how our development is profoundly influenced by our earliest relationships with those around us. Donald Winnicott (discussed in Chapter 2) famously said, 'there is no such thing as a baby', meaning that it makes no sense to think of a baby in isolation; he can only function and be understood in relation to his mother as part of the mother–baby dyad (Winnicott, 1975 [1958]: 99). The sociologist Norbert Elias makes a similar point when he states that:

> The concept 'individual' refers to interdependent people in the singular, and the concept 'society' to interdependent people in the plural. (Elias, 1978: 125)

The infant is socialised first by the mother or primary caregiver, then by the rest of the family – and then by the wider community of extended family, neighbours, friends and social institutions with which he comes into contact. And as he – or she – grows up, he will increasingly play his part in shaping the lives of others in a process of mutual influence and exchange.

Although there is a sense in which Margaret Thatcher was right to point out the danger of talking about society as if it were a concrete, objective entity (she went on to say that there are only individual men and women, and of course this is true), 'society' is a word that describes the way these individuals interact with and relate to each other, and the institutional structures through which those relationships are shaped, and within which they are contained. To fail to take account of the influence of society on the course of human growth and development is a bit like trying to describe learning to swim without mentioning water.

In the rest of this chapter we will look at some of the social mechanisms which shape our understanding of ourselves and the developmental options open to us, and then we will look at some of the aspects of the social world which influence the direction of our development; class, gender and culture.

Bronfenbrenner's Ecological Systems Theory

In Chapter 7 we looked at the lifespan approach to human development, and saw that one of the features of this approach is an understanding of the interaction between the individuals and their environment. The psychologist Urie Bronfenbrenner made an important contribution to this understanding with the development of his ecological systems theory. Working on the frontiers of psychology and sociology, he based his ideas on the work of the sociologist Kurt Lewin, and was also influenced by Piaget. Lewin, writing in 1935, had begun to explore the way that personality and environment react together to influence an individuals behaviour. Bronfenbrenner pointed out that subsequently more attention had been paid by academic theorists and researchers to the individual, psychological perspective than to the environmental, social one (Bronfenbrenner, 1979: 16). This led him to develop his own model of the ecological environment, which he described as 'a set of nested structures, each inside the other, like a set of Russian dolls' (Bronfenbrenner, 1979: 3). You will see the obvious similarity with the notion of 'system levels' we discussed in Chapter 9.

The four structures/levels/settings he identified are:

1. microsystem – the immediate setting in which the individual finds themselves, for example home, school, work
2. mesosystem – the network of relationships between the different interacting microsystems which make up the individual's world
3. exosystem – those settings where the person is not present, but which nevertheless affect them, for example the effect on young children of factors relating to their parents' employment, or the effect of a planning decision taken by the local council on the street where you live
4. macrosystem – the wider cultural context in which the smaller systems are contained, and through which ideology and values are transmitted.

This model offers a way of understanding how individuals relate to the environment in which they find themselves, and how cultural norms and values are transmitted to individuals and played out in relationships. The interconnections and transitions between the different levels of the ecological system are as important as what happens within each level, and movement between them often involves a change of *role* for the individual – a concept to which we will return later. Incidentally, if you are a social work student, you will recognise Thompson's well-known PCS (personal, cultural and structural) model of anti-oppressive practice as a multi-level systemic model of this kind (Thompson, 2006: 26).

Social Construction

What is 'reality'? What determines our perceptions? The idea of 'social construction' offers a perspective on this. This term was first used by Berger and Luckmann (1967) and has become an influential way of looking at the social world. It maintains that most of what we think of as reality is not a matter of objective facts 'out there' waiting to be discovered or perceived, but that it is constructed out of the interactions between individuals and groups in society, and mediated through ideology and culture. Language plays an important part in this process.

> Our sense of who we are depends on what meaning others make of us and how they convey that meaning back to us. This is an essential premise that underpins all of social constructionist thinking: the sense of who one is, the self, the I, are all constructed in the interaction between the individual and others. (Campbell, 2000: 16)

The social model of disability discussed in Chapter 8 is a good example of how social construction operates. The reality of a disabled person's experience is constructed by her interactions with the world around her. For someone who uses a wheelchair, the inability to walk is a physical, personal fact, real in any social context, but the degree to which this is experienced as a disability is dependent on the degree to which the society in which she lives makes it possible, or impossible, for her to interact with it. She will literally be excluded from buildings where there is no provision for wheelchair access, and she will also feel excluded in more subtle ways by a culture which does not reflect positive images of people like herself. If she never sees media images of wheelchair users taking part in mainstream activities along-side non-wheelchair users on an equal basis, and if those around her relate to her in a way that assumes she is unable to do things for herself, she will have a further obstacle to overcome as well as the weakness in her legs – her socially constructed lack of belief in her ability to play a full part in society.

Language is an important part of this process because it is a major medium of social interaction. Language which has negative, patronising or stereotyping connotations is one of the ways in which disability is socially constructed, hence the importance attached to the language used in areas such as disability or ethnicity. So for example we now talk about 'people with disabilities' and not 'the handicapped'. However, the difficulty is that there is also a constant interaction between language and the people who use it. Finding the 'right' word does not make the prejudices and assumptions behind the original 'wrong' word go away, and in time these negative connotations attach themselves to the new words too. 'Handicapped' replaced the even more negative term 'cripple', and was seen as acceptable in its day. So long as the experience of these excluded groups is described in the language of the mainstream world, and the voices of those groups themselves are not heard in the words chosen to speak about them, language will continue to have a tendency to reinforce social exclusion and restrict the developmental pathways available. To some extent language shapes what is possible and what is not.

Social Roles

One of the ways in which social construction operates is through social roles – the cluster of expectations which become attached to a particular position, status or job. In order to make sense of new information about the diverse world in which we find ourselves, we need some kind of map – so we look for a category or a label to tell us what to expect of new people we encounter, or to tell us how to act in new situations. Social roles help us to do this. For example, when we meet someone for the first time one of the first questions we are likely to ask is 'what do you do?' because the answer to that question will tell us a lot more than what their job is. We are trying to find out about their social status, what we have in common with them, and whether we want to get to know them better. Asking about their job role is a short cut to doing this, because we think we know the kind of person who is likely to be a teacher, a policeman or a demolition worker. (Of course, like all short cuts, this can sometimes lead us badly astray!)

The word 'role' comes from the world of the theatre and acting. As Shakespeare says in the well-known passage from *As You Like It* (2008 [1599]:

> All the world's a stage
>
> And all the men and women merely players:
>
> They have their exits and their entrances;
>
> And one man in his time plays many parts … (Act II, Scene vii: 138)

Shakespeare goes on to describe the 'seven ages of man' – a sixteenth-century version of the stages of human development. We see one man passing through and being transformed by a series of roles, from the 'infant mewling and puking in the nurse's arms', and the schoolboy, growing up to become in turn lover, soldier and magistrate, before reaching old age and finally declining into 'second childishness'.

Roles are not just descriptive – they are prescriptive. Shakespeare's description above charts an orderly progression through the life cycle, in which the lover's role belongs only to youth, and it isn't possible to be both a lover and an old man. As we noted in Chapter 7, progress through life is not always as neat as this, but the 'social clock' which tells us what society thinks we ought to be doing at a certain age influences and constrains us. Social roles carry a heavy weight of expectation.

A famous psychology experiment by Zimbardo and colleagues (Haney et al., 1973) showed how powerful the influence of role expectations can be in determining how we act. Two groups of American university students were invited to take the roles of prisoners and guards in a simulated prison situation for a maximum of two weeks. The volunteers were all considered to be mature and well-adjusted. The guards' brief was simply to maintain order in the prison situation. In spite of the fact that there were no pre-existing differences or divisions within the group, within the first few days there was an extreme polarisation between the two groups assigned to the different roles, with the prisoners rebellious, violent and distressed, and the guards behaving towards the prisoners in a brutal and intimidating fashion. This extreme reaction was a surprise to the team conducting the experiment, which had to be concluded early because it was becoming dangerous.

This is a dramatic example of the influence of role expectations on behaviour, showing how frighteningly quickly we can 'grow into' the roles which are assigned to us. You can probably think of everyday examples from your own experience, such as a colleague at work being promoted to a managerial role, resulting in a change in your relationship with them. Some of the roles we play in the course of our lives become a significant and permanent part of our identity, such as parental or professional roles. Others are adopted only briefly, like becoming a member of the audience at the theatre. Some roles may or may not become permanent. For example, we become a patient when we visit our doctor, but if we become chronically ill, the role of patient will become a more central part of our identity. Some roles we choose (like applying for a particular job, or choosing to go to the theatre and become a member of the audience), while others are thrust upon us (like getting ill and becoming a patient). But the distinction between chosen roles and involuntary roles may not always be clear. All kinds of factors, both to do with our individual circumstances and with wider social forces, may limit the choices available to us as we progress through life, or steer our development in a particular direction. Think, for example, about the many steps in the process by which our baby might end up in the very different roles of prime minister or office cleaner, and the choices which might or might not be open to him – or her – along the way.

ACTIVITY 10.1

1. Thinking of yourself at this moment in your life, what roles do you play? Examples might be parent, partner, carer, manager, student, clown, listener, organiser – which are the most important ones? Which ones are you most comfortable with? And which do you find difficult? Are there any roles from which you feel excluded because of your background or other factors? We are not always aware of the different roles we play, but if you have recently experienced a change of role, for example, if you have just become a student, or a new parent, it may be easier to start by thinking about this new role, and then of the other roles you play in your life (we often speak of 'wearing many hats').
2. You are probably reading this book because you have chosen a particular professional role involving caring for others. Have you always played this role in your life? And if so, has it been a chosen role or one you have felt you had to play?

COMMENTS ON ACTIVITY 10.1 ⌋⌋⌋

You will probably have concluded that some roles feel more natural to you, while others sit less comfortably, and you may have considered the reasons for these differences. It may be that some roles are ones you feel you have chosen, while others have been forced on you. Sometimes we are uncomfortable because we feel that we are being asked to reverse roles – for instance, when a teacher signs up for an evening class, and becomes a student, with someone else in the teacher role, or when someone who is used to looking after others – such as a parent, carer, nurse or doctor – themselves needs to be looked after because of illness or incapacity. Often the discomfort comes from the fact that a more powerful role is being exchanged for a less powerful one. We may also be uncomfortable in a new role because we do not know what is expected of us, or are not confident that we can meet expectations. As we described above, social roles are all about what is expected of us by others – 'society' – in specific situations. You may remember that Erikson characterised the adolescent life crisis as identity versus role confusion (see p. 110), and the challenge of the transition to adult life presents us with many new roles all at once. If we are able to meet this challenge and make the right choices, playing these new roles successfully will contribute to our developing a sense of identity.

Stereotyping and Labelling Theory

Stereotyping is what happens when expectations about roles become too rigid, and leads us to lose sight of the fact that roles are played by individual human beings. So we will have a set of assumptions about a particular group of people – what they will be like, how they will act – which will colour our real-life experiences of them. Gender stereotyping is one example; racial stereotyping is another.

Labelling theory describes how those who are stereotyped may respond to the expectations by becoming what they are expected to become, and how, once a label is applied, it becomes very difficult to see beyond it. It was first proposed by Howard Becker (1963) in his work on deviance, and has also been applied to other areas such as mental illness and educational attainment. Rosenthal and Jacobson (1968) demonstrated the effects of teachers' expectations on their students' performance by selecting a group of students at random and telling their teachers that the students showed potential for developing their intelligence. IQ tests then showed that these students had progressed more rapidly than their peers. You may yourself have experienced the effects of being 'labelled' either positively or negatively in the past, perhaps by a teacher, or by some other powerful figure in your life, and be able to reflect on the effect this has had on you. Perhaps you were told you were good at sport, or that you could not sing, or that you were very caring?

ACTIVITY 10.2

Jamie is just about to start a new school, having moved house with his mother after his parents' divorce. His new teacher meets his old teacher at a training day before the beginning of term, and they get talking about Jamie. His old teacher says that she found him very difficult and is glad that he has moved; he was disruptive in class and she doesn't think he is very bright. What effect is this likely to have on Jamie's subsequent progress in his new school?

COMMENTS ON ACTIVITY 10.2

It is likely that Jamie's behaviour in his old school was affected by the family's stress around the break-up of his parents' marriage, and he seems to have given his teacher a hard time. Now he has an opportunity to make a new start, so it is unfortunate that this informal encounter between his teachers took place when it did. Professional written reports would be more likely to confine themselves to factual information and to avoid general judgemental statements. Hopefully his new teacher will have read this book! He will have to work hard to set aside what he has heard and the sinking feeling that will go with the news of a potentially disruptive newcomer to his class, and to approach Jamie's arrival with an open mind. If he accepts the two 'labels' that his colleague has given Jamie – 'disruptive' and 'not very bright' – his behaviour is likely to communicate these expectations to Jamie, and this will have a negative effect on Jamie's ability to put the past behind him and reach his full potential.

When outsiders look at a particular group and make stereotyped assumptions about it, this in turn affects the self-perceptions of those who belong to that group, and what they are able to achieve. Stereotyping is an important aspect of the social model of disability, and it also powerfully affects people with mental health problems. The assumptions that are shared by outsiders and insiders are reflected in the way that society is organised, and the way in which its social institutions function. If you were a woman living in Britain in the nineteenth century, for example, you would have been unlikely to consider yourself capable of achieving a university degree because universities were not open to women. And they were not open to women because of the assumptions of the time about a woman's role, which was exclusively concerned with marriage, homemaking and raising children, and was seen as a subordinate one to the role of the man who was active in the world outside the home. And if you were a working-class woman it would not only be your gender that would have placed a university education beyond your reach, but your class position as well.

While belonging to a particular group within society can make us the object of stereotyping and negative perceptions, it is also a highly significant aspect of our sense of identity. We 'identify with' other members of the same group, and the sense of belonging and solidarity which this gives can empower us and influence the development of our attitudes and opinions. We are members of a group from the first day of our lives, and that family group is held within a system of other groups, as we saw from Bronfenbrenner's model.

There is a difference between those groups where there is actual interaction between group members (clubs, etc.) and those where there is not. The sociological terms for these are *primary* and *secondary* groups (Sprott, 1958: 15). In Bronfenbrenner's terms, primary groups are part of an individual's microsystem and secondary groups belong to the exosystem or the macrosystem. We have more choices about the primary groups we join (church, university class, football team), but the secondary groups we belong to (community, ethnic group, gender) are often those that are more visible to others.

We define ourselves, not only by the groups we belong to, but by those we don't belong to. The psychological defence mechanisms of splitting and projection, which we described in Chapter 2, operate powerfully in group situations and lead people to locate all the good in the group which they belong to, and all the bad in the 'other' group. Divisions and rivalries between different groups in society such as neighbourhoods, gangs, football teams and ethnic and religious groups are common everywhere in the world.

As we have seen, an individual will be part of many different groups, large and small, within society. The groups we belong to are a part of the identity which we recognise for ourselves, and also of the identity which others ascribe to us. Thus our membership of them will affect us in complex ways. These may be positive, adding to our sense of self and belonging, but there may also be a negative effect which undermines our confidence and limits our opportunities. We have considered in previous chapters the effect of the immediate family group on the course of our development, and in the first part of this chapter we have thought about how the development of our identity is also influenced by the wider social systems in our immediate environment: the groups we engage with and the roles we choose, or are assigned. In Bronfenbrenner's terms, we have been focusing on the microsystem and the mesosystem. We will now turn our attention to the exosystem and the macrosystem: those broader aspects of society with which we don't engage directly, and whose influence on us may be less immediately apparent. We will consider, very briefly and broadly, three of the most significant lines along which society divides: gender, class and ethnicity.

Divisions in Society

Gender

In Chapter 5 we explored the processes by which we learn gender roles as we grow up, and we acknowledged that these roles are, at least in large part, socially constructed.

The social construction of gender in Britain, Europe and the USA has changed hugely in the last few generations. Women now take their place alongside men as equal players in the public sphere rather than being confined to the domestic world, although there are still factors which work against them, such as the so-called 'glass ceiling', the process whereby women are often prevented from reaching the top ranks of organisations by prejudices, assumptions and restrictive practices which, like glass, are not readily apparent to the outside observer, but nevertheless create an impenetrable barrier. And women's pay continues to be lower on average than that of men, in spite of equal pay laws (Joshi and Paci, 1998). When it comes to parenthood, in spite of the fact that it is now the cultural norm for both parents to be involved in caring for their children, in practice it is still usually women who carry the majority of the domestic and childcare responsibility, and whose careers and earning potential suffer as a result. This is borne out by research on the gender pay gap showing that it increases as women get older (Dex et al., 2008).

Class

Social class is another factor which can strongly influence the course of individual development, both because of the part it plays in defining identity and because of the extent to which it creates or restricts life choices. Some have declared class to be dead (for example, Paluski and Waters [1996] in *The Death of Class*). Others take a different view; for example, Westergaard (1995) maintains that class inequalities hardened in the late twentieth century, with the richest increasing their share of wealth and income at the expense of the poorest in society. To understand this debate it is important to distinguish between social inequality and a class system. Those who argue that class is no longer relevant do not deny the existence of social inequality, or of hierarchies of power and influence, but would argue that the differentiation is between individuals, and not organised along class lines, and that class no longer creates a barrier to the progress a talented person can make. Income, of course, is not the only factor which defines social class, although it is important, and it is linked with other factors such as education, power and prestige. The definitions of social class that are commonly used for research purposes are organised around the work people do, whether they are professionally qualified and how much responsibility they carry, and broadly speaking, the higher the social class, the higher the income.

This raises the issue of social mobility: how easy it is for an individual to move from one class to another in the course of his or her lifetime. Is equality of opportunity in modern society a reality or merely a slogan? Social mobility has been much studied and debated by sociologists in the last half century, beginning with John Goldthorpe's work in the 1960s (Goldthorpe et al., 1969). More recent research in Britain suggests that an individual's chances of moving from one social class to another have actually declined (Blanden et al., 2004). A press report on these findings summed them up thus:

Britain is 'seizing up' and social mobility is declining. ... Today's middle classes, many of them the sons and daughters of people who climbed the social ladder in the 60s, are consolidating their hold on high status and highly paid jobs and blocking the ascent of children from lower class backgrounds. (Walker, 2002)

Putting these findings in an international context, a further study (Blanden et al., 2005) compared social mobility in eight Western countries and found that it was lowest in Britain, with the USA not far behind, though it was only in Britain that it had actually declined.

So in terms of opportunity, class remains an important factor in today's society. And it is still an important aspect of our identity. An analysis of interviews conducted with a cross-section of Manchester residents in 1997–9 concluded that people wanted to see themselves as 'ordinary' individuals rather than identifying strongly with a particular class, but that the context of social class was still important: 'Class does not determine identity, but it is not irrelevant either. It is a resource, a device, with which to construct identity' (Savage et al., 2001: 888). Class may be a changing phenomenon, but it continues to be a factor that influences our course through life, and helps to determine who we become.

Race and ethnicity

The concept of race is now generally accepted to be a social construct with no scientific basis – the human race is a single species – though its use survives in the term 'racism'. Ethnicity and nationality, however, are important aspects of identity, and of course they can be combined in many different ways. An ethnic African Caribbean person, for example, may be British or American by birth and nationality, and for each individual the relative importance and meaning which they attach to their ethnicity and their nationality will be different, for all sorts of complex reasons to do with family history and relationships and past and current social and cultural experience. Writing from the perspective of social anthropology, Thomas Hylland Eriksen defines ethnicity as concerned with 'aspects of relationships between groups which consider themselves, and are regarded by others, as being culturally distinctive' (2002: 4) though he acknowledges that in everyday usage it has become associated with minority issues in particular. His definition, because it is based on social construction – the way that the identities of self and others are perceived – allows for the possibility of flexibility and change over time. This seems essential in today's rapidly moving and often contradictory world, where globalisation brings us together one minute and drives us apart the next.

Belonging to an ethnic minority group in a society can also have a profound effect on life chances through the forces of stereotyping and social exclusion, as we will see in Activity 10.3 below. British official statistics show that members of ethnic minority groups are significantly more likely to be living in poverty than members of the white population (DWP, 2006).

Poverty, inequality, power and social exclusion

In considering these divisions in society, poverty and inequality emerge as significant factors. These are huge and complex social issues which we can only touch on here. What do we mean by poverty? Definitions of poverty can be absolute or relative; that is, it can be defined in terms of basic human needs like food and shelter, or in relation to what is generally seen in society as an acceptable standard of living. But in fact there is always a social context; even what is considered adequate food and shelter will vary from one time and place to another. For example, in the UK and elsewhere in the first half of the twentieth century having no indoor toilet was quite common, whereas now it would be regarded as unacceptable. Relative definitions of poverty, however, place it firmly in the context of inequality and social exclusion. It means not having the resources and choices that are generally taken for granted, for example, access to the internet or the money for family holidays or school trips. The definition of poverty itself can be a political issue, as is the question of how governments should deal with it. The welfare state in the UK, which was part of the post-war reconstruction and supported consensually by all governments until the 80s, has increasingly come under attack from the neo-liberal right, who believe that it is a factor contributing to poverty rather than a means of addressing it.

Inequality is increasing worldwide. Figures from the Organisation for Economic Co-operation and Development show that it is at its highest level for half a century (OECD, 2015). And a powerful argument can be made that poverty is an issue that has an effect on the development and life chances not just of those who are poor, but of those across the whole of society. In their book *The Spirit Level* Richard Wilkinson and Kate Pickett (2010) present evidence that inequality in a society affects the well-being of all its members. They found that health and social problems were more prevalent across the whole range of income in countries where inequality was greater.

Another recurring theme has been that of power and influence – who has it, where it comes from, how it is exercised in society and what it means to be without it. In our birth scenario we looked at the chances of the baby ending up as prime minister or an office cleaner (see Activity 1.2) and we thought in terms of nature and nurture. In this chapter we have been focusing on aspects of nurture which are beyond the immediate control of parents, and belong to the wider social context. For example, if our baby is the child of the Smiths, a long-term unemployed father and an office-cleaner mother, they will be unable to afford private education for their child, and are unlikely to be in a position to move to the catchment area of a 'good' school, or to provide the extras like music lessons, sports clubs and trips abroad that can supplement a basic education. Statistics show that the overwhelming majority of those going to university are from middle-class backgrounds, and that this is particularly true of the elite universities whose degrees are the passport to careers which command high salaries and a high degree of social influence (Reay et al., 2005). Life is rather like a Monopoly game in which the rules have been changed so that some players start with thousands and others start with almost nothing. Depending on your social class, your ethnic background, your gender and where you were born, there are huge variations in the options that are available to you, which will be affected by how you are seen, and 'labelled' by those around you. Racism, sexism and other assumptions based on stereotypes are powerful forces of social exclusion.

ACTIVITY 10.3

Josh is an 18-year-old who likes to go drinking with his friends. When they have had a bit to drink, they sometimes shout and swear and damage property. How is this behaviour likely to affect his chances in life if he is:

- a white university student?
- unemployed and black?

COMMENTS ON ACTIVITY 10.3

If you concluded that a group of drunken unemployed black youths would be much more likely to attract the attention of the police than a group of drunken white university students, you would be right. And the evidence also shows that if Josh is arrested, he is more likely to be charged and convicted if he is black, thereby acquiring a criminal record which will damage his future prospects of employment. A study of data from 1999 to 2000 by Phillips and Bowling showed that African Caribbean people were significantly more likely to be arrested than white people, and if arrested, were more likely to be given a custodial sentence (Phillips and Bowling, 2002). There are different ways of interpreting the significance of these figures, but Phillips and Bowling conclude that there is evidence that racism is a factor. This kind of institutional racism was defined in the MacPherson Report into the police handling of the murder of the black teenage student Stephen Lawrence in London as:

> the collective failure of an organisation to provide an appropriate and professional service to people because of their colour, culture or ethnic origin. It can be seen or detected in processes, attitudes and behaviour which amount to discrimination through unwitting prejudice, ignorance, thoughtlessness and racist stereotyping which disadvantage minority ethnic people. (MacPherson, 1999)

The authors of this book are both white, so we do not have personal experience of institutional racism, but we have been struck by the fact that for black colleagues of a similar age to us, being stopped by the police is a fact of life. It is something that has never happened to either of us.

Culture and History

The example above shows how the rowdy activities of unemployed black youths are more likely to attract police attention than those of white university students, so they will feature in media crime reports, affecting public perception of risk. The media and popular culture play a key role in the social construction of reality. News reporting gives us a window on the wider world in which we live, in local, national and international dimensions. Marshall McLuhan (1962) used the term 'global village' to describe the way that electronic media have transformed modern society to bring events beyond our own communities alive for us through the use of a combination of words, visual images and different points of view which have a far greater immediacy and intimacy than the written word alone. And, however true that was in 1962, the advent of the internet has brought us into even closer contact with what is happening worldwide on a minute-by-minute basis and the development of social media has given us a whole range of new ways to engage with this, and perhaps to become part of the story ourselves.

But if the media open a window on the world, it is often hard to keep in mind the limitations of the window's frame. There is much that we don't see because it isn't regarded as interesting or important by those who select the news, and news values are determined ultimately by the market – what will sell because people want to read about it or watch it. So there is a reciprocal relationship between those who produce and those who consume the news, and popular culture becomes a kind of mirror. We talk about 'image' – which is a mirror word, and our image is part of our identity formation, reflected back from what we identify with in the wider cultural context. A major preoccupation of popular culture is lifestyle and fashion. It becomes particularly important in adolescence, when we are looking outside the immediate family for role models. It is often expressed through how we look – our haircuts, the clothes we wear, the music we listen to. The history of adolescence in Britain is inextricably linked with the history of popular culture, emerging in the 1950s with teddy boys, beatniks, mods and rockers in an unbroken but constantly changing line of fashions and groupings – to name any currently in vogue would be to risk with certainty their being out of date by the time this book is published.

It is not just in adolescence that image is important to us. Our identity is deeply entwined with popular culture all our lives – where we choose to live, which newspapers we read, where we go on holiday. Advertising of course has its part to play here; it constructs a narrative in which we want to place ourselves. The advertising industry has come a long way from the early days of simple exhortations to buy in bold capitals to become a sophisticated way of speaking to our aspirations and our conscious and unconscious desires for status, and of associating ourselves with particular groups by how we spend our money. And much thought is given to the location of advertising – to careful targeting of the message.

These patterns of cultural identifications and lifestyle preferences were described by the French sociologist Bourdieu (1984) as the 'habitus'. It is a useful concept which represents another way of thinking about social stratification which takes into account differences and distinctions which are more complex and elusive than those relating to occupation and social roles.

Our sense of identity is also bound up with history – both our own individual and family history, as we saw in Chapters 7 and 9, and the wider currents of national and international affairs and social and political change. And the interaction between culture and history is a powerful one. As an example of this, consider the way in which the history of the Second World War has been kept alive in Britain, although most of those who experienced it as adults are now dead. Watching *The Great Escape* on Christmas day was for years as much part of the traditional British Christmas as turkey and tinsel. This kind of reworking of the past owes more to myth than to history. The narrative is one in which heroes are larger than life and good and bad are clearly delineated, with no room for moral ambiguity – a bit like the myth of the American West, as portrayed in countless films. It is the way in which the present tries to make a relationship with the past, and so construct a coherent narrative of identity. Often, there are competing narratives which contribute to this process. The Vietnam war, for example, has inspired a wide range of film interpretations over time, from the heroic, patriotic treatment of *The Green Berets* to the horrific and crazy fantasy world depicted in *Apocalypse Now*.

As well as the stories we are told, we have our own personal experience of history, which becomes a part of our identity. For example, the generation who can remember wartime and post-war rationing and shortages have a different attitude to consumption and waste from those generations who have grown up later, and those gay men who grew up when homosexual activities were still illegal are likely to find it much more difficult to be open about their sexuality than younger men. These differences in historical experience can make it difficult for different generations to understand each other, and living in a rapidly changing, post-modern society increases the difficulty of dialogue between the generations. It also affects the status of older people, as we will discuss in the next chapter. In cultures where the process of change is slower, the life experience of the older generation is a valuable resource to be drawn on, while in societies like our own, their knowledge and experience is more likely to be dismissed as outdated and irrelevant.

The so-called life course perspective (Hunt, 2005) takes account of the fact that, as we have seen throughout this book, all kinds of distinctions which seemed clearer in the past are becoming more uncertain and shifting. This applies particularly to age and life stages, but also to social status, family, community and value systems. It emphasises the social construction of human experience, as opposed to the biological processes of growth, development and ageing. The term 'life course' is seen as one that '... does not assume a stable social system, but one that is constantly changing' (Hunt, 2005: 21). The experience of adolescence or old age, for example, will be very different for different generations. This is a perspective with a long history; the Greek philosopher Heraclitus said that 'everything flows' and 'you cannot step twice into the same river' (Plato, 1998). The following activity gives you an opportunity to consider how social change can affect the experience of individuals.

ACTIVITY 10.4

Sally is an 18-year-old who has been going out with her boyfriend for six months when she discovers that she is pregnant. Think about the differences in her experience if this happened in 1955, 1969, 1985 or 2015. What choices would she have? What effect will this have on the rest of her life, her boyfriend's and her baby's? How will she be seen by her family, friends and neighbours? And what might her experience be in 2025?

COMMENTS ON ACTIVITY 10.4

You will probably have identified many differences. In terms of choices, in Britain, abortion was not legal until 1967. Before 1970, when the age of majority was lowered from 21 to 18, Sally would not have been legally adult. In 1955 Sally's choices would have been marriage (with her parents' consent), illegal abortion, leaving home to have her baby in secret in an institution and having it adopted, or social disgrace. Her family might also have taken the option of passing the child off as her mother's – a not uncommon solution to the dilemma for that generation. By 1969 abortion would have been a legal option, though one which would have been more readily available if she had the money to pay for it privately than if she had to rely on the NHS. And it was just beginning to be socially acceptable to bring up a child alone, or to live with a partner outside marriage, though this still varied hugely between individual families and communities. The stigma attached to unmarried motherhood continued to decrease, and by 1985 terminating the pregnancy, being a single parent, living with a partner and marriage would all have been seen as possible options in this situation. Today marriage would be much less likely to be chosen as an option; in 2013 only just over half of births occurred within marriage or civil partnership as opposed to just under 80 per cent in 1986 and over 90 per cent in 1963 (ONS, 2014b). There will still be consequences for the young parent – such as the interruption of education and career plans or the foreclosure of adolescent identity formation which we discussed in Chapter 6 – but an unplanned pregnancy is unlikely to lead to the kind of social exclusion that was common in the past. Yet the experiences of the past can still be a factor in the present; the Sallys of previous generations are the mothers and grandmothers of today's young parents, and are supporting them, or not, in their decisions.

In speculating about how attitudes and choices might change in the future, we might expect the trend towards greater choice and less stigma to continue, and perhaps for advances in medical science to play a part in it. But other factors may work against this. Objections and challenges to legal abortion are regularly raised, and, particularly in the USA, this has led to changes of the law to reverse previous steps towards liberalisation. And the world we live in today is full of political and economic uncertainty which seems likely to continue; young people who have been unable to get educational qualifications and are less flexible because of parental responsibilities will be particularly disadvantaged by limited job opportunities and decreasing social support.

In this chapter we have tried to put individual human development into a social context. We have only been able to outline a few sociological concepts, and to touch on some complex ideas which make links with history, philosophy, politics and cultural studies. We hope that you will be inspired to read more. The developing human being is always a figure in a landscape, and to study the one without some awareness of the other is to miss an essential dimension.

Chapter Summary

- In this chapter we have been looking at the wider social factors which influence human growth and development.
- We explored what it means to look at the individual from a sociological point of view, and saw the importance of the framework of social structures and relationships within which we live.
- We looked at Bronfenbrenner's ecological systems theory as a way of understanding how social systems influence the individual.
- We considered the idea of social construction; that the way we see ourselves and our lives is strongly influenced by the individuals and institutions around us and our interactions with them.
- We discussed social roles, stereotyping and labelling theory and explored how they influence the development of our identity and our life chances. We looked at the ways in which the groups we belong to contribute to defining our identity.
- We considered some of the lines along which society is divided, and looked at aspects of gender, class and ethnicity which relate to our identity formation and our life chances, in the context of power and social exclusion.
- We explored the significance of the cultural and historical setting in which an individual grows up, and how this can affect intergenerational relationships.

Further Reading

Berger, P. and Luckmann, T. (1967) *The Social Construction of Reality*. London: Penguin.
Haralambos, M. and Holborn, M. (2013) *Sociology Themes and Perspectives*, 3rd edn. London: HarperCollins.
This basic textbook gives a good general overview of sociology, including the topics we have touched on in this chapter.

11 COMING TO A CONCLUSION

DIMENSIONS OF OLD AGE

- Physical changes — 210
- Cognitive changes — 211
- Tasks and challenges — 212
- Old age and society — 215
- Cultural differences — 219

We concluded the previous chapter by observing that the developing human being is always a figure in a landscape, and certainly it would make no sense to describe the experience of 'growing old' without reference to the landscape in which it occurs, for the role and status of old people varies enormously from one society to another, as does the age at which a person is seen as being 'old'. It is, as Pat Thane points out in her survey of social histories of old age and ageing,

> … The stage of life which encompasses greater variety than any other. It can be seen, in any time period, as including people aged from their fifties to past one hundred; those possessing the greatest wealth and power, and the least; those at a peak of physical fitness and the most frail. In consequence of this variety many different histories and fragments of histories of old age are emerging. (2003: 93)

There are, of course, biological factors in ageing which are general to all societies, and there are also existential issues which seem likely to come to the fore in later life in whatever culture. (As we grow older, we are increasingly faced with the fact of our mortality, just as in early childhood we must come to terms with finding ourselves in a strange new world.) But how society manages these biological changes and existential questions – and the ways that are open to us to deal with them as individuals – varies from one social context to another.

In the UK and other industrialised countries, for instance, retirement from work is an important transition point in the process of growing old. But retirement is not a universal human phenomenon. It is an entirely culture-specific event.

> Until the development of public welfare schemes in the second half of the twentieth century, older people seldom had a chance to retire from work, and in most cases that meant being dependent on family support or individual savings … It was only in the second half of the twentieth century that retirement became such a general phenomenon but nowadays it is a key part of the modern life-course and widely taken for granted. (Künemund and Kolland, 2007: 167)

These authors go on to observe that retirement is an example of what Kohli (1986) called 'the institutionalisation of the life course' – 'the evolution of a chronologically standardised sequence of life phases and life events … arranged according to the labour force needs of the economies of industrialised societies' (Künemund and Kolland, 2007: 167). Another example would be the phenomenon of adolescence which, we suggested in Chapter 6, has become seen as a distinct stage of life partly as a result of the advent of compulsory secondary schooling. And as with adolescence, retirement is not only a modern phenomenon but a phenomenon of industrialised countries. In much of the non-industrialised world there is no compulsory retirement and no state pension, just as there is no compulsory secondary schooling. Even within the industrialised world, there are large variations in the age at which retirement occurs, as Künemund and Kolland discuss (2007: 168). In the UK legislation governing compulsory retirement and payment of state pensions has changed considerably over the last decade. The default retirement age of 65 was abolished in 2011, and from 2010 the age at which the state pension is paid is gradually being increased. This means that people will be able to carry on working for longer, and will need to do so in order to provide an income for themselves. This is good news for those who enjoy their jobs and want to continue working beyond the age of 65, but not for others, maybe working in physically demanding or stressful jobs, who will struggle to maintain their effectiveness into their late 60s.

In broad terms, it makes sense to distinguish between the earlier and later stages of old age, and such a distinction is not new. In the England of several hundred years ago a distinction was drawn between 'green' old age and later old age (Thane, 2003: 98). Peter Laslett's book *A Fresh Map of Life* (1989) popularised the term 'third age' to describe the post-retirement phase of life, when people have the time and energy for learning and contributing to society, as distinct from the 'fourth age' of failing health and intellectual powers which may come towards the end of life. The term developed in the context of the University of the Third Age, a voluntary educational organisation in which older people share their skills and knowledge with each other.

We will now look in more detail at the changes involved in old age, but you might first like to consider the case example in the following activity. We should add that this example is not meant to represent a *typical* old person, but is intended to give an instance of the kind of issue that can arise for professionals working with old people.

ACTIVITY 11.1

Consider the following case study and ask yourself what position you might take, if you were a professional involved in the situation it describes – the general practitioner, a social worker, a community nurse, a member of the hospital staff …

Miss Kipling (aged 82) lives in a house on her own with a large number of cats. She is very isolated, venturing out once a week for her shopping, but avoiding almost all social interaction with her neighbours. A niece, Mrs Yeats, who lives some way away, visits her a few times a year. Miss Kipling is physically quite frail. On several occasions, neighbours have had to call out the police on hearing her shouting, to find her lying on the floor where she has fallen and been unable to get up. On these occasions the police and neighbours have always been concerned about the dirty conditions of the house, and its poor state of repair.

A recent fall resulted in a broken leg, and Miss Kipling is now in hospital. Mrs Yeats has been summoned as next of kin, and there is a strong feeling on the part of Mrs Yeats and the neighbours that Miss Kipling should not return to her own house, but should be found a place in a residential care home. The arguments given for this are that:

- Miss Kipling is clearly not safe, and could fall and lie for a long time without being found. It would be irresponsible to allow her to return, since it could easily result in a fatal accident.
- Miss Kipling's house and her cats are now a health hazard.
- Miss Kipling would be happier with company and others around her.
- It is not fair on Mrs Yeats or the neighbours to have the worry of her – and it is difficult for Mrs Yeats to keep coming at short notice.
- Miss Kipling is increasingly confused. According to Mrs Yeats, Miss Kipling showed no sign of recognition at first when she visited her in hospital, and seemed unsure as to where she was. It is suggested that she is growing 'senile'.

Having considered this case, and decided what stance you would take on it, ask yourself whether your thoughts would have been different if Miss Kipling had been aged 32.

COMMENTS ON ACTIVITY 11.1

You may have noticed that Miss Kipling's physical safety was assumed by the neighbours not to be Miss Kipling's own responsibility, but a responsibility that is being placed, unreasonably, on themselves. It seems to us that with younger people, we are more ready to accept that the taking of risks is a matter of personal choice.

It may have struck you too that, if Miss Kipling had been a young woman, the health hazard allegedly posed by her cats and living conditions might be a matter that neighbours would deal with by complaining to Miss Kipling herself, or by taking the matter up legally. They would be less likely to suggest that Miss Kipling is not fit to have a home of her own.

Finally, it may have struck you that the neighbours are very quick to assume that Miss Kipling is growing 'senile'. A younger person might well be confused in similar circumstances – a fall resulting in a broken bone, a long wait to be discovered, and then a hospital admission – but this would not, anything like so readily, be considered to be evidence of permanent mental decline.

Physical Changes

Physical decrepitude and poor health is not inevitable in old age. As Christina Victor observes, describing British data:

> The popular stereotype of old age as a time of universal and inevitable chronic health [problems] and impaired activity, is somewhat inaccurate. While the reported prevalence of a longstanding limiting illness increases with age, it is not a universal characteristic of later life. A little over half of men and women aged 85 and over living in the community report that they do not have a long-standing disability or illness that impairs their activity levels. (Victor, 2005: 141)

Victor goes on to note that the extent of chronic health problems in old age is linked to other factors such as class, gender, ethnicity and former occupation, which further undermines the notion that steep physical decline and ageing are necessarily linked. Citing Meltzer et al. (2000), she notes that there is a 20 per cent difference in the prevalence of disability between people who had manual or non-manual occupations. This finding is in line with the statistics from the World Health Organisation Commission on the Social Determinants of Health previously quoted in Chapter 10 (p. 190).

It is important to avoid having an expectation of inevitable poor health in old age, because such an expectation can be a self-fulfilling prophecy. If we receive negative messages when we are old such as 'Well, what do you expect at your age?' this is likely to actually discourage us from remaining active, resulting in a deterioration in our fitness. Nevertheless, some physical decline is of course a normal part of ageing, and the incidence of disability, physical and sensory, becomes higher as later life progresses, so that managing it becomes for many part of the challenge of this stage of life:

> I did think about moving because I wanted a walk-in shower, because I cannot get ... I mean before my husband died I couldn't get in the bath ... well, I could but I couldn't get out. But when he died I thought I couldn't have a bath, so my son fixed a shower up over the bath. But now since I have done this, and my back again, I can't get in to have a bath. And I have put in to the council to see whether I could have a walk-in shower, but oh no that was it, I am not disabled enough. ... ('Nancy', quoted by Peace et al., 2006: 143)

As the quotation also illustrates, another challenge of old age is the loss of others. Here the speaker is focusing on the loss of practical support when her husband was no longer there to help her get out of the bath, and this is an important aspect of bereavement for many older people with disabilities, adding to the difficulties they face with the activities of daily living. But, of course, the emotional impact of bereavement is also huge, as we will discuss in the next chapter, and the longer people live the more often they are likely to have to face this as they outlive their partner, siblings, relatives and friends.

Cognitive Changes

Some old people suffer severe short-term memory loss as a result of specific forms of dementia such as Alzheimer's disease or vascular dementia. It is sometimes assumed that such problems are a natural consequence of ageing, but in fact as Ian Stuart-Hamilton observes, '... dementia is not totally a condition that occurs in old age – it is simply far more *probable* that if a person develops dementia it will be in late rather than early adulthood.' (2012: 219, his emphasis). He also notes, drawing on research carried out for the Alzheimer's Society, that severe dementia becomes more common as people live to an older age, rising from around 6 per cent in 65–69-year-olds to around 23 per cent for those aged 95 or older (2012: 220). However, psychological research confirms what most old people report: there is generally some deterioration in memory in old age, even in the majority of old people who do not suffer from any form of dementia. The problem seems to lie particularly in the area of retrieving items from memory. That is to say, the memories are still there, but are harder to locate, so that old people are more prone than younger people to the experience 'I know I know it, but I can't put my finger on it'. This is demonstrated by the fact that old people fare less well – in comparison to younger people – on tests of recall than they do on tests of recognition (Marcoen et al., 2007: 50).

This difficulty with retrieval may reflect a more general slowing down of some cognitive processes linked to changes in the brain. It is known that there is a loss of brain volume associated with ageing, but it is not clear exactly how this relates to psychological functioning (Stuart-Hamilton, 2012: 83–4) Old people do less well on tests of 'fluid intelligence', which are tests involving finding solutions to problems not previously encountered, as opposed to tests of 'crystallised intelligence' (Cattell, 1971), which involve problems that draw on accumulated knowledge (Marcoen et al., 2007: 51).

One type of intelligence that is traditionally associated with old age is the kind that is known as 'wisdom'. (Our guess is that if you were asked to call to mind an image of a 'wise man' or a 'wise woman', then that image would be of an older person.) Wisdom is a hard quality to define, however, with the result that it doesn't lend itself very readily to psychological tests, with their characteristic multiple-choice questions and puzzles. Nevertheless, some researchers have attempted to do so, by posing problems to subjects involving long-term issues and complex and ambiguous situations open to more than one interpretation. Interestingly, while not all old people did better on these tests, old people were more highly represented than other age groups among those who did do well (Baltes et al., 1992).

While there is a biological basis for some cognitive decline, external pressures also have a major effect on old people's cognitive functioning. Most professionals who work with elderly people will probably have noticed how old people can become dramatically more 'confused' (like 'Miss Kipling' in Activity 11.1) as the result of an admission to residential care or hospital – a form of psychological defence at a time of frightening loss of control over one's own life. This question of loss of control is a topic that we'll return to below.

Tasks and Challenges

Late adulthood – old age – is the last of Erikson's eight stages (see Table 2.2, p. 39) and he assigns to it a sort of summing-up task. You may recall that Erikson's model envisages that to understand a person at any stage of life you need to understand the challenges that they have had to confront at earlier stages, and the extent to which they have successfully or unsuccessfully resolved them. What is different about old age is that if we fail to negotiate *this* stage successfully, there will not be further opportunities later. Hence *integrity versus despair* is what Erikson (1995 [1951]) identified as the 'crisis' of this particular stage. A successful outcome would include: acceptance of one's life for what it has been, freedom from the burden of regret that it had not been different, and acceptance that one's life is one's own responsibility. Erikson referred to this as the achievement of 'ego integration'. An acceptance of one's own small place in the scheme of things could be said to be part of what is commonly referred to as 'wisdom', a quality which, as we noted above, is commonly associated with old age. So perhaps Erikson's 'ego integration' could be seen as the achievement of a kind of wisdom.

This statement from the British politician Lord (Denis) Healey at the age of 83, seems to us to illustrate what might be entailed in achieving 'ego integration':

> Personally, I did not notice much change until I was 75. From that age on, I have found my memory deteriorating and my senses getting less acute. … I can distinguish between different vowels, but all consonant sounds are the same to me. I can fail to see something I am looking at when it is staring me in the face.

There is a saying that when you are old, you either widen or wizen. ... Physically I have wiz-ened; I lost two stones in weight between the ages of 75 and 77. I can no longer run upstairs as I used to do. I find travel very tiring. Psychologically I have widened. I am much more interested in people as human beings and can imagine them at every age from childhood onwards when I see them.

I have lost all interest in power and position and no longer worry about making money. I still enjoy my work, but only what I want to do. ...

I am much more sensitive to colours, shapes and sounds. My eye will automatically compose a clump of flowers or a corner of a landscape into a picture. ... I get greater pleasure out of the sound of different instruments.

I have become exceptionally sensitive to sunlight, which immediately moves me to pleasure. ... I love my wife, my children and my grandchildren more than ever. ... (Healey, 2000: 3)

But Lord Healey had many advantages. He was no doubt comfortably off financially, he clearly had a caring family around him and he could look back on a distinguished career in which he had many interesting experiences, met many interesting people and had ample opportunity to develop and use his talents. Not everyone adjusts so contentedly to the final stage of life. And for those who do not reach the state of 'ego integration', Erikson suggests, there can be despair, a sense that life has not been as it should have been and that it is now too late to change it.

This despair may be expressed as a contempt for people, institutions or the world in general, or as a retreat into a passive, helpless role. Successful ageing depends on the satis-factory resolution of issues raised earlier in life, but it also depends on external factors: the opportunities and encouragement available in a person's environment. And one of the aims of those who work with the elderly must surely be to maximise those opportunities, and to recognise the scale of the task that is involved in growing old.

The challenges of growing old require adaptation not just from old people themselves but from those around them. From a systems perspective (as discussed in Chapter 9), a successful transition into old age requires adjustments from the entire family system. Elderly couples, for instance, may need to renegotiate their relationship, and not just their individual lives, if they are to cope comfortably with the changing roles and more time together that result from retirement. The couple relationship may not always survive this transition, and separa-tion and divorce in later life are becoming more common. Statistics in the UK show that the number of people over 60 getting divorced has increased since the 1990s, although it has fallen for the population as a whole (ONS, 2013). This is partly due to a higher proportion of older people in the general population and increased life expectancy, and also because divorce has become more socially acceptable, and women are less likely to be economically dependent on their husbands, and therefore have more choices open to them. And the wider family too needs to make changes. An ideal adjustment would perhaps be one in which the members of the extended family were sensitive to the possibility that it might be necessary to reduce their demands on ageing family members (for help in looking after grandchildren, for example), and to offer them additional support when necessary, yet without at the same time characterising them as more helpless or incapable than they really are. But how easily the family is able to make this adjustment will depend on family history (vertical stressors) and on the other challenges now facing the family as a whole (horizontal stressors).

The following activity looks at a fictional instance of a family struggling to cope with some of the challenges of old age.

ACTIVITY 11.2

What horizontal and vertical stressors can you identify in the family described in the family described in the following case example? (See p. 176 for a reminder about these terms.)

Mr and Mrs Patel (aged 80 and 75) came to Britain in the 1970s as refugees from Uganda, where Mr Patel ran a chain of grocery shops. When they arrived, they had no money, because their home and property in Uganda had been confiscated during the Idi Amin era. However, they were able to set up a new business (a convenience store), which is now run by their two daughters. Mr and Mrs Patel have no sons.

Mr Patel has always been reliant on his wife to provide for him in the home, and she is no longer really able to do this as she suffers from severe arthritis and is in fact physically much frailer than Mr Patel.

He is suffering from mild dementia as result of arteriosclerotic illness, with the result that he forgets things after even a few minutes and is often muddled about who he is talking to. He sometimes imagines that he is back in Uganda, or even in India where he was born. He constantly imagines that his wife and daughters are plotting against him. He also requires pretty constant supervision from a safety point of view. He has turned a gas fire on without lighting it and has been picked up wandering in the street, not knowing where he is.

Mr and Mrs Patel have never had a very happy marriage. Both of them are rather 'highly strung', volatile people, and Mr Patel in particular can be domineering and 'bullying'. He has always found it difficult to come to terms with what happened in Uganda.

Mrs Patel's daughters say that she is being made ill by the worry and stress of trying to cope with Mr Patel and she is now on anti-depressant medication. Neither of the daughters is willing to have Mr Patel living with them, though they do try to provide support to Mrs Patel. Both daughters insist that for his own safety and his wife's health, Mr Patel should now be in residential care.

However, confused as he is, Mr Patel is still able to state, absolutely adamantly, and tearfully, that he does not want to have to leave his home. His one supporter in the family is his son-in-law Sanjay (now separated from Mr and Mrs Patel's older daughter), who says that Mr Patel has worked hard all his life to provide for the family, has had to cope with the constant nagging and attempts to undermine him of his wife and daughters – and does not deserve to be pushed out.

COMMENTS ON ACTIVITY 11.2

Among the possible vertical stressors you may have noticed are marital problems and a possible tendency for the family to polarise into male and female camps. The family's expulsion from Uganda, associated with a loss of property and prestige, may well also be relevant here, and may make the suggestion of giving up his family home especially distressing for Mr Patel.

Among the horizontal stressors you might have included: Mrs Patel's arthritis, Mr Patel's arteriosclerotic illness, the current marital difficulties between the daughter and son-in-law, and perhaps the demands of running the family business.

Professionals providing services to older people (as might be the case, for example, if you were a care coordinator, a GP or a community nurse) really need to have some understanding of these family dynamics if they are to accurately assess the needs of old people and their carers in any given situation.

Old Age and Society

As we have already observed, old age is, like adolescence (or adulthood, or childhood) as much a social construction as a biological fact. So what old age means to an individual will depend not only on factors like physical health and level of cognitive functioning, but on the messages she receives from those around her and from society at large. Even physical health and cognitive functioning are themselves directly affected by external circumstances and messages received from others (see the discussion in the previous chapter on 'labelling'). It is important not to assume that, because old people happen to behave in a certain way under certain circumstances, that behaviour is in some way inevitable. The debate about 'disengagement', which we'll describe shortly, illustrates this point very well.

Having noted that the way old people perceive themselves will be shaped by the world around them, one must bear in mind that the world is also changing. For instance:

- Demographic changes resulting from a declining birth rate and longer lifespans mean that old people are a larger proportion of the population than in most other periods of history, particularly in the industrialised world, where an estimated 29.9 per cent of the population of Europe will be over 65 by the year 2050 (Peace et al., 2007: 2). This is likely to have huge consequences for the status of older people in society and their relationship with the rest of the population.
- Differences in the average lifespan of men and women also mean that there are more elderly women than men.

- Rapid social and technological change in society generally, as well as longer lifespans, means that the world in which old people find themselves is vastly different from the one in which they grew up. This would not have been true to anything like the same extent in many pre-industrial cultures, where technology and social mores might remain relatively unchanged for generations.

- Social expectations about the participation of older people in the economy change over time (for example, retirement age) as do welfare provisions for old people (pensions, social care).

- The political 'clout' of older people may increase. People over 65 could constitute well over a third of the European electorate by 2050.

Disengagement

The term 'disengagement' was coined in the 1960s by Cumming and Henry (1961) to describe the generally reduced involvement of old people in the outer world. Models of ageing tended at that time to be *medical* models expressed in terms of deteriorating functioning, and the term 'disengagement' was supposed to provide a more positive way of describing – and thinking about – the process of letting go of external involvement that is typical of many older people.

Cumming and Henry suggested that this disengagement from external interests – along with other personality changes such as a preference for simple and familiar situations – does not represent any sort of reduced functioning, but rather a way of preserving energy for other tasks which have become more important. These tasks, in their view, were really of the kind envisaged by Erikson, to do with reflecting on, reviewing and coming to terms with one's life as a whole.

One obvious criticism of disengagement is that not all old people conform to that pattern. We can probably all think of elderly people who are just as engaged with the world around them as they would have been when young. Other critics of the idea, such as Estes et al. (1982), have pointed out that disengagement is often forced upon old people, for example by compulsory retirement or by institutional care. Old people do not necessarily *want* to give up their involvement in the world. The theory of disengagement, according to this view, simply lends legitimacy to a process by which society chooses to marginalise its elderly people and, so to speak, to tidy them away out of sight.

There is no reason, incidentally, why both Cumming and Henry *and* Estes should not be right. Disengagement could indeed be a normal and necessary psychological characteristic of old age, and yet also be exploited as a concept for political ends. You may remember from Chapter 3 that Bowlby's attachment theory may likewise have been taken on board by those wishing for political reasons to get women out of the industrial workforce, but this does not invalidate the theory itself.

Control

In the discussion of learning theory in Chapter 5, we mentioned evidence that ability to control events in the environment is linked directly to indicators of stress. We also discussed the idea that passivity and helplessness can itself be a form of behaviour that is learned in situations where we have no control. Many old people do experience a sense of reduced control over their environment for a variety of reasons, and this can lead to anxiety, depression and low self-esteem, and even to reduced physical health.

One study (Langer, 1983) demonstrated the importance of a feeling of control in a residential home setting. A group of residents was addressed by the home administrator with speeches that placed an emphasis on their responsibility for their own lives. The speaker encouraged them to make decisions and gave them actual decisions to make as well as asking them to take responsibility for things in the home environment other than themselves. Another group of residents was addressed by the same person with speeches that emphasised the responsibility of the staff of the establishment to provide care for them and meet their needs. Of the latter group, 71 per cent were found to become more debilitated in a period as short as three weeks, while in the former group, 93 per cent showed overall improvement.

The fear of losing control of one's own life is common in old age, but it is not necessarily an inevitable feature of old age. After all, some of the most powerful people have been old people. (For instance, Deng Xiaopeng became the leader of China – containing a quarter of the world's population – in his mid-70s and continued to hold this position into his 80s.) Just as disability is not only a result of impairments but also of society's attitude to people with impairments, so the feeling of losing control is in part a product of society's attitude to old people. Langer's experiment illustrates how a feeling of losing control – even if the feeling is as a result of no more than different *words* – can have a very dramatic effect on general well-being. Old people experience many difficulties which can lead to a feeling of loss of control. They may have limited financial resources, compared to people in work, and limited life choices as a result. Some, though not all, have to deal with physical impairments. All will be aware of at least some loss of their physical power, and be aware that younger people around them are physically more capable (old people may feel more vulnerable to crime, for example). And even if they are mentally and physically in very good shape, old people may have to deal with the *assumption* that this is not the case.

Indeed, in some contexts old people are treated as if they are not adults at all (infantilised) and spoken to as if they were dependent children ('Have we been to the toilet yet, Mrs Jones?'). Sachweh (1998, cited by Westerhof and Tulle, 2007: 246) found in a study of German nursing homes that 'baby talk', the high pitch and exaggerated intonation that is used in talking to small children, was used by staff in over half of the interactions with residents, and that 'we' as opposed to 'you' (as in 'have we been to the toilet?') was used in nearly two thirds of interactions.

Ageism

'Ageism' is a word coined by analogy with 'sexism' and 'racism' to mean the unwarranted application of negative stereotypes to old people. We've just mentioned the example of old people being patronised and infantilised, as if by being old they had ceased to be adult. The assumptions that are made about old people can be like the assumptions that are made by racists or sexists in that they result in judgements being made about old people which are not the same as those that would be made about younger people in the same situation.

We do not wish to portray all old people as necessarily victims of oppression and injustice. Many old people would not see themselves in such a light at all, and, as we have seen, there are positive as well as negative stereotypes of old age, and powerful old people as well as powerless ones. But negative stereotypes do exist and they do have an effect on people. If old people are labelled as 'bad-tempered', 'inflexible', 'senile' or whatever else, then they are likely to live up to the expectations created. Westerhof and Tulle (2007: 249), discussing the evidence for the effects of expectations on performance and self-perceptions, note that there is an extra twist when we impose negative labels on old people, since most of us eventually become old people ourselves. 'It has been argued', they write, 'that as individuals age, the stereotypes they previously held about older people are turned towards themselves'. Ageism rebounds on the ageist! Like all stereotypes, stereotypes of old age are a 'short-cut' to try and make sense of something of which we have no direct experience, or to avoid thinking about it. Old age will always remain unknown territory until we reach it ourselves.

Certainly there *are* numerous negative images of old people. There are far more demeaning terms for old people than there are for other age groups. Think of 'wrinkly', 'fuddy-duddy', 'old dear', 'old fart', 'old crow' or 'old bat'. Indeed, only children seem to be comparable with the elderly in having derogatory terms (like 'brat') which are specific to their age group. A number of unwarranted generalisations are also made about old people's health and mental capacity, though the majority of old people are *not* sick or demented and there is no medical condition that is exclusive to old age. For example, as mentioned earlier, developing dementia tends to be associated with old age and is sometimes talked about as if it was an inevitable part of the ageing process (with terms such as 'going gaga' and 'losing her marbles' being used), though in fact it happens to only a minority of elderly people and can happen, albeit more rarely, to younger people also.

Another common assumption is that old people are no longer sexually active. Given that sexual activity is generally seen as one of the prerogatives of adulthood, this is perhaps an instance of the way that old people are 'infantilised' as a result of ageism. The fact is that old people tend to remain sexually active well into 'old age.' An American survey found for instance that, among the over-70s, 79 per cent of men and 65 per cent of women reported that they were sexually active (Brecher, 1984).

In the political arena, old people are also sometimes negatively characterised as an unsustainable burden on the public purse, a 'burden' (to use a word which some old people seem to use about themselves) because of the cost of pensions, social security benefits, health and social care (see Westerhof and Tulle, 2007: 239). In the UK in recent years, as benefits and other financial support for younger people have been cut, a potential for intergenerational conflict is emerging as the so-called 'baby boomer' generation (those born in the years following the second world war) reach old age and are perceived to have 'had it all' as beneficiaries of the welfare state in the course of their lives – student grants, affordable mortgages and now earlier retirement, and good pensions and associated benefits.

If we contrast the active, positive attitude of famous and successful elderly people – such as Lord Healey quoted earlier – with that of those who seem to have accepted, or felt forced into, a passive, dependent, childlike role, we can perhaps get some sense of the impact of ageism on old people who do not have the same advantages. Social attitudes to old people, however, are not fixed, and this is evidenced by the fact that in different societies, old people are viewed in different ways.

Cultural Differences

Old people are traditionally seen as repositories of wisdom, but Western industrialised society does not place the value on the wisdom of old age that is, or was, given to it in other cultures. David Gutmann (1987), an anthropologist who compared attitudes to ageing in industrialised societies with attitudes in the Middle East and Central America, suggested that old age flourishes in a stable, coherent culture with well-defined traditions. In such a culture, women become more powerful in the extended family as they enter old age. Older men tend to disengage from day-to-day decision making and action, but become custodians for the values of their culture. In less industrialised societies, there is also likely to be more interdependency between generations as land is farmed together, and inherited by the next generation, while 'modern societies in contrast have pursued change and innovation, and moved away from intergenerational dependency' (Gilleard and Higgs, 2000: 43).

The constantly changing circumstances of modern society make these authoritative roles much harder to play because old people are a bit like time travellers. As discussed at the end of the previous chapter, old people at the beginning of the twenty-first century were brought up in a society vastly different from the one in which they now find themselves, with very different values and social mores. Though they will of course have adjusted to new developments over the years, the values they were brought up with were the product of a very different context. In a rapidly changing world, we may seem to have somewhat less to offer as we grow old than would have been the case if we lived in a society which did not change so very quickly, for the lessons we have learnt will quite often come from experiences which are no longer relevant to present-day experience.

This book is intended for those working in or studying for the caring professions, so we will end this chapter with an activity in which we invite you to reflect on how such professionals work with old people. It is worth remembering that our attitudes to older people are really our attitudes to our own future selves.

ACTIVITY 11.3

Erikson described the central task of old age as resolving the 'crisis' of integrity versus despair. Think of old people you've known or worked with, and try to think of instances of people who have managed to achieve some sense of integrity in old age – and others who have not. (The latter might be evident either as a resigned passivity or as a general hostility.) Can you see any common factors among those who manage to achieve integrity, and those who do not?

What role can professionals and others play in helping old people accomplish this task?

COMMENTS ON ACTIVITY 11.3

You have probably been able to think of some examples, though of course many old people will fall somewhere in between the two extremes. Resolving any 'crisis' (in Erikson's sense) is ultimately something that a person can do only for themselves, but it may have occurred to you that the modern welfare system is full of attitudes which can hardly help old people to feel positive about the last stage in their lives. Perhaps you felt that if we treated old people as (a) human beings (rather than merely logistical problems), and (b) adults (rather than quasi-children), this might help. One of the things that seems to be important in achieving integrity is to be able to look back on one's life with a sense of achievement and not too many regrets. But too often care workers dealing with older people, who may be the only social contacts they have, have little time for anything but their present-day care needs and never get to hear about the lives they have led, or the roles and relationships that have made up their past.

Chapter Summary

- In this chapter, we looked at the changes that occur in old age, including physical and cognitive changes. While some common changes may be biological in origin, we should be careful not to assume that they apply equally to all old people. An assumption that all old people have poor health, for instance, would not only be unwarranted by the facts, but could also have the effect of being a self-fulfilling prophecy.

- We then looked at the particular tasks and challenges in old age, using Erikson's idea of old age as a time when our principal task is to come to terms with, or reconcile ourselves to, our lives as a whole. We also looked briefly at the challenges that old age poses not only to individuals but to families.
- We then looked at old age in a social context. We looked at the idea of 'disengagement', relating it to Erikson's model, but also asking the question as to what extent an old person's disengagement from the world is a psychological necessity, and to what extent it is actually imposed by society.
- We also discussed the diminished control over the rest of the world that commonly occurs in old age and its impact on the individual.
- We considered the impact of prejudice against old people: ageism.
- Finally, we briefly considered cultural differences and the consequences of living to old age in a very rapidly changing society.

In the next and final chapter, we will consider dying and death.

Further Reading

Bond, J., Peace, S., Dittman-Kohli, F. and Westerhof, G. (eds) (2007) *Ageing in Society*, 3rd edn. London: Sage.
A particularly comprehensive collection of writings on many different aspects of the psychology and sociology of old age.
Stuart-Hamilton, I. (2012) *The Psychology of Ageing: An Introduction*, 5th edn. London: Jessica Kingsley.

12 THAT GOOD NIGHT

DEATH, DYING AND BEREAVEMENT

- Death and society   223
- Death and others   227
- The individual experience of death   234
- The end   237

We have put this chapter on death after the chapter on old age, so we should start by acknowledging that of course death is not the exclusive property of the old. Though death is the end of life, as birth, with which we started this book, is the beginning, we can die at any age. We may have to cope with the death of others at any age too, although as Sidell (1993: 151) observes, 'death has become increasingly unfamiliar to young people' in modern industrialised society. Most people live to old age and most people die in the relatively segregated environment of the hospital with the result that many people, for much of their lives, have little direct exposure to death. Many adults, for example, have lived through their lives without ever actually seeing a dead person.

It is certainly the case that in the UK, most people who die are old, and most die away from home. Of those who died in England and Wales in 2013, 84 per cent were 65 or older, and 68 per cent had passed their 75th birthday. Out of all deaths (at whatever age) in England and Wales during that year, just 22 per cent took place at home (figures derived from ONS, 2014c).

As with other events which we have discussed, death is both a biological event and a social one. Death occurs when the body ceases to function as a biological entity, but the meanings attached to it, both by the individual concerned and by those around her, are dependent on the complex web of personal and social circumstances in which the death occurs, as well as on the way of dying itself. Indeed, Clive Seale (1998: 34) makes the point that biological death and social death need not necessarily coincide:

The material end of the body is only roughly congruent with the death of the social self. In extreme old age, or in diseases where mind and personality disintegrate, social death may precede biological death. Ghosts, memories and ancestor worship are examples of the opposite: a social presence outlasting the body.

Caroline Currer adds that there is actually quite a widespread fear of social death prematurely preceding actual death: 'There is evidence in certain cemeteries … of mausolea with bell-towers with a connecting wire through into the coffin to enable the allegedly deceased person to ring the bell in the event of waking' (Currer, 2001: 25).

Here we are going to look at death at three 'system levels' (to use a term which we discussed in Chapter 9). We will consider first death in the context of society as a whole, then (under the heading 'Death and others') death at the level of family and community, and finally death as an individual experience. But, as ever, dividing the subject up in this way is in the end an artificial device. All the topics under these headings could in fact be discussed with reference to each of these three levels. Religious belief, for example, can have a very direct impact on the individual experience of death, but religions are something developed and maintained at the level of society as a whole. Death itself is not just an event, but an existential question, one with which we struggle at every level and in every culture and social context.

Death and Society

Dying takes place in a social context and how we deal with it is shaped in part by the society in which we live. Among the many areas of difference between different cultures and different epochs, are the following:

- The extent to which death and dying or dead people are a matter of everyday experience.
- Beliefs as to the existence and nature of an afterlife. (All the world's major religions include some conception of an afterlife, but its components vary greatly. Consider, for instance, the ideas of heaven, hell, purgatory and limbo in Roman Catholic theology, the widespread belief in ghosts, or the Buddhist idea of a soul being reborn again and again on earth in different human and animal forms. In modern secular industrial cultures, many people do not believe in any kind of continuation of personal existence after death, but many still do.)
- Cultural beliefs regarding acceptable and appropriate expressions of grieving. (In some cultures an extravagant display of grief is encouraged, while in others restraint and containment of emotion are admired and seen as decorous.)
- Funeral rituals and the treatment of human remains. (The different practices that exist for the latter include cremation, burial, mummification and even 'sky burial', as practised in some Native American cultures, where human remains are placed on a platform to be consumed by birds.)

- The extent to which dying people are made aware of the fact that they are dying. (This is now the norm in Britain, for example, but is less common in Japan, apparently, where relatives may be informed about the fact that the dying person has a terminal illness, although this news is kept from the dying person herself, according to Seale, 1998: 111.)

We shall not attempt here to cover all these topics. What we will do now is look at two themes in current thinking about death.

The denial of death

According to one view of contemporary attitudes to death, we live in a society that denies death – and death is now a taboo subject in the way that sex once was.

According to this view, death is hidden in hospitals or institutions and we no longer know how to talk about death, or to help the bereaved, or to mourn properly for the dead.

A leading exponent of this perspective has been Ariès (1976), a French historian, who argued that in medieval times people were much more at home with death, which was visible all around them. He argues that in modern times medical science has led to the idea of controlling illness and controlling nature. Instead of believing in an afterlife, we comfort ourselves with the illusion that *this* life can be prolonged indefinitely by defeating death. So death becomes something to be battled against, as illustrated by the media cliché: 'X finally lost her courageous battle against cancer.' In modern times, it is argued, the doctor fighting disease has replaced the priest fighting for the salvation of the soul. Writing about how society copes with anxiety about death at an organisational level, Anton Obholzer also draws a parallel between the role of doctors and that of priests in the past:

> I believe that many of the organisational difficulties that occur in hospital settings arise from a neglect of the unconscious psychological impact of death or near-death on patients, their relatives and staff. Hospitals are as much an embodiment of a social system that exists to defend society and its citizens against anxieties about death as are churches; from a psychic point of view, doctors occupy a similar niche to priests. (Obholzer, 1994: 171)

He also suggests that 'our health service might more accurately be called a "keep-death-at-bay" service'.

But, as doctors ultimately cannot abolish death, death has become segregated, hidden away. People avoid others who are bereaved or dying. Dying people are isolated as a result and deprived of support which they might otherwise receive.

This idea can be extended also to our treatment of old people. In the previous chapter, we discussed the concept of 'disengagement' (Cumming and Henry, 1961), and the debate as to whether disengagement in old age reflected a psychological need on the part of old people, or merely a need on the part of the rest of society to justify the marginalisation of old people. Kearl (1989) takes the latter argument further by suggesting that the purpose of disengagement is to remove from society those who are likely to die, so that the rest of us need not be confronted by the fact of death. There are two views on disengagement, and it is also possible to argue, as does Kalish (1985) that disengagement is a useful psychological preparation for dying, on the part of the individuals concerned. Kalish argues that disengagement is one reason that old people tend to find it easier to accept their own imminent death than do younger people: they have already begun the work of letting go.

This difference of view on disengagement reflects a difference of view on the whole 'denial of death' thesis. Many commentators would dispute whether the 'denial of death' in modern times is really as extreme as Ariès (1976) argued, or whether there has been such a fundamental change as he suggests in comparison with previous periods of history. Some degree of denial of death is surely inevitable to allow us to get on with our own lives, and probably always has been at any stage in history. Indeed, Seale (1998: 211) argues that our whole social and cultural life – the stories we tell ourselves about the nature and meaning of life – can be seen as defences against death:

> Social institutions which are reflected in the minutiae of conversational exchanges, are based on a successful but continuing active defence against disorder and decay, the root cause of which is the temporal nature of bodily existence.

Some psychoanalytic thinkers would argue that we battle not only against the fact of death but against our own 'death instinct', an innate drive towards annihilation:

> Besides the instinct to preserve living substance and to join it into ever larger units, there must exist another, contrary instinct to dissolve those units and to bring them back to their primeval, organic state. (Freud, 1961 [1930]: 118–19)

Melanie Klein in particular draws heavily on this concept and speaks of two instincts at war with each other. The ego is 'faced at the very beginning of its development with the task of mobilizing libido [life-instinct] against its death instinct' (Klein, 1975 [1933]: 250). If we look at it this way, death becomes, not just an external enemy to be kept at bay, but a drive within ourselves to be managed, as we have to manage our other drives and longings.

'Revivalist death'

In the latter part of the twentieth century something of a reaction occurred to the medicalised model of death so that we now also have what Walter (1994) calls a 'revivalist' model, in which death is seen as an important stage of life to be, if not celebrated, at any rate experienced to the full. There would seem to be a close parallel here with changes of attitude to childbirth where, during the same period, there was a similar reaction against an excessively medicalised approach and towards a more personal one in which the individual concerned, rather than the professionals, is placed at centre stage. This changing view of death was reflected in the growth of the hospice movement.

In the 'revivalist' view the dying person herself is seen as choosing her own way of dealing with her own death, rather than subjecting herself to the control of doctors, and death is seen as a psychological process, rather than just a medical event – something to be worked through, rather than blotted out. Dying, in this model, is a process of coming to terms with the end of one's life, the final culmination of the process of integration which we discussed in the previous chapter. We should note, however, that the logical consequence of giving more choice to dying people about the manner of their dying means that some might actually *choose* the more medicalised model. The 'revivalist' approach is itself only one way of looking at things.

Society's attitudes to dying seem to fluctuate between several different perspectives. The practical implications of this for those working with dying or bereaved people would seem to be that it is important to have thought through one's own attitude on these matters, but it is also important to be aware that there is no one 'right' approach, and that others may have very different views about the social context of death.

You may like to use the following activity to consider your own thoughts on this:

ACTIVITY 12.1

Should dying people always be informed that they are dying? And if not, under what circumstances should they not be informed, and who should take the decision not to inform them?

Suppose you are a doctor and your patient Mr J is dying of cancer. His daughter, who is his only surviving relative, has been told that the disease is terminal and untreatable. She insists that Mr J should not be informed of this, saying that it would be cruel and would cause him quite unnecessary distress.

On the other hand, Nurse B who is also caring for Mr J, feels very strongly that Mr J should be informed. She says that, if it was her, she would certainly wish to be informed and would be very angry if she was not informed, and was therefore deprived of the opportunity to say her goodbyes to life. Nurse B does not consider that her daughter, or anyone else, would have any right to deny her this information. To deny Mr J this information, she says, would be to deny him his right to be treated as an adult.

What would you do? Would it make any difference to you if Mr J came from another country, and if his daughter informed you that in their country dying people were not normally told the nature of their illness?

COMMENTS ON ACTIVITY 12.1

The question of whether or not to tell dying people that they are dying is not one that has a final definitive answer, because in different societies at different times, there have been different views about what is appropriate, and because different individuals have different needs and different ways of handling things. Your decision might be simpler if you were able to establish what Mr J's own views on this matter had been in the past, or if you were able to find out what was the norm in the country from which he had come. (If Mr J came from a country where dying people were not normally told, it is likely that he himself would be aware that this was the norm, and would not himself expect to be told.) But, ultimately, you would need to try to find some way of exploring what Mr J's own wishes were. Does he really want frankness, or does he cope better by keeping his distance from the facts? If you could take time to encourage him to talk about his situation in an open-ended way you might well pick up some clues to help you decide how best to deal with the issue.

Death and Others

In Chapter 6, we discussed the psychological stages that are involved in transitions, moving from initial shock and incredulity through depression and self-doubt to eventual letting go. In Chapter 9, when we looked at the family life-cycle from a systems perspective, we presented the idea that every transition that occurs is not just a challenge for the individual but also for every other member of their family network. This is true of marriage or the formation of a couple relationship, the birth of a child, puberty, retirement, and the onset of old age. All of these events require, to a greater or lesser extent, that a whole group of people have to find a way of letting go of an old and familiar order of things, and (whether they wish it or not) to re-establish themselves as best they can in new and unfamiliar territory. And this is also true of death.

There are a few very isolated people whose death has little significant impact on anyone else, and some unloved people whose death is not mourned. There are also some people who are loved but whose death is felt to be a welcome release by all concerned. But in most cases, for family and friends, the corollary of a death is bereavement and grief. In the case of deaths which are predictable, that grief does not just follow on from the death, but includes the 'anticipatory grieving' which can also be experienced by the dying person herself.

Grief is a reaction to what can be a massive disruption in one's social world. When we grieve for someone we loved, we are also grieving for the part of ourselves that we invested in that person. More generally, Seale (1998: 211) suggests that grief:

> is in fact an extreme version of an everyday experience of 'grief' which is routinely worked upon
> in order to turn the psyche away from awareness of mortality and towards continuation in life.

In other words, Seale is suggesting that it is in the nature of life that we are constantly struggling with the possibility of death and loss. An actual bereavement simply brings our worst fears to the fore. We might use the analogy of a flood occurring in a landscape, such as the Cambridgeshire Fens, which is normally kept dry by constant pumping. The flood itself is an exceptional event but the possibility of it has never been far away.

The nature and extent of grief, and the ability of the bereaved person to come to terms with their loss, will depend of course on a whole range of factors, including the personal history of the grieving person, the nature of the relationship and the manner and timing of the death (see the discussion below, on timely and untimely deaths).

Attachment and loss

In thinking about bereavement, it is useful to go back to attachment theory. You may remember that John Bowlby's major works were entitled *Attachment, Separation and Loss* (1997, 1998a, 1998b), and it is of course sadly the case that the risk of loss is the inevitable price to be paid for the many benefits of forming an attachment. Colin Murray Parkes, in his study of bereavement, puts it like this:

> The pain of grief is just as much a part of life as the joy of love; it is, perhaps, the price we pay for love, the cost of commitment. (Murray Parkes and Prigerson, 2010: 6)

Murray Parkes worked closely with Bowlby, coming at the attachment theory from the perspective of studying bereavement, which has been his lifetime's work. Insights from his research and writing have been hugely influential in developing ways of working with those who have been bereaved, for example, through the charity Cruse in the UK. The major aspects of bereavement reactions he identifies are:

1. an alarm reaction of anxiety and restlessness which feels physiologically like fear
2. anger and self-reproaches
3. post-traumatic stress reactions
4. pining and searching for the lost person
5. finding a continuing bond with the lost person
6. excessive, prolonged or distorted grief
7. a sense of dislocation between the world that is and the world that should be
8. a process of realisation, moving towards acceptance of the loss
9. helplessness and hopelessness; depression.

(Murray Parkes and Prigerson 2010: 253)

Clearly, not all of these features will be present in every case. Every bereavement is different, as every individual and their history is different. It is not a stage model, though the earlier features on the list relate more to the initial, traumatic stages of loss, moving through the process of grieving to an adjustment, or not, as the case may be. You will notice echoes here of the model of transition described in Chapter 6 and summarised below, and of Kübler-Ross's description of how people react to the news of their own impending death, which we will discuss shortly. There are also, of course, links with the stages that young children go through in separation from their parents, which we described in Chapter 3 (p. 48).

According to attachment theory, people who as children had a secure attachment with their carers are able to internalise the security that came from that relationship (the 'secure base') and this will not only help them to form satisfactory adult relationships, but will help them to withstand the pain of loss in the future. Sable (1989) undertook a study of widows who had lost their husbands in the previous one to three years. She found that women whose early attachment histories had been relatively secure coped better with their bereavement than women with histories of insecure attachment, experiencing less distress and less depression.

Writers on attachment theory suggest that we can identify characteristic grieving patterns for the avoidant attachment style and for the ambivalent attachment style. Avoidant individuals, who try to be self-reliant, often display delayed grief reactions.

> The typical attempts to be emotionally self-reliant and wary about forming intimate relationships means that the loss of someone close … triggers the usual defence mechanisms of emotional shut-down and distancing. In the short term at least the person suffering the loss may not cry or appear to be unduly upset. Those who fail to grieve remain vulnerable to future losses. Seemingly exaggerated grief reactions to a loss experience … can sometimes be accounted for when it is realised that the individual never really acknowledged or adjusted to the earlier loss of a significant attachment relationship. (Howe, 1995: 136)

On the other hand, *ambivalently* attached people seem to be more than averagely vulnerable to 'severe protracted grief' (Murray Parkes, 2006: 79). Howe suggests that people who have internalised anxious/ambivalent patterns tend to experience relationships in which there are 'equal measures of desperate clinging and resentful anger'. As a result, if the other partner dies, the bereaved person may experience 'guilt and self-blame (because anger and hostility had been a constant feature of the relationship) and acute pain (because there is now no one emotionally available)' (Howe, 1995: 136). In cases of *chronic grief*:

> individuals cannot seem to escape their feelings of despair and depression. It may be that their relationship with the lost other was characterised by deep feelings of ambivalence. … The simmering resentment that may have lurked beneath the surface of the relationship is still difficult to acknowledge and so the true range of feelings associated with the grief fail to receive proper expression and therefore remain unresolved. (Howe, 1995: 137)

Narratives of grief

From a sociological perspective, Seale (1998), as we have already mentioned, sees society constructing various discourses or narratives with which somehow to contain or combat the fact of death. This takes place at the system level of society as a whole. He suggests that 'in late modern society medicine and psychiatry offer one of a number of discourses that people have constructed as a sheltering canopy against the adverse consequences of embodiment' (Seale, 1998: 211). ('Embodiment' refers to the fact that we are physical, biological entities, the consequence of which is that we cannot avoid dying.) But he also describes ways in which individuals construct their own narratives to deal with their own feelings in particular circumstances. Each of us when bereaved has to deal with the fact that a loved or familiar person is no longer available, and to make some sense perhaps of the suffering and indignities that person may have suffered at the end. Often there is also guilt or regret about not having been there, or not having done more to help, or of having left things unsaid or unresolved until it was too late.

Coming to terms with a death may in part be seen as the construction of a narrative which in some ways lays these distressing feelings to rest. You may remember from the discussion of transitions in Chapter 6 that the latter stages in the model we presented there were:

- *Letting go* of the old order of things as they existed prior to the new event (which have been clung onto up to now in defiance of the new circumstances).
- *Testing and exploring* the new circumstances, trying out new identities and starting to form new attachments.
- *Searching* for meaning by looking back at the past from the new viewpoint of it being in the past, reappraising it and trying to make sense of it.
- *Integration*, when the transition process is complete and we feel 'at home' in the new reality. New behaviours and new ideas about ourselves have become part of our sense of our own identity.

Many people who have lost someone to whom they have been very close would say that they never 'feel at home' in the new reality. But constructing a narrative, an explanation to oneself about what has occurred and how it makes sense in the scheme of things, would seem to be part of the work involved in being able to find a way into a future life of which the lost other person will no longer be a part, except in memory.

A very simple and rudimentary example of this process, perhaps, is the common custom in Britain in recent times of laying flowers at the site of fatal accidents and murders. The people who do this do not necessarily know the deceased person personally, but it is as if they are seeking to cover up the image of tragedy and violence associated with a particular spot, with a new image of beauty and growth.

Loss and restoration

Another account of the process of coping with bereavement is offered by a 'dual process model' (Stroebe and Schut, 2001). They suggest that two types of coping are involved in bereavement, which they call respectively 'loss-orientated' and 'restoration-orientated' (see Figure 12.1).

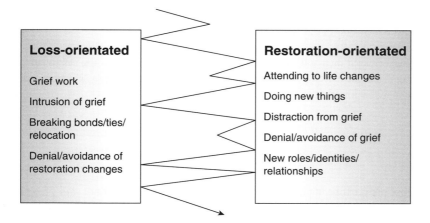

FIGURE 12.1 Bereavement: oscillation between loss-orientated and restoration-orientated tasks (from Stroebe and Schut, 2001: 396)

While other models imply a chronological sequence in which coming to terms with loss is followed by 'building a new life', these authors suggest that a 'waxing and waning' occurs and that grieving people typically oscillate between grieving and getting on with life. They point out that in reality bereaved people do take 'time off from grieving' (1999: 212), and have to address themselves to the practical adjustments that are required in the wake of a death (financial arrangements, for example) and indeed to other matters.

Loss-orientation and restoration-orientation, then, are two separate kinds of work, or stressor, that bereaved people face, though the former is what is conventionally seen as grieving, and has received much more attention. It is interesting that the model illustrated above envisages that to get on with *either* of these tasks requires a degree of denial. Loss work involves turning away from the here and now, while restoration work involves turning away from the pain of grief. This is a reminder that while denial (or 'defensive exclusion') can be harmful and counter-productive in its effects, it is also a very necessary psychological mechanism.

Stroebe and Schut (2001) suggest that there are individual differences as to how people allocate their time between loss-orientation and restoration-orientation, and that this can lead to conflict between survivors. For example, following the death of a child, the parent who focuses more on restoration may be seen by the other parent as not grieving, whereas in fact this person simply has a different *way* of grieving. These authors also suggest that typically men are more restoration-orientated when bereaved, while women are more loss-orientated. Female grief has, it seems, historically been studied more than male grief, in contrast to other areas that we have discussed in this book where generalisations have sometimes been made from a mainly male perspective.

Stroebe and Schut postulate that oscillation between loss-orientation and restoration-orientation is likely to be psychologically more healthy than going to either extreme.

In one study (Schut et al., 1997), they tried out different kinds of grief counselling with widows and widowers. What they found was that:

> 'Teaching' bereaved men and women to cope in the way that the opposite sex usually adopts (teaching men to be more emotion-orientated and women to be more problem-orientated) was associated with a lowering of distress. (Stroebe and Schut, 1999: 219)

ACTIVITY 12.2

Tony lost his partner Michael a year ago to cancer, when Michael was 75 and Tony was 63. They'd been together as a couple for more than thirty years, but it had always been a fractious and difficult relationship, and Tony had always felt a little in Michael's shadow. Friends invariably referred to them as 'Michael and Tony', for instance, never the other way round. Michael, twelve years older than Tony, was the more flamboyant and confident one of the two. They'd moved across the country twice in order to accommodate Michael's career, with Tony simply falling in with this and finding the best job he could in the new area. And somehow they'd both fallen into the pattern whereby Tony took responsibility for almost all of the domestic tasks. Tony was resentful about this, but had never quite found a way of effectively challenging it. Sometimes he'd wondered why he stayed with Michael at all, and wondered if this reflected his own lack of self-confidence as much as anything else, his own doubt that he would ever again find someone as attractive and interesting as Michael to be his partner. There were times too, when he sensed that Michael was disappointed in him, and would have wished for a partner more like himself.

In the latter stages of Michael's long and drawn-out illness, Tony had been faced with a choice of either taking retirement earlier than he'd intended in order to care for Michael, or allowing Michael to enter a nursing home. It had been a hard decision. He was in a job that he enjoyed and one where, after a somewhat unsatisfying career, he felt that he'd finally found his niche. But he felt he couldn't just abandon Michael in his time of need, and he gave up his job and became a full-time carer to Michael, who, after a busy, active and productive life, hated the sick role, and proved an awkward and cantankerous person to care for. Tony resented the fact that his sacrifice hadn't been appreciated, coming as it did after a lifetime of playing second fiddle, but he contained his resentment. It didn't seem fair to be angry with Michael when he was so obviously desperate and frail.

After Michael's death, Tony grieved horribly. His former employers would have been willing to take him back, but even a year on, he simply doesn't emotionally feel up to it. Friends who were supportive are starting to fall away, and some of them have spoken quite sharply to Tony about the need to move on, but he simply doesn't know how to do this. Tony visits his GP who refers him to a counsellor attached to the GP practice. What kinds of things might the counsellor need to think about, and what reasons might there be for Tony's difficulties in coming to terms with his loss?

COMMENTS ON ACTIVITY 12.2

Part of Tony's difficulty is likely to be bound up with the complicated and ambiguous feelings he always had about the relationship. He is aware that he sometimes wanted to get out of the relationship completely. He knows he only cared for Michael at the end with reservations and with resentful feelings that, yet again, he was having to take second place to Michael's needs. He perhaps worries now that he didn't love Michael enough, or that he did love him very much, but never really let Michael know it. If 'grief is the price we pay for love' perhaps Tony feels that he must carry on grieving to prove that he really did love Michael, or to recompense Michael for not having loved him enough. Or perhaps part of the grief that is pushing up to the surface is a long-standing grief for the happier relationship that he'd always hoped for, and which it may now be too late to find. This may well be connected not just with his experience of relationships as an adult, but with his childhood attachment relationships; the history of his relationship with Michael suggests the pattern of ambivalent attachment which we have described above and in Chapter 3.

The popular expression 'moving on' in relation to grief can be unhelpful, with its implications that the loss can somehow be left behind and forgotten. Mourning actually involves a slow process of integrating the experience of loss into one's life, and finding a new direction, not just carrying on as before after a brief interruption. Tony is not unusual in still grieving at the end of the first year, though, as we have seen, there are good reasons why the process may be a more difficult one for him than it is for some. It will be hard for his friends to witness this, as they will feel powerless to help, and being too close to Tony's grief may remind them of the fragility of their own lives and happiness.

Counselling would offer Tony a space to express his grief without having to worry about it being too much for the counsellor to hear. It would also give him the opportunity to talk about his relationship with Michael and to try to make sense of his conflicting feelings through constructing a narrative. A counsellor could give him permission to express the anger he feels with Michael, which he has struggled to repress for so long, rather than turning it in on himself in the form of the depression from which he now seems to be suffering. Hopefully this will free him to also access the loving feelings he had for Michael, and his sense of loss will become more about the loss of his partner rather than of the part of himself that had confidence, competence and a sense of agency. At present these feelings of low self-worth are preventing him from feeling he can return to work, and, in terms of Stroebe and Schut's model, keeping him firmly on the loss-oriented side of the balance, and preventing him from engaging with the restoration-oriented tasks of building a future for himself. The counsellor might also explore whether there are prototypes of Tony's ambivalent relationship with Michael in his early attachment history, (maybe a parent who made it difficult for him to express what he needed, or whose own needs often took priority, or who often seemed disappointed in him). If this is the case, working with Tony on these earlier relationships may help him to disentangle his feelings about the more distant past from his response to his present loss.

The Individual Experience of Death

People deal with the fact of their own death in many different ways, depending on their own personality, their culture and the actual circumstances.

Predictable and unpredictable deaths

Some deaths – such as death from cancer – can be predicted in advance by the person who is dying as well as by others. It is these deaths which the 'revivalist' model and the hospice movement, which we discussed above, really address. In such circumstances, the dying person herself can go through a grieving process for her *own* life.

Kübler-Ross (1970), a psychiatrist who worked extensively with terminally ill patients, has described the reaction to news of a terminal illness as going through several stages:

1. *denial* ('It can't be true. You've made a mistake …')
2. *anger* (against doctors, family members, God … someone must be blamed)
3. *bargaining* (the dying person attempts to make some kind of deal with fate: 'just let me live to see my grandchild …')
4. *depression* (feelings of guilt, fear of dying, loosening of relationships, preoccupation with a sense of loss)
5. *acceptance* (letting go, the end of the struggle …).

You can see that although not divided up in exactly the same way, this is very much the same pattern as the transition model which we discussed in Chapter 6.

Not all deaths can be predicted in this way. There are many sudden, unexpected deaths. Many deaths occur as a result of heart disease, often involving a sudden heart attack. Fatal accidents are another kind of sudden unexpected death. There are also chosen deaths, not only suicides, but also less clear-cut choices to let go of life, perhaps after a long illness. (There is currently an ethical debate in the UK about whether the law should be changed to legalise assisted dying in some of these circumstances; at present people suffering from terminal and disabling conditions who choose to die must travel to countries like Switzerland, where assisted dying is legal, to obtain medical assistance to die in dignity with the support of family and friends at a time and in a manner of their choosing). And, though 'old age' per se is not a cause of death, many old people die as a result of a series of health problems, so that the actual cause of death is quite hard to define. In such cases there may not be a moment at which the dying person is clearly faced with the knowledge that she is dying. There are cases too where others may know that a person is dying but the knowledge has been withheld from the dying person herself. As we noted earlier, this may be more common in some cultures than others.

Timely and untimely deaths

The way we experience death – and the way also that it is experienced by others – may be greatly influenced by whether we see the death as timely or premature. In the case of old people, death is often accepted as inevitable and even as 'fair'. In England, when a person dies at quite an old age, it is commonplace for others to remark: 'Well, he had a good innings.' (For readers who do not come from the cricket-playing part of the world, we should explain that the reference is to the game of cricket and a batsman's 'innings' is the time he lasts on the pitch.) We also speak of a 'ripe old age', where the connotations of the word 'ripe' are of fruit or corn that has reached the time where it is ready to be gathered or reaped. Death itself, of course, is traditionally the 'grim reaper'.

And dying does seem, in general terms, to be a rather different experience for the old person than it is for younger people. Young people who learn that they are dying may feel cheated of life, just as their friends and relatives may feel that they have been stolen prematurely from them. One study of attitudes to dying among old people found that older people most often personified death as 'gentle, well-meaning' (Kastenbaum and Alsenburg, 1976). 'Speaking generally, one of the many benefits … of living well into old age', write Young and Cullen (1996: 27), who interviewed dying people and their relatives in the East End of London, 'was that death was easier to accept'. As an 80-year-old interviewee of theirs remarked:

> When I was your age … I'd have been terrified of dying but not now. As you grow older it becomes inevitable. I'm not afraid of dying, no, nor the manner of dying. I just don't think about it. It doesn't trouble me at all. (Young and Cullen, 1996: 25–6)

One reason for this resignation seems to be that in old age, most people will increasingly have experienced the death of friends and loved ones. 'I do my book at Christmas and it's crossing out such a lot', said one old person (quoted in Sidell, 1993).

We do not wish to suggest that this degree of acceptance is characteristic of *all* old people. But, as Sidell puts it (1993: 155), many old people do not seem to follow the famous advice of the poet Dylan Thomas to his father:

> Do not go gentle into that good night,

> Old age should burn and rave at close of day;

> Rage, rage against the dying of the light.

> (Thomas, 1973: 474)

On the contrary, many seem to yield to the 'good night' of death without a fight. The implication of this is that old people tend to reach Kübler-Ross's stage of *acceptance* in relation to their own death more easily than younger people, if 'easily' can ever be an appropriate word when talking about this most fundamental of tasks.

People dying at a younger age seem to spend more time at the earlier of Kübler-Ross's stages (*denial*, *anger*, *bargaining* and *depression*). For the younger people in Young and Cullen's study, 'their general inclination … was to struggle against the onset of death (or the unseemly acceleration of ageing that death implies) with all the vigour they could muster' (1996: 27).

> Whether a fighting spirit makes final death any easier or more difficult we do not know, and even those who are very close to the end can do no more than guess. But during the period which leads up to it, such a spirit certainly does give something to live for. (Young and Cullen, 1996: 36)

But we should be careful not to overgeneralise about younger people, any more than about older ones. Even for those who die before old age, the approach of death may be accepted, even if not welcomed.

'Things are both more trivial than they ever were, and more important than they ever were', said the playwright Denis Potter, dying at 59, in an interview with Melvyn Bragg, 'and the difference between the trivial and the important doesn't seem to matter – but the *nowness* of everything is absolutely wondrous' (Channel 4, 1994 cited by Seale, 1998: 129).

Death and the afterlife

Death, for many people, is not necessarily the end. We would guess that the vast majority of the population of the world still subscribes to belief systems which include the idea of an afterlife. Carl Jung was quite open to the idea of an afterlife and he considered that the idea was a useful one for many people. Acknowledging that some 'feel no craving for immortality, and … shudder at the thought of sitting on a cloud and playing the harp for ten thousand years', he nevertheless thought that:

> for most people it means a great deal to assume that their lives will have an indefinite continuity beyond their present existence. They live more sensibly, feel better and are more at peace. (Jung, 1995 [1961]: 332)

Freud by contrast saw religious beliefs in general in a very negative light:

> The whole thing is so patently infantile, so foreign to reality, that to anyone with a friendly attitude to humanity it is painful to think that the great majority of mortals will never be able to rise above this view of life. (Freud, 1961 [1930]: 261)

Researchers have looked into the question of whether a belief in an afterlife helps us to face death and found, not surprisingly, that a simple 'yes' or 'no' answer is not forthcoming. Kalish and Reynolds (1976) found that people with strong religious convictions showed the least anxiety about death, though people with confused religious beliefs, interestingly, showed *more anxiety* than did atheists. Wink and Scott (2005: 212) found that 'moderately religious individuals feared death more than individuals for whom religion played either a central or a marginal role in life'. They observe that:

> individuals who do not have a definite (either religious or secular) view of mortality as suggested by a moderate or lukewarm religious engagement or a disjunction between religious beliefs and practices are particularly vulnerable to fear of death in late adulthood. (2005: 212)

Whether or not a belief in an afterlife is helpful to the dying is of course a very different question than that of whether an afterlife actually exists, but this is a question that we will not attempt to address.

The End

We began this book with the image of a baby's birth, and so it seems appropriate to conclude it like this:

> *In a bed in a side room on a hospital ward, an elderly woman is drawing close to death. It is some hours since she last spoke and it is not clear whether she is entirely conscious. There are four other people in the room: a son, a daughter, a daughter-in-law and a nurse. They can all see that the end is very near. The son and the daughter are holding their mother's hands. The daughter is murmuring 'Dear mum, dear, dear mum …'*
>
> *And then she stops. 'She's gone', she says, and they all know it is so. There were five people in the room a moment ago, but now there are only four.*

Chapter Summary

- In this chapter we looked at the social context of death, drawing attention to the many cultural differences that exist in relation to death. We have drawn attention in particular to two approaches within secular industrialised society: the medicalised approach (which some suggest represents a 'denial of death') and the 'revivalist' approach which places an emphasis on dying as a part of life to be experienced by the individual concerned.
- We then looked at the impact of death on those around the dying person, discussing the nature of grief and bereavement.
- Finally we looked at the ways that death is experienced by the dying person, looking at different factors and focusing in particular on the differences between deaths that could be predicted in advance and those that could not, and between deaths in old age and deaths at other ages. Finally, we mentioned the impact of different beliefs in the possibility of an afterlife.

Further Reading

Currer, C. (2001) *Responding to Grief: Dying, Bereavement and Social Care.* Basingstoke: Palgrave.
A book aimed specifically at social care workers with dying and bereaved people.
Murray Parkes, C. and Prigerson, H.G. (2010) *Bereavement: Studies of Grief in Adult Life.* London: Penguin.
Seale, C. (1998) *Constructing Death: The Sociology of Dying and Bereavement.* Cambridge: Cambridge University Press.

REFERENCES

A Two Year Old Goes to Hospital 1952, film, Robertson Films, London. Available on DVD from Concord Media, Ipswich.

Ainsworth, M. (1967) *Infancy in Uganda: Infant Care and the Growth of Love*. Baltimore, MD: Johns Hopkins University Press.

Ainsworth, M., Blehar, M., Aters, E. and Wall, S. (1978) *Patterns of Attachment: A Psychological Study of the Strange Situation*. Hillside, NJ: Lawrence Erlbaum.

Anderson, E.S., Dunlea, A. and Kekelis, L. (1993) 'The impact of input: language acquisition in the visually impaired', *First Language* 13: 23–49.

Appleyard, K., Egeland, B., Van Dulmen, M. and Sroufe, A. (2005) 'When more is not better: the role of cumulative risk in child behaviour outcomes', *Journal of Child Psychology and Psychiatry* 46: 235–45.

Ariès, P. (1976) *Western Attitudes Towards Death*. London: Marion Boyars.

Arnett, J.J. (2004) *Emerging Adulthood: The Winding Road from the Late Teens through the Twenties*. New York: Oxford University Press.

Azrin, N.H. (1959) 'Punishment and recovery during fixed ratio performance'. *Journal of the Experimental Analysis of Behavior* 2: 303–5.

Baillargeon, R. (1987) 'Object permanence in 3.5- and 4.5-month-old infants', *Developmental Psychology* 23: 655–64.

Baillargeon, R., Li, J., Gertner, Y. And Wu, D. (2011) 'How do infants reason about physical events?' in U. Goswami (ed.), *The Wiley-Blackwell Handbook of Childhood Cognitive Development*, 2nd edn. Chichester: Wiley-Blackwell, pp. 11–48.

Balbernie, R. (2001) 'Circuits and circumstances: the neurobiological consequences of early relationship experiences and how they shape later behaviour', *Journal of Child Psychotherapy* 27 (3): 237–55.

Baltes, P.B. (1987) 'Theoretical propositions of lifespan developmental psychology', *Developmental Psychology* 23: 611–28.

Baltes, P.B., Smith, J. and Staudinger, U.M. (1992) 'Wisdom and successful ageing', in T.B. Sonderegg (ed.), *Nebraska Symposium on Motivation* 39. Lincoln, NE: University of Nebraska Press, pp. 123–67.

Bandura, A. (1977) *Social Learning Theory*. Englewood Cliffs, NJ: Prentice-Hall.

Barber, B. (1992) 'Family, personality and adolescent problem behaviours', *Journal of Marriage and the Family* 56: 375–86.

Barker, P. (2007) *Basic Family Therapy*, 5th edn. Oxford: Blackwell.

Barnes, C. (2012) 'Understanding the social model of disability: past, present and future' in N. Watson, A. Roulstone and C. Thomas (eds), *Routledge Handbook of Disability Studies*. Abingdon: Routledge, pp. 12–29.

Barnes, G. (2004) *Family Therapy in Changing Times*, 2nd edn. Basingstoke: Palgrave.

Baron-Cohen, S. (1989) 'The autistic child's theory of mind: a case of specific developmental delay', *Journal of Child Psychology and Psychiatry* 30 (2): 285–97.

Baron-Cohen, S. (1997) *Mindblindness: An Essay on Autism and Theory of Mind*. Cambridge, Massachusetts: MIT Press.

Barone, l. and Guiducci, V. (2009) 'Mental representations of attachment in eating disorders: a pilot study using the Adult Attachment Interview', *Attachment and Human Development* 11 (4): 405–17.

Bateson, G. (1973) *Steps to an Ecology of Mind*. St Albans: Paladin.

Baum, W. (2005) *Understanding Behaviorism: Behavior, Culture and Evolution*. Oxford: Blackwell.

Baumrind, D. (1991) 'The influence of early parenting style on adolescent competence and substance abuse', *Journal of Early Adolescence* 11: 56–95.

Beardslee, W. and Podorefsky, D. (1988) 'Resilient adolescents whose parents have serious affective and other psychiatric disorders: importance of self-understanding and relationships', *American Journal of Psychiatry* 145 (1): 63–9.

Beck, A.T. (1963) 'Thinking and depression. 1: Idiosyncratic content and cognitive distortions', *Archives of General Psychiatry* 9: 324–33.

Beck, A.T. (1964) 'Thinking and depression. 2: Theory and Therapy', *Archives of General Psychiatry* 10: 561–71.

Becker, H.S. (1963) *Outsiders*. New York: Free Press.

Beckett, C. (2010) *The Holy Machine*. London: Corvus.

Berenbaum, S.A. and Hines, M. (1992) 'Early androgens are related to sex-related toy preferences', *Psychological Science* 3: 202–6.

Berger, P. and Luckmann, T. (1967) *The Social Construction of Reality*. London: Penguin.

Berlin, L., Ziv, Y., Amaya-Jackson, L. and Greenberg, M.T. (eds) (2005) *Enhancing Early Attachments: Theory, Research, Intervention and Policy*. New York: Guilford Press.

Bernstein, D., Atance, C., Meltzoff, A. and Loftus, G. (2007) 'Hindsight bias and developing theories of mind', *Child Development* 78 (4): 1374–94.

Berthoud, R. (2006) *The Employment Rates of Disabled People* (research report 298). London: Department for Work and Pensions. Accessed online October 2015 at www.researchgate.net/publication/247867179_The_Employment_Rates_of_Disabled_People

Blakemore, J.E.O. (2003) 'Children's beliefs about violating gender norms: boys shouldn't look like girls and girls shouldn't act like boys', *Sex Roles* 48: 411–19.

Blanden, J., Goodman, A., Gregg, P. and Machin, S. (2004) 'Changes in intergenerational mobility in Britain', in M. Corak (ed.), *Generational Income Inequality*. Cambridge: Cambridge University Press.

Blanden, J., Gregg, P. and Machin, S. (2005) *Intergenerational Mobility in Europe and North America*. London: Centre for Economic Performance.

Boden, M. (1994) *Piaget*. London: Fontana.

Bond, J., Peace, S., Dittman-Kohli, F. and Westerhof, G. (eds) (2007) *Ageing in Society*, 3rd edn. London: Sage.

Boswell, J. (1996) *The Marriage of Likeness: Same-Sex Unions in Pre-Modern Europe*. London: Fontana.

Bouchard, T.J., Lykken, D.T., McGue, M., Segal, N.L. and Tellegen, A. (1990) 'Sources of human psychological differences: the Minnesota study of twins reared apart', *Science* 250: 223–8.

Bourdieu, P. (1984) *Distinction: A Social Critique of the Judgement of Taste*. London: Routledge and Kegan Paul.

Bowlby, J. (1940) 'The influence of early environment in the development of neurosis and neurotic character', *International Journal of Psychoanalysis* 21: 154–78.

Bowlby, J. (1951) *Maternal Care and Mental Health*. Geneva: World Health Organisation.

Bowlby, J. (1990 [1953]) *Childcare and the Growth of Love*. Harmondsworth: Penguin.

Bowlby, J. (1997 [1969]) *Attachment*. London: Pimlico.

Bowlby, J. (1998a [1973]) *Separation*. London: Pimlico.

Bowlby, J. (1998b [1980]) *Loss*. London: Pimlico.

Brambring, M. (2007) 'Divergent development of manual skills in children who are blind or sighted', *Journal of Visual Impairment & Blindness* 101 (4): 212–14.

Brecher, E.M. (1984) *Love, Sex and Aging: A Consumers' Union Report*. Boston: Little, Brown.

Bronfenbrenner, U. (1979) *The Ecology of Human Development*. Cambridge, MA: Harvard University Press.

Bronstein, P., Fitzgerald, M., Briones, M., Pienadz, J. and D'Ari, A. (1993) 'Family emotional expressiveness as a predictor of early adolescent social and psychological adjustment', *Journal of Early Adolescence* 13: 448–71.

Brooks-Gunn, J. and Paikoff, R. (1997) 'Sexuality and developmental transitions during adolescence', in J. Schulenberg, J. Maggs and K. Hurrelmann (eds), *Health Risks and Developmental Transitions during Adolescence*. Cambridge: Cambridge University Press, pp. 190–219.

Burman, E. (1994) *Deconstructing Developmental Psychology*. London: Routledge.

Bussey, K. (2011) 'Gender Identity Development', in S.J. Schwartz, K. Luyckx and V.L. Vignoles, (eds), *Handbook of Identity Theory and Research*. London: Springer, pp. 603–28.

Campbell, D. (2000) *The Socially Constructed Organisation*. London: Karnac Books.

Carers UK (2014) *Policy Briefing – Facts about Carers*. Accessed online October 2015 at www.carersuk.org/for-professionals/policy/policy-library/facts-about-carers-2014

Carr, A. (2012) *Family Therapy: Concepts, Processes and Practice*, 3rd edn. Chichester: Wiley-Blackwell.

Carskadon, M. and Acebo, C. (2002) 'Regulation of sleepiness in adolescence: updates, insights and speculation', *Sleep* 25: 606–16.

Carter, B., McGoldrick, M. and Petkov, B. (2011) 'Becoming parents: the family with young children', in M. McGoldrick, B. Carter and N. Garcia Preto (eds), *The Expanded Family Life Cycle: Individual, Family and Social Perspectives*, 4th edn. Boston: Pearson, pp. 211–31.

Casey, B., Galvan, A. and Hare, T. (2005) 'Changes in cerebral functional organization during cognitive development', *Current Opinion in Neurobiology* 15 (2): 239–44.

Cattell, R. (1971) *Abilities, their Structure, Growth and Action*. New York: Houghton Mifflin.

Channel 4 (1994) *An Interview with Dennis Potter*. London: Channel 4 TV.

Chappell, A.L. (1998) 'Still out in the cold: people with learning difficulties and the social model of disability', in T. Shakespeare (ed.), *The Disability Reader*. London: Cassell, pp. 211–20.

Chassin, L., Hussong, A. and Beltran, I. (2009) 'Adolescent substance use', in R.M Lerner and L. Steinberg (eds), *Handbook of Adolescent Psychology*. Hoboken, NJ: Wiley, pp. 723–63.

Chen, Z., Sanchez, R.P. and Campbell, T. (1997) 'From beyond to within their grasp: analogical problem solving in 10- and 13-month-old infants', *Developmental Psychology* 33: 790–801.

Chodorow, N. (1978) *The Reproduction of Mother*. Berkeley: University of California Press.

Cione, G., Paolicelli, P.B., Sordi, C. and Vinter, A. (1993) 'Sensorimotor development in cerebral palsied infants assessed with the Uzgiris-Hunt scales', *Developmental Medicine and Child Neurology* 35: 1055–66.

Clinton, H. (1996) *It Takes a Village*. New York: Simon and Schuster.

Clulow, C. and Mattinson, J. (1989) *Marriage Inside Out*. Harmondsworth: Penguin.

Cobb, N. (1995) *Adolescence: Continuity, Change and Diversity*, 2nd edn. Mountain View, CA: Mayfield.

Colby, A., Kohlberg, L., Gibbs, J. and Lieberman, M. (1983) 'A longitudinal study of moral judgement', *Monographs of the Society for Research in Child Development* 48: 1–24.

Coleman, J. (2011) *The Nature of Adolescence*, 4th edn. London: Routledge.

Compas, B. (1995) 'Promoting successful coping during adolescence', in M. Rutter (ed.), *Psychosocial Disturbances in Young People: Challenges for Prevention.* Cambridge: Cambridge University Press, pp. 247–73.

Compas, B. and Reeslund, K. (2009) 'Processes of risk and resilience during adolescence', in R.M. Lerner and L. Steinberg (eds), *Handbook of Adolescent Psychology*. Hoboken, NJ: Wiley, pp. 561–617.

Cox, M.V. (1991) *The Child's Point of View*, 2nd edn. Hemel Hempstead: Harvester.

Crawford, M. and Popp, D. (2003) 'Sexual double standards: a review and methodological critique of two decades of research', *The Journal of Sex Research* 40 (1): 13–26.

Crawley, A.C. (ed.) (1992) *Geoffrey Chaucer: The Canterbury Tales*. London: David Campbell Publishing.

Crews, F., He, J. and Hodge, C. (2007) 'Adolescent cortical development: a critical period of vulnerability for addiction', *Pharmacology, Biochemistry and Behavior* 86 (2): 189–99.

Crittenden, P.M. (2008) *Raising Parents: Attachment, Parenting and Child Safety*. Cullompton: Willan Press.

Crittenden, P.M. and Newman, L. (2010) 'Comparing models of borderline personality disorder: mothers' experience, self-protective strategies and dispositional representations', *Clinical Child Psychology and Psychiatry* 15 (3): 433–51.

Crockett, L., Bingham, C., Chopak, J. and Vicary, J. (1996) 'Timing of first sexual intercourse: the role of social control, social learning and problem behaviour', *Journal of Youth and Adolescence* 25 (1): 89–111.

CSDH (Commission on the Social Determinants of Health) (2008) *Closing the Gap in a Generation: Health Equity through Action on the Social Determinants of Health. Final Report of the Commission on the Social Determinants of Health*. Geneva: World Health Organisation.

Cumming, E. and Henry, W. (1961) *Growing Old: The Process of Disengagement*. New York: Basic Books.

Currer, C. (2001) *Responding to Grief: Dying, Bereavement and Social Care*. Basingstoke: Palgrave.

Currie, C., Zanotti, C., Morgan, A., Currie, D., de Looze, M., Roberts, C., Samdal, O., Smith, O.R.F. and Barnekow, V. (eds) (2012) *Social Determinants of Health and Well-being among Young People. Health Behaviour in School-aged Children (HBSC) Study: International Report from the 2009/2010 Survey*. Copenhagen, WHO Regional Office for Europe (Health Policy for Children and Adolescents, No. 6).

Dale, N. and Salt, A. (2007) 'Early support developmental journal for children with visual impairment: the case for a new developmental framework for early intervention', *Childcare, Health and Development* 33 (6): 684–90.

Daniels, H. (ed.) (2005) *An Introduction to Vygotsky*. Hove: Routledge.

Dennison, C. and Coleman, J. (1998) *Adolescent Motherhood: The Relation between a Young Mother and her Mother*. Research report. Brighton: Trust for the Study of Adolescence.

Dex, S., Ward, K. and Joshi, H. (2008) 'Gender differences in occupational wage mobility in the 1958 cohort', *Work, Employment and Society* 22: 263–80.

Diamond, L.M. and Savin-Williams, R.C. (2009) 'Adolescent sexuality', in R.M. Lerner and L. Steinberg (eds), *Handbook of Adolescent Psychology*. Hoboken, NJ: Wiley, pp. 479–523.

Dillenburger, K. and Keenan, M. (1997) 'Human development: a question of structure and function', in K. Dillenburger, M. O'Reilly and M. Keenan (eds), *Advances in Behaviour Analysis*. Dublin: University College Dublin Press.

Dillon, F.R., Worthington, R.L. and Moradi, B. (2011) 'Sexual identity as a universal process', in *S.J. Schwartz, K. Luyckx, and V.L. Vignoles, (eds) Handbook of Identity Theory and Research*. London: Springer, pp. 649–70.

Dinnerstein, D. (1987) *The Rocking of the Cradle and the Ruling of the World*. London: The Women's Press.

Docherty, D., Hughes, R., Phillips, P., Corbett, D., Regan, B., Barber, A., Adams, M., Boxall, K., Kaplan, I. and Izzidien, S. (2010) 'This is what we think', in L.J. Davis (ed.), *The Disability Studies Reader* (3rd edn.) Abingdon: Routledge, pp. 432–40.

Doidge, N. (2007) *The Brain that Changes itself: Stories of Personal Triumph from the Frontiers of Brain Science*. London: Penguin.

Donne, J. (1962 [1624]) 'Meditation XVII (from Devotions Upon Emergent Occasions)', in G.R. Potter and E.M. Simpson (eds), *Sermons of John Donne*, Vol. 7. Berkeley: University of California Press, p. 369.

Durkin, K. (1995) *Developmental Social Psychology*. Oxford: Blackwell.

DWP (Department for Work and Pensions) (2006) *Households Below Average Income 2004/5*. London: DWP.

Elbert, T., Pantev, C., Wienbruch, C., Rockstroh, B. and Taub, E. (1995) 'Increased cortical representation of the fingers of the left hand in string players', *Science* 270 (5234): 305–7.

Elias, N. (1978) *What is Sociology?* London: Hutchinson.

Eliot, L. (2001) *Early Intelligence: How the Brain and Mind Develop in the First Years*. London: Penguin.

Elliot, A. (2002) *Psychoanalytic Theory: An Introduction*. Oxford: Oxford University Press.

Epstein, C.F. (1997) 'The multiple realities of sameness and difference: ideology and practice' *Journal of Social Issues* 53: 259–278.

Eriksen, T.H. (2002) *Ethnicity and Nationalism: Anthropological Perspectives (Anthropology, Culture and Society)*, 2nd edn. London: Pluto Press.

Erikson, E. (1980 [1959]) *Identity and the Life Cycle*. New York: W.W. Norton.

Erikson, E. (1994 [1968]) *Identity, Youth and Crisis*. New York: W.W. Norton.

Erikson, E. (1995 [1951]) *Childhood and Society*. London: Vintage.

Ernst, M. and Spear, L.P. (2009) 'Reward systems', in M. de Haan and M.R. Gunnar (eds) *Handbook of Developmental Social Neuroscience*. New York: Guilford.

Estes, C.C., Swan, J.S. and Gerard, L.E. (1982) 'Dominant and competing paradigms in gerontology', *Ageing and Society* 2: 151–64.

Family Relations Institute (2011–2014). Accessed online October 2015 at http://family relationsinstitute.org/include/dmm_model.htm

Farrell, M.P. and Rosenberg, S.D. (1981) *Men at Mid-life*. Boston, MA: Auburn House.

Flores, P.J. (2004) *Addiction as an Attachment Disorder*. Lanham, MD: Jason Aronson.

Fodor, J. (1983) *The Modularity of Mind*. Cambridge, MA: MIT Press.

Fonagy, P. and Target, M. (2005), 'Bridging the transmission gap: An end to an important mystery of attachment research?', *Attachment & Human Development*, 7 (3): 333–43.

Fonagy, P., Gergely, G., Jurist, E. and Target, M. (2002) *Affect Regulation, Mentalisation and the Development of the Self*. New York: Other Press.

Foucault, M. (1980) *Power/Knowledge*. London: Harvester Wheatsheaf.

Franklin, C. and Warren, K. (1999) 'Advances in systems theory', in C. Franklin and C. Jordan (eds), *Family Practice*. Pacific Grove, CA: Brooks/Cole, pp. 397–425.

Freeman, W.J. (1999) *How Brains Make up their Minds*. London: Wiedenfeld and Nicholson.

Freud, A. (1968 [1937]) *The Ego and the Mechanisms of Defence*. London: Hogarth Press.

Freud, S. (1959 [1926]) *The Question of Lay Analysis*, standard edn, Vol. 20. London: Hogarth Press.

Freud, S. (1961 [1923]) *The Ego and the Id*, standard edn, Vol. 19. London: Hogarth Press.

Freud, S. (1961 [1930]) *Civilization and its Discontents*, standard edn, Vol. 21. London: Hogarth Press.

Freud, S. (1963 [1916–17]) *Introductory Lectures on Psychoanalysis*, standard edn, Vol. 16. London: Hogarth Press.

Freud, S. (1964 [1933]) *New Introductory Lectures in Psychoanalysis*, standard edn, Vol. 22. London: Hogarth Press.

Freud, S. (2003 [1949]) *An Outline of Psychoanalysis*. London: Penguin.

Freud, S. and Breuer, J. (1955 [1895]) *Studies on Hysteria*, standard edn, Vol. 2. London: Hogarth Press.

Frosh, S. (1997) *For and Against Psychoanalysis*. London: Routledge.

Frydenberg, E. (2008) *Adolescent Coping: Advances in Theory, Research and Practice*. Hove: Routledge.

Gallagher, H. and Frith, C. (2003) 'Functional imaging of "theory of mind"', *Trends in Cognitive Science* 7 (2): 77–83.

Garcia Preto, N. (2011) 'Transformation of the family system during adolescence', in M. McGoldrick, B. Carter and N. Garcia Preto (eds), *The Expanded Family Life Cycle: Individual, Family and Social Perspectives*, 4th edn. Boston: Pearson, pp. 232–46.

Garmezy, N. and Rutter, M. (eds) (1983) *Stress, Coping and Development in Children*. New York: McGraw Hill.

Gath, A. (1977) 'The impact of an abnormal child upon the parents', *British Journal of Psychiatry* 130: 405–10.

Gay, P. (1988) *Freud: A Life for our Time*. London: Macmillan.

Gerhardt, S. (2004) *Why Love Matters: How Affection Shapes a Baby's Brain*. Hove: Routledge.

Giedd, J.N. (2008) 'The teen brain: insights from neuroimaging', *Journal of Adolescent Health* 42: 335–43.

Gilleard, C.J. And Higgs, P. (2000) *Cultures of Ageing: Self, Citizen and the Body*. Harlow: Prentice Hall.

Gilligan, C. (1982) *In a Different Voice: Psychological Theory and Women's Development*. Cambridge, MA: Harvard University Press.

Golding, K. (2008) *Nurturing Attachments: Supporting Children who Are Fostered and Adopted*. London: Jessica Kingsley.

Goldthorpe, J.H., Lockwood, D., Bechofer, F. and Platt, J. (1969) *The Affluent Worker in the Class Structure*. Cambridge: Cambridge University Press.

Golombok, S. and Fivush, R. (1994) *Gender Development*. Cambridge: Cambridge University Press.

Goswami, U. (2011a) 'Inductive and Deductive Reasoning', in U. Goswami (ed.), *The Wiley-Blackwell Handbook of Childhood Cognitive Development*, 2nd edn. Chichester: Wiley-Blackwell, pp. 399–419.

Goswami, U. (ed.) (2011b) *The Wiley-Blackwell Handbook of Cognitive Development*, 2nd edn. Oxford: Blackwell.

Graber, T. and Brooks-Gunn, T. (1996) 'Transitions and turning points: managing the passage from childhood through adolescence', *Developmental Psychology* 32: 768–76.

Green, J. and Goldwyn, R. (2002) 'Annotation: attachment disorganisation and psychopathology: new findings in attachment research and their potential implications for developmental psychopathology in childhood', *Journal of Child Psychology and Psychiatry* 43 (7): 835–46.

Greenberg, M.T. and Kushe, C. (1989) 'Cognitive, personal and social development of deaf children and adolescents', in M. Wang, M. Reynolds and H. Walberg (eds), *The Handbook of Special Education: Research and Practice*, Vol. 3, pp. 95–129. New York: Pergamon.

Grossman, F.K. (1972) *Brothers and Sisters of Retarded Children*. Syracuse, NY: Syracuse University Press.

Gullotta, T., Adams, G. and Markstrom, C. (2000) *The Adolescent Experience*, 4th edn. San Diego: Academic Press.

Gutmann, D.L. (1987) *Reclaimed Powers: Towards a New Psychology of Men and Women in Later Life*. New York: Basic Books.

Halford, G.S. and Andrews, G. (2011) 'Information-processing models of cognitive development' in U. Goswami (ed.), *The Wiley-Blackwell Handbook of Childhood Cognitive Development*, 2nd edn. Chichester: Wiley-Blackwell, pp. 697–722.

Haney, C., Banks, C. and Zimbardo, P. (1973) 'Interpersonal dynamics in a simulated prison', *International Journal of Criminology and Penology* 1: 69–97.

Haralambos, M. and Holborn, M. (2013) *Sociology Themes and Perspectives*, 3rd edn. London: HarperCollins.

Hare, T.A., Tottenham, N., Galvan, A., Voss, H.U., Glover, G.H. and Casey, B.J. (2008) 'Biological substrates of emotional reactivity and regulation in adolescence during an emotional go-nogo task', *Biological Psychiatry* 63 (10): 927–34.

Harlow, H. (1963) 'The maternal affectional system', in B.M. Foss (ed.), *Determinants of Human Behaviour*. London: Methuen, pp. 3–29.

Healey, Lord, D. (2000) 'Golden oldies', *The Guardian ('Society' supplement)*, 27 September, p. 3. Accessed online October 2015 at www.theguardian.com/society/2000/sep/27/guardiansocietysupplement

Heard, D.H. and Lake, B. (1986) 'The attachment dynamic in adult life', *British Journal of Psychiatry* 149 (4): 430–38.

Herrnstein, R.L., Loveland, D. and Cable, C. (1976) 'Natural concepts in pigeons', *Journal of Experimental Psychology: Animal Behaviour Processes* 2: 285–302.

Hodapp, R.M. (1998) *Development and Disabilities: Intellectual, Sensory and Motor Impairments*. Cambridge: Cambridge University Press.

Hodapp, R.M. and Krasner, D.V. (1995) 'Families of children with disabilities: findings from a national sample of eighth-grade students', *Exceptionality* 5: 71–81.

Holmes, J. (1993) *John Bowlby and Attachment Theory*. London: Routledge.

Holmes, T.H. and Rahe, R.H. (1967) 'The social readjustment rating scale', *Journal of Psychosomatic Research* 11: 213–18.

Hopson, B. (1981) 'Response to the papers by Schlossberg, Bramner and Abrego', *Counselling Psychologist* 9 (2): 36 ff.

Howe, D. (1995) *Attachment Theory for Social Work Practice*. London: Macmillan.

Howe, D. (2005) *Child Abuse and Neglect: Attachment, Development and Intervention*. Basingstoke: Palgrave Macmillan.

Howe, D. (2011) *Attachment across the Lifecourse*. Basingstoke: Palgrave Macmillan.

Howe, D., Brandon, M., Hinings, D. and Schofield, G. (1999) *Attachment Theory, Child Maltreatment and Family Support*. London: Macmillan.

Howells, G. (1997) 'A general practice perspective', in J. O'Hara and A. Sperlinger (eds), *Adults With Learning Disabilities*. Chichester: Wiley, pp. 61–79.

Hunt, S.J. (2005) *The Life Course: A Sociological Introduction*. Basingstoke: Palgrave Macmillan.

Huxley, A. (1955 [1932]) *Brave New World*. Harmondsworth: Penguin.

Iwaniec, D. (2004) *Children who Fail to Thrive: A Practice Guide*. Chichester: Wiley.

Jacobs, M. (2003) *Sigmund Freud*. London: Sage.

Jaques, E. (1965) 'Death and the mid-life crisis', *International Journal of Psychoanalysis* 46: 502–14.

Jensen, G.D. and Tolman, C.W. (1962) 'Mother–infant relationship in the monkey, *Macaca Nemestrina*: the effect of brief separation and mother–infant specificity', *Journal of Comparative Physiological Psychology* 55: 131–6.

Jessor, R. and Jessor, S. (1979) *Problem Behaviour and Psychosocial Development: A Longitudinal Study of Youth*. New York: Academic Press.

Joshi, H. and Paci, P. (1998) *Unequal Pay for Women and Men: Evidence from the British Birth Cohort Studies*. Cambridge, MA: MIT Press.

Juffer, F. and Bakermans-Kranenberg, M.J. (2008) *Promoting Positive Parenting: An Attachment-based Intervention*. London: Psychology Press.

Jung, C. (1995 [1961]) *Memories, Dreams, Reflections*. London: Fontana.

Kahn, S., Zimmerman, G., Csikszentmihalyi, M. and Getzels, J.W. (1985) 'Relations between identity in young adulthood and intimacy at mid-life', *Journal of Personality and Social Psychology* 9: 117–26.

Kail, R. (2004) 'Cognitive development includes global and domain-specific processes', *Merrill–Palmer Quarterly* 50 (4): 445–55.

Kalish, R.A. (1985) 'The social context of death and dying', in R.H. Binstock and E. Shanas (eds), *Handbook of Ageing and the Social Sciences*. New York: Van Nostrand Reinhold, pp. 149–70.

Kalish, R.A. and Reynolds, D.K. (1976) *Death and Ethnicity: A Psychocultural Study*. Los Angeles: University of Southern California Press.

Karmiloff-Smith, A. (1995) *Beyond Modularity*. Cambridge, MA: MIT Press.

Kastenbaum, R. and Alsenburg, R. (1976) *The Psychology of Death*. New York: Springer.

Kearl, M. (1989) *Endings: A Sociology of Death and Dying*. Oxford: Oxford University Press.

Kielhofner, G. (2008) *Model of Human Occupation: Theory and Application*. Baltimore: Lippincott Williams and Wilkins.

Kierkegaard, S. (2001 [1843]) *The Kierkegaard Reader*. Edited by J. Chamberlain and J. Rée. Oxford: Blackwell.

Klein, M. (1975 [1933]) 'The early development of conscience in the child', in M. Klein, *Love, Guilt and Reparation and other Works*. London: The Hogarth Press, pp. 248–57.

Klein, M. (1986 [1946]) *The Selected Melanie Klein*. Edited by J. Mitchell. Harmondsworth: Penguin.

Kobak, R., Cassidy, J. and Ziv, Y. (2004) 'Attachment related trauma and Post-traumatic Stress Disorder', in W.S. Rholes and J.A. Simpson (eds), *Adult Attachment: Theory, Research and Clinical Implications*. New York: Guilford Press, pp. 388–407.

Kohlberg, L. (1980) 'Stages of moral development as a basis for education', in B. Munsey (ed.), *Moral Development, Moral Education and Kohlberg*. Birmingham, AL: Religious Education Press.

Kohli, M. (1986) 'The world we forgot: a historical review of the life course', in V. Marshall (ed.), *Later Life: The Social Psychology of Aging*. London: Sage, pp. 271–303.

Kroger, J. (2000) *Identity Development: Adolescence through Adulthood*. London: Sage.

Kroger, J. (2004) *Identity in Adolescence: The Balance Between Self and Other*, 3rd edn. London: Routledge.

Kroger, J. and Marcia, J. (2011) 'The identity statuses: origins, meanings and interpretations', in S.J. Schwartz, K. Luyckx, and V.L. Vignoles (eds), *Handbook of Identity Theory and Research*. London: Springer, pp. 603–28.

Kübler-Ross, E. (1970) *On Death and Dying*. London: Tavistock.

Künemund, H. and Kolland, F. (2007) 'Work and retirement', in J. Bond, S. Peace, F. Dittman-Kohli and G. Westerhof (eds), *Ageing in Society*, 3rd edn. London: Sage, pp. 167–85.

L'Engle, K., Brown, J. and Kenneavy, K. (2006) 'The mass media are an important context for adolescents' sexual behavior', *Journal of Adolescent Health* 38 (3): 186–92.

Laflin, M., Wang, J. and Barry, M. (2008) 'A longitudinal study of adolescent transition from virgin to nonvirgin status', *Journal of Adolescent Health* 42 (3): 228–36.

Langer, E. (1983) *The Psychology of Control*. London: Sage.

Langlois, J.H. and Downs, A.C. (1980) 'Mothers, fathers and peers as socialization agents of sex-typed play behaviors in young children', *Child Development* 51: 1237–47.

Laslett, P. (1989) *A Fresh Map of Life*. London: Weidenfeld and Nicholson.

Lazarus, R.S. (1993) 'Coping theory and research: past, present and future', *Psychosomatic Medicine* 55: 234–47.

Lazarus, R.S. and Folkman, S. (1984) *Stress, Appraisal and Coping*. New York: Springer.

Leaper, C. and Friedman, C.K. (2007) 'The socialisation of gender', in J.E. Grusec and P.D. Hastings (eds), *Handbook of Socialisation: Theory and Research*. New York: Guilford Press, pp. 561–87.

Lerner, J.V., Phelps, E., Forman, Y. and Bowers, P. (2009) 'Positive youth development', in R.M. Lerner and L. Steinberg (eds), *Handbook of Adolescent Psychology*. Hoboken, NJ: Wiley, pp. 524–58.

Levinson, D. (1978) *The Seasons of a Man's Life*. New York: Ballantine.

Levinson, D. and Levinson, J. (1996) *The Seasons of a Woman's Life*. New York: Knopf.

Lewin, K. (1935) *A Dynamic Theory of Personality*. New York: McGraw-Hill.

Lewis, V. (2003) *Development and Disability*, 2nd edn. Oxford: Blackwell.

Lollar, D.J. (1994) *Social Development and the Person with Spina Bifida*. Washington, DC: Spina Bifida Association of America.

Lowenthal, M., Thurnher, M. and Chiriboga, D. (1975) *Four Stages of Life: A Comparative Study of Women and Men Facing Transitions*. San Francisco: Jossey-Bass.

Maccoby, E. and Martin, J. (1983) 'Socialisation in the context of the family: parent–child interaction', in E. Hetherington (ed.), *Handbook of Child Psychology*. New York: Wiley.

MacPherson, Sir W. (1999) *The Stephen Lawrence Inquiry*. London: Stationery Office.

Main, M. and Goldwyn, R. (1994) 'Adult attachment rating and classification systems', version 6.0, unpublished manuscript, University of California at Berkeley.

Main, M. and Hesse, E. (1990) 'Parents' unresolved traumatic experiences are related to infant disorganised attachment status: is frightened and/or frightening parental behaviour the linking mechanism?', in M.T. Greenberg, D. Cicchetti and E.M. Cummings (eds), *Attachment in the Pre-school Years: Theory, Research and Intervention*. Chicago: University of Chicago Press, pp. 161–84.

Mallory, M. (1984) 'Longitudinal analysis of ego identity status', unpublished doctoral dissertation, University of California, Davis.

Marcia, J. (1966) 'Development and validation of ego identity status', *Journal of Personality and Social Psychology* 3: 551–8.

Marcoen, A., Coleman, P. and O'Hanlon, A. (2007) 'Psychological ageing', in J. Bond, S. Peace, F. Dittman-Kohli and G. Westerhof (eds), *Ageing in Society*, 3rd edn. London: Sage, pp. 38–67.

Mareschal, D., Johnson, M.H., Sirois, S., Spratling, M.W., Thomas, M.D.C. and Westermann, G. (2007). *Neuroconstructivism: How the Brain Constructs Cognition*. Oxford: Oxford University Press.

Marx, K. (1986 [1845]) Extract from *The German Ideology*, in J. Elster (ed.), *Karl Marx: A Reader*. Cambridge: Cambridge University Press.

Masson, J. (2003) *The Assault on Truth: Freud's Suppression of the Seduction Theory*. New York: Ballantine Books.

McAdams, D. (1997) *Stories we live by: Personal Myths and the Making of the Self*. New York: Guilford Press.

McAdams, D. (2005) *Redemptive Self: Stories Americans Live by*. Cary, NC: Oxford University Press.

McAdams, D. (2010) 'Personality development: continuity and change over the life course', *Annual Review of Psychology* 61 (1): 517–42.

McCrae, R.R. and Costa, P.T. (2003) *Personality in Adulthood: A Five-Factor Theory Perspective*, 2nd edn. New York: The Guilford Press.

McGoldrick, M. (2011) 'Becoming a couple', in M. McGoldrick, B. Carter and N. Garcia Preto (eds), *The Expanded Family Life Cycle: Individual, Family and Social Perspectives*, 4th edn. Boston: Pearson, pp. 193–210.

McGoldrick, M. and Carter, B. (2011) 'Families transformed by the divorce cycle: reconstituted, multinuclear, recoupled and remarried families', in M. McGoldrick, B. Carter and N. Garcia Preto (eds), *The Expanded Family Life Cycle: Individual, Family and Social Perspectives*, 4th edn. Boston: Pearson, pp. 317–35.

McGoldrick, M., Carter, B. and Garcia Preto, N. (2011) 'Overview: the life cycle in its changing context', in M. McGoldrick, B. Carter and N. Garcia Preto (eds), *The Expanded Family Life Cycle: Individual, Family and Social Perspectives*, 4th edn. Boston: Pearson, pp. 1–19.

McGoldrick, M., Carter, B. and Garcia Preto, N. (eds) (2011) *The Expanded Family Life Cycle: Individual, Family and Social Perspectives*, 4th edn. Boston: Pearson.

McLuhan, M. (1962). *The Gutenberg Galaxy: The Making of Typographic Man.* Toronto: University of Toronto Press.

Meltzer, D., McWilliams, B., Brayne, C. and Johnson, T. (2000) 'Profile of disability in elderly people: estimates from a longitudinal study', *British Medical Journal* 318: 1108–11.

Meristo, M., Falkman, K., Hjelmquist, E., Tedoldi, M., Surian, L. and Siegal, M. (2007) 'Language access and theory of mind reasoning: evidence from deaf children in bilingual and oralist environments', *Developmental Psychology* 43 (5): 1156–69.

Mind (2013) 'Postnatal depression'. Accessed online October 2015 at www.mind.org.uk/information-support/types-of-mental-health-problems/postnatal-depression

Minnes, P. (1988) 'Family stress associated with a developmentally handicapped child', *International Review of Research on Mental Retardation* 15: 195–226.

Mitchell, J. (2003) *Siblings.* Cambridge: Polity Press.

Moore, S. and Rosenthal, D. (2006) *Sexuality in Adolescence: Current Trends*, 2nd edn. Hove: Routledge.

Murray Parkes, C. (2006) *Love and Loss.* London: Routledge.

Murray Parkes, C. and Prigerson, H.G. (2010) *Bereavement: Studies of Grief in Adult Life.* London: Penguin.

Music, G. (2011) *Nurturing Natures: Attachment and Children's Emotional, Sociocultural and Brain Development.* Hove: Psychology Press.

National Scientific Council on the Developing Child (2010) Working paper 10: Early experiences can alter gene expression and affect long-term development. Accessed online Oct 2015 at http://developingchild.harvard.edu/resources/reports_and_working_papers/working_papers/wp10/

Neugarten, B.L., Moore, J.W. and Lowe, J.C. (1965) 'Age norms, age constraints and adult socialisation', *American Journal of Sociology* 70: 710–17.

Neugarten, B.L., Wood, V., Kraines, R.J. and Loomis, B. (1963) 'Women's attitudes towards the menopause', *Vita Humana* 6: 140–51.

Obholzer, A. (1994) *The Unconscious at Work*. London: Routledge.

OECD (Organisation for Economic Co-operation and Development) (2015) 'Inequality'. Accessed online June 2015 at www.oecd.org/social/inequality.htm

ONS (Office of National Statistics) (2013) *Older People Divorcing, 2011*. Accessed online August 2015 at www.ons.gov.uk/ons/rel/family-demography/older-people-divorcing/2011/index.html

ONS (Office of National Statistics) (2014a) *Live Births in England and Wales by Characteristics of Mother 1, 2013*. Accessed online, June 2015, at www.ons.gov.uk/ons/dcp171778_380800.pdf

ONS (Office of National Statistics) (2014b) *Births in England and Wales, 2013*. Accessed online, June 2015, at www.ons.gov.uk/ons/dcp171778_371129.pdf

ONS (Office of National Statistics) (2014c) *Mortality Statistics: Deaths Registered in England and Wales (Series DR), 2013*. Accessed online September 2015 at www.ons.gov.uk/ons/rel/vsob1/mortality-statistics--deaths-registered-in-england-and-wales--series-dr-/2013/index.html

Paluski, J. and Waters, M. (1996) *The Death of Class*. London: Sage.

Pantev, C., Roberts, L.E., Schultz, M., Engelien, A. and Ross, B. (2001) 'Timbre-specific enhancement of auditory cortical representations in musicians', *NeuroReport* 12 (1): 169–74.

Peace, S., Dittman-Kholi, F., Westerhof, G. and Bond, J. (2007) 'The ageing world', in J. Bond, S. Peace, F. Dittman-Kohli and G. Westerhof (eds), *Ageing in Society*, 3rd edn. London: Sage, pp. 1–14.

Peace, S., Holland, C. and Kellaher, L. (2006) *Environment and Identity in Later Life*. Maidenhead: Open University Press.

Perosa, L.M., Perosa, S.L. and Tam, H.P. (1996) 'The contribution of family structure and differentiation to identity development in females', *Journal of Youth and Adolescence* 25: 817–37.

Perry, D. and Bussey, K. (1979) 'The social learning theory of sex difference: imitation is alive and well', *Journal of Personality and Social Psychology* 37: 1699–712.

Petitto, L. and Marentette, P.F. (1991) 'Babbling in the manual mode: evidence for the ontogeny of language', *Science* 251: 1493–6.

Phillips, C. and Bowling, B. (2002) 'Racism, ethnicity, crime and criminal justice', in M. Maguire, R. Morgan and R. Reiner (eds), *The Oxford Handbook of Criminology*, 3rd edn. Oxford: Oxford University Press.

Phinney, J.S. (1989) 'Stages of ethnic identity development in minority group adolescents', *Journal of Early Adolescence* 9: 34–49.

Phinney, J.S. (1993) 'A three-stage model of ethnic identity development', in G.P. Knight and M.E. Bernal (eds), *Ethnic Identity, Formation and Transmission among Hispanics and Other Minorities*. Albany, NY: State University of New York Press, pp. 61–79.

Phinney, J.S. and Alipuria, L.L. (1990) 'Ethnic identity in college students from four ethnic groups', *Journal of Adolescence* 13: 171–83.

Piaget, J. (1930) *The Child's Conception of Physical Causality*. London: Routledge.

Piaget, J., Montangero, J. and Billeter, J. (1977) 'Les correlats', in *L'Abstraction réfléchissante*. Paris: Presses Universitaires de France.

Pierce, W.D. and Cheney, C.D. (2004) *Behavior Analysis and Learning*, 3rd edn. Mahwah, NJ: Lawrence Erlbaum Associates Inc.

Pinker, S. (2007) *The Language Instinct*. New York: HarperCollins.

Pinkstinks (2008). Accessed online October 2015 at www.pinkstinks.org.uk

Plato (1973) *Phaedrus and Letters VII and VIII* (trans. Walter Hamilton). Harmondsworth: Penguin.

Plato (1998) *Cratylus* (trans. C.D.C. Reeve). Cambridge: Hackett.

Polivy, J., Herman, C.P., Mills, J. and Wheeler, H. (2003) 'Eating disorders in adolescence', in G. Adams and M. Berzonsky (eds), *Blackwell Handbook of Adolescence*. Oxford: Blackwell, pp. 523–49.

Powell, R., Symbaluk, D. and Macdonald, S. (2002) *Introduction to Learning and Behaviour*. Belmont, CA: Wadsworth.

Quinn, P. (1998) *Understanding Disability – A Lifespan Approach*. London: Sage.

Reay, D., David, M.E. and Ball, S. (2005) *Degrees of Choice: Class, Race, Gender and Higher Education*. Stoke-on-Trent: Trentham Books.

Reicher, S. and Emler, N. (1986) 'The management of delinquent reputations', in H. Beloff (ed.), *Getting into Life*. London: Methuen.

Ridley, M. (2004) *Nature via Nurture: Genes, Experience and What Makes us Human*. London: Harper Perennial.

Riesz, E. (2004) 'Loss and transitions: a 30-year perspective on life with a child who has Down Syndrome', *Journal of Loss and Trauma* 9 (4): 371–82.

Roberts, P. and Newton, P.M. (1987) 'Levinsonian studies of women's adult development', *Psychology and Aging* 2: 154–63.

Robertson, J. and Bowlby, J. (1952) 'Responses of young children to separation from their mothers', *Courier of the International Children's Centre* 2: 131–42.

Rosenbaum, J.E. (2006) 'Reborn a virgin: adolescents' retracting of virginity pledges and sexual histories', *American Journal of Public Health*, 96: 1078-103.

Rosenthal, R. and Jacobson, L. (1968) *Pygmalion in the Classroom*. New York: Holt, Rinehart and Winston.

Rutter, M. (1981) *Maternal Deprivation Reassessed*, 2nd edn. Harmondsworth: Penguin.

Rutter, M. and the English and Romanian Adoptees Study Team (1998) 'Developmental catch-up, and deficit, following adoption after severe global early privation', *Journal of Child Psychology and Psychiatry* 39 (4): 465–76.

Ryan, R.M. and Lynch, J.H. (1989) 'Emotional autonomy versus detachment: revisiting the vicissitudes of adolescence and young adulthood', *Child Development* 60: 340–56.

Rycroft, C. (1995) *A Critical Dictionary of Psychoanalysis*, 2nd edn. London: Penguin.

Sabatier, C. (2008) 'Ethnic and national identity among second-generation immigrant adolescents in France: the role of social context and family', *Journal of Adolescence* 31: 185–205.

Sable, P. (1989) 'Attachment, anxiety and loss of husband', *American Journal of Orthopsychiatry* 59 (4): 550–56.

Sachweh, S. (1998) 'Granny darling's puppies: secondary babytalk in German nursing homes for the aged', *Journal of Applied Communication Research* 26: 52–65.

Santrock, J.W. (2012) *Adolescence*, 14th edn. New York: McGraw Hill.

Sartre, J.-P. (2001 [1943]) *Basic Writings* (edited by Stephen Priest). London: Routledge.

Savage, M., Bagnall, G. and Longhurst, B. (2001) 'Ordinary, ambivalent and defensive: class identities in the northwest of England', *Sociology* 35 (4): 875–92.

Savin-Williams, R.C. (2011) 'Identity development among sexual minority youth', in S.J. Schwartz, K. Luyckx, and V.L. Vignoles, (eds), *Handbook of Identity Theory and Research*. London: Springer, pp. 671–89.

Savin-Williams, R.C. and Ream, G.L. (2007) 'Prevalence and stability of sexual orientation components during adolescence and young adulthood', *Archives of Sexual Behavior* 36: 385–94.

Sayers, J. (1998) *Boy Crazy*. London: Routledge.

Schindler, A., Thomasius, R., Sack, P-M., Gemeinhardt, B., Küstner, U. and Eckert, J. (2005) 'Attachment and substance abuse disorders', *Attachment and Human Development* 7 (3): 207–28.

Schofield, G. and Beek, M. (2006) *Attachment Handbook for Foster Care and Adoption*. London: BAAF.

Schore, A. (2000) 'Attachment and the regulation of the right brain', *Attachment and Human Development* 2 (1): 23–47.

Schore, A. (2001) 'Effects of a secure attachment relationship on right brain development, affect regulation and infant mental health', *Infant Mental Health Journal* 22 (1–2): 7–66.

Schore, J.R. and Schore, A.N. (2008) 'Modern attachment theory: the central role of affect regulation in development and treatment', *Clinical Social Work Journal* 36: 9–20.

Schut, H., Stroebe, M., de Keijser, J. and van den Brout, J. (1997) 'Intervention for the bereaved: gender differences in the efficacy of grief counselling', *British Journal of Clinical Psychology* 36: 63–72.

Seale, C. (1998) *Constructing Death: The Sociology of Dying and Bereavement*. Cambridge: Cambridge University Press.

Segal, J. (2004) *Melanie Klein*, 2nd edn. London: Sage.

Seigal, D.J. (1999) *The Developing Mind: Towards a Neurobiology of Interpersonal Experience*. New York: Guilford.

Seligman, M. (1975) *Helplessness: On Depression, Development and Death*. San Francisco: Freeman.

Seroczynski, A., Jacquez, F. and Cole, D. (2003) 'Depression and suicide during adolescence', in G. Adams and M. Berzonsky (eds), *Blackwell Handbook of Adolescence*, Oxford: Blackwell, pp. 550–72.

Shakespeare, T. (2014) *Disability Rights and Wrongs Revisited*, 2nd edn. Abingdon: Routledge.

Shakespeare, W. (2008 [1599]) 'As you like it', in S. Greenblatt, W. Cohen, J. Howard and K. Maus (eds), *The Norton Shakespeare*, 2nd edn. New York: Norton.

Sidell, M. (1993) 'Death, dying and bereavement', in J. Bond, P. Coleman and S. Peace (eds), *Ageing in Society*, 2nd edn. London: Sage, pp. 151–79.

Skinner, B.F. (1953) *Science and Human Behaviour*. New York: Macmillan.

Skinner, B.F. (1960) 'Pigeons in a pelican', *American Psychologist* 15: 28–37.

Skinner, B.F. (1974) *About Behaviorism*. London: Jonathan Cape.

Solnit, A. and Stark, M. (1961) 'Mourning and the birth of a defective child', *Psychoanalytic Study of the Child* 16: 523–37.

Sophocles (1984) *The Theban Plays* (trans. Robert Fagles). Harmondsworth: Penguin.

Spear, L. (2000) 'The adolescent brain and age-related behvioral manifestations', *Neuroscience and Biobehavioral Reviews*, 24 (4): 417–63.

Sperlinger, A. (1997) 'Introduction', in J. O'Hara and A. Sperlinger (eds), *Adults With Learning Disabilities*. Chichester: Wiley, pp. 3–16.

Sprott, W.J.H. (1958) *Human Groups*. Harmondsworth: Penguin.

Steen, R.G. (1996) *DNA and Destiny: Nature and Nurture in Human Behavior*. New York: Plenum Press.

Steinberg, L. and Silverberg, S.B. (1986) 'The vicissitudes of autonomy in early adolescence', *Child Development* 57: 841–51.

Storr, A. (1973) *Jung*. London: Fontana.

Stroebe, M. and Schut, H. (1999) 'The dual process model of coping with bereavement', *Death Studies*, 23: 197–224.

Stroebe, M. and Schut, H. (2001) 'Models of coping with bereavement: a review', in M.S. Stroebe, R.O. Hansson, W. Stroebe and H. Schut (eds), *Handbook of Bereavement Research*. Washington: American Psychological Association.

Stuart-Hamilton, I. (2012) *The Psychology of Ageing: An Introduction*, 5th edn. London: Jessica Kingsley.

Sugarman, L. (2001) *Life-Span Development: Frameworks, Accounts and Strategies*, 2nd edn. Hove: Psychology Press.

Sullivan, P. and Knutson, J. (2000) 'Maltreatment and disabilities: a population-based epidemiological study', *Child Abuse & Neglect* 24 (10): 1257–73.

Taylor, L. (2005) *Introducing Cognitive Development*. Hove: Psychology Press.

Thane, P. (2003) 'Social histories of old age and aging', *Journal of Social History* 37 (1): 93–111.

Thatcher, M., interviewed by Douglas Keays (1987) 'Aids, education and the year 2000!', *Woman's Own*, 31 October, pp. 8–10.

Thomas, D. (1973) 'Do not go gentle into that good night', in P. Larkin (ed.), *The Oxford Book of Twentieth Century English Verse*. Oxford: Clarendon Press, p. 474.

Thompson, N. (2006) *Anti-discriminatory Practice*. Houndmills: Palgrave Macmillan.

Tupuola, A.M. (1993) 'Critical analysis of adolescent development – a Samoan woman's perspective', unpublished masters thesis, cited by Kroger (2004).

Umaña-Taylor, A.J. (2011) 'Ethnic identity', in S.J. Schwartz, K. Luyckx and V.L. Vignoles, (eds), *Handbook of Identity Theory and Research*. London: Springer, pp. 791–809.

UN (2006) *Convention on the Rights of Persons with Disabilities.* Accessed online Aug 2015 at www.un.org/disabilities/convention/conventionfull/s html

UPIAS (1976) *Fundamental Principles of Disability.* London: Union of the Physically Impaired Against Segregation.

Victor, C. (2005) *The Social Context of Ageing: A Textbook of Gerontology.* London: Routledge.

von Bertalanffy, L. (1971) *General System Theory: Foundations, Development, Application.* London: Allen Lane.

Vygotsky, L.S. (1962) *Thought and Language.* New York: Wiley.

Vygotsky, L.S. (1978) *Mind in Society.* Cambridge, MA: Harvard University Press.

Walker, D. (2002) 'New breed of middle class closes ranks: social mobility suffers as poorer children kept off ladder', *The Guardian*, 18 May. Accessed online, October 2015 at www.theguardian.com/uk/2002/may/18/britishidentity.socialsciences

Walker, S. (1984) *Learning Theory and Behaviour Modification.* London: Methuen.

Walter, T. (1994) *The Revival of Death.* London: Routledge.

Warren, D.H. (1994) *Blindness and Children: An Individual Differences Approach.* Cambridge: Cambridge University Press.

Watson, J.B. (1931) *Behaviourism*, 2nd edn. London: Kegan Paul, Trench and Trubner.

Webster, R. (2005) *Why Freud Was Wrong: Sin, Science and Psychoanalysis*, 3rd edn. Oxford: Orwell Press.

Westbrook, D., Kennerley, H. and Kirk, J. (2011) *An Introduction to Cognitive Behaviour Therapy*, 2nd edn. London: Sage.

Westergaard, J. (1995) *Who Gets What? The Hardening of Class Inequality on the Late Twentieth Century.* Cambridge: Polity Press.

Westerhof, G. and Tulle, E. (2007) 'Meanings of ageing and old age: discursive contexts, social attitudes and personal identities', in J. Bond, S. Peace, F. Dittman-Kohli and G. Westerhof (eds), *Ageing in Society*, 3rd edn. London: Sage, pp. 235–54.

Westermann, G., Thomas, M.S.C. and Karmiloff-Smith, A. (2011) 'Neuroconstructivism' in U. Goswami (ed.), *The Wiley-Blackwell Handbook of Childhood Cognitive Development*, 2nd edn. Chichester: Wiley-Blackwell, pp 723-48.

Whitaker, D.J. and Miller, K.S. (2000) 'Parent–adolescent discussions about sex and condoms: impact on peer influences of sexual risk behaviour', *Journal of Adolescent Research* 15 (2): 251–73.

Whitbourne, S.K. (1996) *The Aging Individual: Physical and Psychological Perspectives.* New York: Springer-Verlag.

White, J., Essex, S. and O'Reilly, P. (1993) 'Family therapy, systemic thinking and child protection', in J. Carpenter and A. Treacher (eds), *Using Family Therapy in the 90s.* Oxford: Blackwell, pp. 57–86.

WHO (2011) *World Report on Disability.* Accessed online August 2015 at whqlibdoc.who.int/publications/2011/9789240685215_eng.pdf?ua=1

Wilkinson, R.G. and Pickett, K. (2010) *The Spirit Level.* London: Penguin.

Willemsen, E.W. and Waterman, K.K. (1991) 'Ego identity status and family environment: a correlational study', *Psychological Reports* 69: 1203–12.

Windle, M., Miller-Tutzauer, C. and Domenico, D. (2000) 'Adolescence, suicidal behaviour and risky activities among adolescents', in G. Adams (ed.), *Adolescent Development: The Essential Readings*. Oxford: Blackwell, pp. 261–74.

Wink, P. and Scott, J. (2005) 'Does religiousness buffer against the fear of death and dying in late adulthood? Findings from a longitudinal study', *Journal of Gerontology*, 60B (4): 207–14.

Winnicott, D. (1975 [1958]) *Through Paediatrics to Psychoanalysis*. London: Karnac.

Winnicott, D.W. (2005 [1971]) *Playing and Reality*, 2nd edn. London: Tavistock/Routledge.

Wolfensberger, W. (1998) *A Brief Introduction to Social Role Valorization*. Syracuse, NY: Training Institute for Human Services, Syracuse University.

Wolfgang, M.E., Thornberg, T.R. and Figlio, R.M. (1987) *From Boy to Man, from Delinquency to Crime*. Chicago: University of Chicago Press.

Wood, D., Bruner, J. and Ross, G. (1976) 'The role of tutoring in problem solving', *Journal of Child Psychology and Psychiatry*, 17: 89–100.

Young Children in Brief Separation 1967–71, film, Robertson Films, London. Available on DVD from Concord Media, Ipswich.

Young, M. and Cullen, L. (1996) *A Good Death: Conversations with East Londoners*. London: Routledge.

INDEX

abortion 205
acceptance stage of transition 108
accommodation 72
addictive behaviours 60
Adler, Alfred 33
adolescence 30, 105
    biology-culture interaction 106–7
    coping skills and resilience 125–6
    and disability 162–5
    family context 123–5, 183–4
    identity development 138
    identity versus role confusion 110–16
    moral development 114–15
    neurological development in 113–14
    and popular culture 203
    problems in 121–3
    relating to others 116–17
    and sexuality 118–21
    and transition 109–10
Adult Attachment Interview 134
adulthood
    defining 130–2
    development, continuity and change 132–6
    and disability 165–7
    generativity 140
    identity and intimacy 138–9
    leaving home 145, 181–2
        and disability 166–7
    middle adulthood 140, 144–9
    stages and transitions 136–8
    young adulthood 141–2
afterlife 223, 236–7
ageing 184
    see also old age
ageism 218–19
Ainsworth, Mary 58–62, 63
alcohol consumption 122
Alzheimer's disease 211
ambivalence 37
ambivalent attachment 59, 61
American Sign Language (ASL) 156
anal stage 30, 31

animal experiments
    on attachment 50
    on conditioning 88–9, 90, 91, 92, 93, 94, 94–5
anorexia 31–2
anxiety 28
anxious-ambivalent attachment 59, 61
anxious-avoidant attachment 58–9, 61, 229
Ariès, P. 224
aristocracy 11
Arnett, Jeffrey 141
assimilation 71
assisted dying 234
assumptions 5
    see also stereotyping
attachment
    and adolescence 123–4
    and adulthood 134
    animal experiments 50
    and loss 228–9
    stages of 54–5
attachment behaviour 50–1, 134–5
attachment behavioural systems 52–3
attachment classification system 58–62
attachment-in-the-making 54–5
attachment theory 45–7
    Ainsworth's attachment classification system
        58–62
    and bereavement 228–9
    biological origins of 49–51
    Bowlby and maternal deprivation 47–9
    criticisms of 64–5
    developments of 61–4
    growth of 54–5
    internal working models 52, 55–8
    parenting and adolescence 124–5
    secure base 51–3
autism 9, 13
autonomy
    and adolescence 116–17
    and disability 163
    psychological 122
avoidant attachment 58–9, 61, 229

babies
  and blindness 155–6
  bonds with mothers 49
  with impairments 159
  love/hate relationship with mothers 36–7
  separation from mothers 49
  social interaction 54–5
Baillargeon, Renée 81
Baltes, P.B. 133
Bandura, Albert 97–8, 100–1
Barnes, C. 187
Baron-Cohen, Simon 76–7
Beck, Harry 5
Becker, Howard 196
behaviour 3–4
  attachment 50–1
  criminal 3–4, 122
  environmental influences 12–13, 14
  genetic inheritance 8, 10, 14
behaviour analysis 86
behaviourism 85–7, 89–90
  classical conditioning 88–9, 90, 100
  cognitive factors 95–6
  gender roles 99–102
  learning theory 102
  observation 97–9
  operant conditioning 90–5, 97
  social learning theory 98, 101, 102
bereavement 107, 159–60, 211, 227–32
  and the afterlife 236–7
  attachment and loss 228–9
  loss and restoration 230–2
  narratives of grief 229–30
biology
  biological death 222–3
  biological origins of attachment 49–51
  interaction with culture 106–7
  see also nature
birth 1–2, 7, 189–90
blind children 155–6
Bourdieu, Pierre 203–4
Bowlby, John 45, 47–51, 52, 62, 64, 64–5
  on attachment behaviour 56–7
  on separation 49
brain development 14, 62–3, 76–7, 82–3
  in adolescence 113–14
Brave New World (Huxley) 89–90
breasts 36–7
Breuer, Josef 22
British Sign Language (BSL) 156
Bronfenbrenner, Urie 192, 198
Brooks-Gunn, Jeanne and Paikoff, Roberta 118, 119
building blocks analogy 71–3, 81–2

Bulger, James 17
bulimia nervosa 122
Burman, Erica 50

Campbell, D. 193
Canterbury Tales (Chaucer) 16
career change 145
carers 132
Carr, Alan 181
Casey *et al.* 83
CBT (cognitive behaviour therapy) 87, 96
centration 74
cerebral palsy 155, 167
change
  career 145
  first- and second- order 181
  in old age 210–11
  in transitions 137–8
Chaucer, Geoffrey 16
choice 16–17
circular causality 173, 176
circularity 171–2
class *see* social class
classical conditioning 88–9, 90, 100
classification 77, 78
clear-cut attachment 55
click training 92
closed systems 171
Clulow, C. and Mattinson, J. 135
cognitive behaviour therapy (CBT) 87, 96
cognitive changes in old age 211–12
cognitive development 55, 60, 67–8, 68
  in adulthood 141
  assimilation, accommodation and equilibration 71–3
  building blocks analogy 71–3, 81–2
  link with emotional development 62, 63–4
  making sense of the world 70–1
  Piaget's model 54, 67–8, 70–9
    challenges to 79–83
  stages of 70–1, 73–9
cognitive psychology 68–9
  theory of mind 76–7
cognitive stimulation 62
Coleman, J. 106
Commission on Social Determinants of Health (CSDH) 190
compulsive behaviour 60
concrete operation stage 77–8
conditioning
  classical 88–9, 90, 100
  operant 90–5
congenital adrenal hyperplasia 101

connections *see* behaviourism
conservation 77
continuity 134–5
control
    and family systems 178
    Freudian theory of 31–2
    in old age 217
coping skills 57, 125–6
countertransference 29
couple relationships 139, 182–3
Crawford, Mary and Popp, Danielle 120
criminal behaviour 3–4, 122
crystallised intelligence 212
cultural differences, and old age 219–20
cultural specificity 43
culture 203–6
    interaction with biology 106–7
    see also nurture; social context
Cumming, E. and Henry, W. 216
Currer, Caroline 223
cyclical models 176

Dali, Salvador 33
deaf children 156
deaf languages 156
deafness 152
death 16, 222–3
    bereavement 227–32
    biological 222–3
    individual experience of 234–7
    social 222–3
    social context of 223–6
        denial of death 224–5
        revivalist death 225–6
    of younger people 235, 236
decentration 77
defence mechanisms 26–8
defensive exclusion 57, 58
delinquency 122, 123
dementia 211, 218
denial 27, 28
    of death 224–5
depression 121
depressive position 38
deprivation, maternal 47–9
desires, suppressed and repressed 23–4
developmental cognitive psychology *see* cognitive
        development
developmental pathways, impairment 153–8
deviancy 122, 123
Diamond, L.M. and Savin-Williams, R.C. 120
In a Different Voice (Gilligan) 117
Dillon, F.R. 121

Dinnerstein, Dorothy 42
disability
    and adolescence 162–5
    and adulthood 165–7
    compared with impairment 152
    defining 151–3
    family context 159–61
    and identity 162–5
    integrated model of 153
    medical model of 152
    reactions to 150–1
    social model of 152, 153, 193
    see also impairment
discriminating social responsiveness 54–5
discrimination 89, 94
disengagement 216, 224–5
dismissing adults, narratives of 134
disorganised attachment 59–60, 64
dissuagement 52
divorce 183
    in old age 213
Donne, John 169
Down syndrome 154, 159, 160, 161, 167
dreams
    following 139
    letting go of 145
drug use 121–2
dual process model 230–1
Dynamic Maturational Model 60
dysfunctional coping 126

eating disorders 31–2, 122
Ecological Systems Theory 192
education 190
ego 24, 25, 25–6
Ego and the Mechanisms of Defence, The (Freud) 28
ego development 30, 34–40
ego integration 212, 213
egocentrism 74, 77, 80, 81
electric shocks 90, 91, 94–5
Elias, Norbert 191
emerging adulthood 141
emotion-focused coping strategies 125, 126
emotional autonomy 116
emotional detachment 117
emotional development 29, 63–4, 68, 156–8
    see also attachment theory
empty nest 145, 175
environment
    Ecological Systems Theory 192
    impact on 7–8, 11–13, 14, 17
    see also family context; social context
epistemology 70

equilibration 72
equilibrium 172
Eriksen, Thomas Hylland 200
Erikson, Erik 78
    adolescence 110–11
    adulthood 137
    on early childhood 36
    ego integration 212, 213
    on generativity 140
    on intimacy 138, 139
    stages model 38–40, 110, 112, 117, 137, 157, 177
    on trusting adults 35
Estes *et al.* 216
ethnicity 115–16, 200
events 18
evil 17
existential questions 15–16
exosystem 192
extinction 88

false self 36
family context
    adolescence in 123–5, 183–4
    disability in 159–61
family life cycle 176–8
family life, stages in 180–5
family systems 169–70
    and adolescence 183–4
    and couple relationships 139, 182–3
    and impairments 160
    leaving home 145, 166–7, 181–2
    new members of 183
    and old age 184, 213–14
    stressors 176–8
    see also systems theory
family systems theory 172–6, 184–5
    limitations of 187–8
fantasies 23, 36, 45, 47
faulty working models 57–8
    attachment classification system 58–62
feedback loops 171–2
femininity 99, 117
feminism 42
fertility 144–5
first-order change 181
fixation 30
fluid intelligence 211
Fodor, Jerry 82
formal operation stage 78–9
Foucault, Michel 6
Franklin, C. and Warren, K. 172
free association 22
free will 16–18

A Fresh Map of Life (Laslett) 208
Freud, Anna 28, 42
Freud, Sigmund 4, 12, 65, 78, 225, 236
    criticisms of 41–3
    influence of 33–4
    preconceptions about 20–1
    psychosexual stages 29–33
    scientific method 41
    sexuality 21
    structure of personality 24–9
    the unconscious 22–4, 24
friendships 139
Frydenberg, E. 126
funeral rituals 223

gay identity 99, 121
Gay, P. 42
gender differences 101–2, 117
    coping strategies 126
    and sexual behaviour 119–20
    social construction of 199–200
gender roles 99–102
generalisation 88
generativity 140, 167
    see also parenthood
genetic inheritance 7–9, 10, 14
genital phase 31, 32
Gilligan, Carol 117
glass ceiling 199
global village 203
global warming 172
Graber, T. and Brooks-Gunn, T. 110
Green, J. and Goldwyn, R. 59–60
grief 227–32
gross early privation 62
groups 198
Gullotta *et al.* 111, 112
Gutmann, David 219

habitus 203–4
handicap 151, 193
Harlow, H. 50, 54
Hawking, Stephen 164
Healey, Lord Denis 212–13
health, in old age 210–11
health inequality 190
Heinz dilemma 115
Heraclitus 204
higher order analytical thinking 79
history, culture, identity and 204, 204–6
Hodapp, R.M. 154, 160
Holmes, T.H. and Rahe, R.H. 137
homeostasis 51, 172

homosexuality 32, 99
horizontal stressors 159, 176–7, 177–8, 179, 214
hormones 113–14, 119, 145
hospice movement 226, 234
Howe, D.
    on ambivalent attachment 229
    on avoidant attachment 229
    on unresolved disorganised attachment 64
Howells, G. 158
Human Genome Project 9
hypnosis 22
hysteria 22, 23

id 24, 25, 26
ideas 2–6
identity
    and adolescence 110–16, 117, 138
    and deviancy 122, 123
    and disability 162–5
    and ethnicity 115–16, 200
    and groups 198
    and intimacy 138–9
    occupational 164
    versus role confusion 110–16
    role of culture and history in 203–4
    sexual 119–21, 164
    status 111–12
identity achievement 112
identity diffusion 111, 112, 122, 123
identity foreclosure 111, 112, 121, 122
illusion of omnipotence 35
image 203
immobilisation stage of transition 107
impairment 150, 152
    babies and children 159–60
    compared with disability 152
    and developmental pathways 153–8
    and family systems 159–61
    see also disability
independence 167
individual, and society 191
individual experience of death 234–7
individuality 16
individuation 144
inequality
    health 190
    impact of 201
    social 199
infantilised adults 151, 217
    and disability 165–6
influence 201
inheritance see genetic inheritance
inner capital 111

insecure attachment 53, 56, 124–5
institutional racism 202
integration stage of transition 108
intelligence 9
    in old age 211–12
internal working models 52
intimacy 138–9, 167

Jaques, Elliott 144
Jung, Carl 33, 144, 236

Kahn *et al.* 138
Kalish, R.A. 225
Kearl, M. 225
Klein, Melanie 36–8, 225
Kohlberg, Lawrence 114–15
Kohli, M. 208
Kroger, J. 106, 115, 138
    on middle adulthood 140
Kroger, J. and Marcia, J. 111
Kübler-Ross, E. 234, 236
Künemund, H. and Kolland, F. 208

labelling theory 196–8
Lacan, Jacques 33
Langer, E. 217
language 80, 193
    deaf languages 156
latency phase 32, 78
learning
    building blocks analogy 71–3
    classical conditioning 88–9, 90, 100
    operant conditioning 90–5
    social learning theory 98, 101, 102
    see also behaviourism; conditioning
learning impairments 154, 154–5, 158
learning theory 86–7, 102
learnt helplessness 95
leaving home 145, 181–2
    and disability 166–7
lesbian identity 121
Levinson, Daniel 133, 136, 144
    tasks in early adulthood 139
Lewin, Kurt 192
life chances 190
life course perspective 204
life cycle, family 176–8
life expectancy 166–7
lifespan psychology 133–4
linear causality 173, 176
linear models 176
living systems 171
Lollar, D.J. 164

London Underground map 5
loss 228–9, 230–2
loss-orientated bereavement 230–1
Lowenthal *et al.* 136

MacPherson Report 202
macrosystem 192
magical thinking 75
Main, Mary 134
Mallory, M. 146
maps
   London Underground 5
Marcia, J. 111
marriage 137, 182
Martha's Vineyard 152
Marx, Karl 11
masculinity 99, 117
maternal deprivation 47–9, 62
McAdams, Dan 135–6
McGoldrick, M. 182
McLuhan, Marshall 203
meaning state of transition 108
means of production 11
media 203
medical model 152
memory, in old age 211
menopause 145
mental illness 158
mentor relationships 139
mesosystem 192, 198
microsystem 192, 198
mid-life crisis 144
middle adulthood 140, 144–9
Minnesota Study of Twins Reared Apart 9
mirror, and object relations 35–6
modularity 82
monkeys, research on separation 49–50, 54, 68
monotropic mother-child bond 64, 65
moral development 114–15, 117
moral judgements 3
moratorium 111, 112, 121
morphine 94
motor impairments 154, 155
myelination 113

narrative 135–6
narratives of grief 229–30
nature
   and gender 99–102
   nature-nurture debate 6–16
   see also biology
needs, of children 35–6

negative feedback loops 171, 172
negative reinforcement 91
neuroconstructivism 83
neuroscience 14, 62–4
non-attachment 60
nurture
   and gender 99–102
   nature-nurture debate 6–16
   see also culture; social context

Obholzer, Anton 224
object permanence 73–4, 80, 81
object relations theory 34–40
   see also attachment theory
observation, and learning 97–9, 100–1
occupational identity 139
   and disability 164
Oedipus complex 31, 42
Oedipus Rex 41
old age
   ageism 218–19
   and baby talk 217
   cognitive changes 211–12
   control in 217
   cultural differences 219–20
   disengagement 216, 224–5
   impact on family system 184
   physical changes 210–11
   retirement 208
   social context of 207–9, 215–19
   stages of 208–9
   stereotyping 218
   tasks and challenges in 212–14
open systems 171
operant behaviour 91
operant conditioning 90–5, 97, 100
operations, Piaget's concept of 75, 77
opportunity 199–200
oral stage 30

paranoid-schizoid position 37, 38
parenthood
   adjustments 183
   and adolescence 123–5
   and gender differences 199
Parkes, Colin Murray 228
partners, choosing 134–5
patriarchy 42
Pavlov, Ivan 88–9
peer groups 116–17
penis envy 31, 42
personality 8, 26, 134, 136

phallic sexual behaviour 32
phallic stage 31
Phinney, J.S. 116
physical appearance 15
physical changes in old age 210–11
physical health, decline in 144
physical maturation 71
Piaget, Jean 54
    cognitive development
        building blocks analogy 71–3, 81–2
        challenges to 79–83
        making sense of the world 70–1
        stages of 67–8, 73–9
Plato 41
pleasure principle 24
Pol Pot regime 13
political arena 10–11, 13
positive feedback loops 171–2
positive reinforcement 91, 94
Potter, Dennis 236
poverty 201
power 10–11, 186–7, 201
pre-attachment stage 54
pre-operational stage 74–7
preconscious 23
predetermination 16–18
predictable deaths 234
predictable events 176–7
pregnancy 123
preoccupied adults, narratives of 134
primary groups 198
privation 62
problem-focused coping strategies
        125, 126
projection 28, 37, 198
psychoanalysis 21, 47
psychodynamic insights 20–1
    criticisms of 41–3
    influence of Freud 33–4
    object relations theory 34–40
    psychosexual stages 29–33
    structure of personality 24–9
    the unconscious 22–4, 24
psychological autonomy 122
psychological defences 26–8
psychosexual stages 29–33
psychosocial stages 38–40
    see also Erikson, Erik
punishment 91

qualitative research 41
Quinn, Peggy 167

race 200
racism 202
reaction stage of transition 107–8
reality principle 24, 193
reasoning
    experimental data 71
    making sense of the world 70–1
    see also cognitive development; thinking
reciprocal relationship stage 55
regulatory theory 63
reinforcement 91–2, 92
    cognitive behaviour therapy (CBT) 87, 96
    schedules of 93
    strength of reinforcers 94–5
relationship, understanding of concept 78
relationships
    choosing partners 134–5
    couple 139, 182–3
    forming 135, 138, 139
    love 139
    mentor 139
religion, and death 236–7
reparation 37
repressed desires 23
repression 26, 48
resilience 18, 125–6
respondent behaviour 91
responsibility 16, 17, 18, 132
restoration-orientated bereavement 230–1
retirement 208
reversibility 74–5, 77
revivalist death 225–6
Ridley, M.
    on free will 18
    on genes 14
Robertson, James 48
role confusion, in adolescence 110–16
role models 98, 100–1
roles, social 194–5
Rosenthal, R. and Jacobson, L. 196
Rutter, Michael 61–2, 64
Ryan, R.M. and Lynch, J.H. 117

Sable, P. 229
sadism 31
Sartre, Jean-Paul 16
Sayers, Janet 119
scaffolding 80, 81
schedules of reinforcement 93
schemas 71
schizophrenia 13
Seale, Clive 222–3, 225, 227, 229–30

Seasons of the Man's Life, The (Levinson) 136
second-order change 181
secondary groups 198
secure attachment 50, 53, 56, 57, 58, 124
secure base 51–3, 124
secure relationships 56
security, adult narratives 134
seduction theory 23, 42
self
   false 36
   new 118
   true 35
   turning against 27
   see also ego; identity
self-doubt stage of transition 108
Seligman, Martin 94–5
sensori-motor stage 73–4
sensory impairments 154, 155–6
separation 183
   Bowlby's work on 48–9, 49–51, 52
separation (Bowlby) 52
sexism 6
sexual abuse 22–3, 42
sexual activity 118–19, 120
   in old age 218
sexual drive, Freud's focus on 21, 29–31
sexual gratification 29–30
sexual identity 119–21
   and disability 164
sexual imagery 89
sexual orientation 120
sexual practices 120
sexuality
   and adolescence 118–21
   Freud 21, 29–31
Shakespeare, Tom 152
Shakespeare, William 194
shaping 93–4
sign language 156
Skinner, B.F. 91, 92, 93
social class 102, 199–200
social construction 193
   and ethnicity 200
   of gender 199–200
   of human experience 204
social context
   of adolescence 105, 122, 123–4
   of death 222–3
   of disability 152, 159, 193
   of old age 207–9
   and poverty 201
   see also society

social death 222–3
social exclusion 193, 201–2
social inequality 199
social interaction 54, 193
social learning theory 98, 101, 102
social mobility 199–200
social model 152, 153
social perspectives
   and language 193
   stereotyping and labelling theory 196–8
social reform 49
social responsiveness 54–5
social roles 194–5
social transmission 71
society 191
   and death 223–6
   and old age 215–19
   see also social context
sociological perspectives 191–2
   culture and history 203–6
   Ecological Systems Theory 192
   social construction 193
   social roles 194–5
   societal divisions 199–202
   stereotyping and labelling theory 196–8
Solnit, A. and Stark, M. 159
Sophocles 41
Sperlinger, A. 166
spina bifida 155, 164
Spirit Level, The (Wilkinson and Pickett) 201
splitting 28, 37, 58, 198
spontaneous recovery 88
stages model of development 133
   adulthood 136–8
   attachment 54–5
   cognitive development 67–8, 70–1, 73–9
   impairment and 157
   psychosexual stages 29–33
   psychosocial stages 38–40
   see also Erikson, Erik
Steinberg, L. and Silverberg, S.B. 116
stereotyping 196–8
   of old age 218
stimulation 62
Strange Situation Test 58
stress 125, 137, 159
stressors 159, 176–8
   see also horizontal stressors; vertical
      stressors
Stroebe, M. and Schut, H. 231
Stuart-Hamilton, Ian 211
sublimation 28

Sugarman, L. 107–8, 141
suicide 122
superego 24, 25
suppressed desires 23–4
system levels 176–8
systems theory 169–72, 174
    family 172–6
    larger systems 186–7
    and old age 184
    whole systems approach 184–5

terminal illness 224, 234
testing stage of transition 108
Thane, Pat 207
Thatcher, Margaret 191
theories 4–6
    nature-nurture 6–16
    see also psychodynamic insights
theory of mind 76–7
thinking 74–5
    higher order 79
    see also reasoning
third age 208–9
Thomas, Dylan 235
Thomson, Robert 17
timely deaths 235–6
toilet training 30–1, 158
transference 28–9
transitional objects 36
transitions 18, 107–10
    and adolescence 109–10
    and adulthood 136–8
    in family life 184–5
    see also adolescence; death
true self 35
trust 35
truth 6
twin studies 8–9

unconscious 21, 22–4, 24
undiscriminating social responsiveness 54
Union of the Physically Impaired against Segregation (UPIAS) 152
United Nations Convention on the Rights of Persons with Disabilities 153
unpredictable deaths 234
unpredictable events 177
unresolved states of mind, adulthood 134
untimely deaths 235–6

Venables, Jon 17
vertical stressors 159, 177, 178–9, 180, 184
vested interests 6, 7
Victor, Christina 210
visual perception 63
von Bertalanffy, Ludwig 170
Vygotsy, Lev 79–81

Walker, D. 200
Walter, T. 225
Watson, J.B. 89–90
Webster, R. 41
Westergaard, J. 199
Westerhof, G. and Tulle, E. 218
Williams syndrome 155
Wink, P. and Scott, J. 237
Winnicott, Donald 35, 35–6, 57
wisdom 212, 219
World Health Organisation (WHO) 48, 122
World Report on Disability (WHO) 153, 164

young adulthood 141–2
    see also adolescence
Young, M. and Cullen, L. 235, 236

Zimbardo, P.G. 194
zone of proximal development 80, 81